open

4 Editorial

Jorinde Seijdel

ESSAYS

6 Languishing in Securityscape
The Interpassive Transformation of the Public Sphere

Gijs van Oenen

18 A Short Archaeology of the New Fear

Lieven De Cauter

26 Temporary Occupation, 2003
A Visual Essay
by Sean Snyder

50 Surveillance and the Ludic Reappropriation of Public Space

Thomas Y. Levin

72 Parklife

Sven Lütticken

88 Architecture in Control Societies
Security as a Selling Point

Harm Tilman

open

104 Insecurity
by Design
WTC New York

Mark Wigley

COLUMN

120 Creation

Hans Boutellier

PROJECTS

122 Beware of
the Dog!
*The Public Domain in
the Information Society*

Jouke Kleerebezem

130 Insecurity as
Absolute Zero
*<re-start> by Jan van
Grunsven and
Ineke Bellemakers,
Kanaleneiland, Utrecht*

Willem van Weelden

142 Emotional
Landscapes in the City
*D-Tower in
Doetinchem by
Q.S. Serafijn and
NOX/Lars Spuybroek*

Q.S. Serafijn

open

152 Cabin Fever

The Home of the Unabomber

Mark Wigley

BOOKREVIEWS

160 Slow-Motion Film with Crash-Test Dummies

Julian Stallabrass, *Internet Art, The Online Clash of Culture and Commerce*
Willem van Weelden

161 Das War Einmal

Reflect #01, New Commitment: In architecture, art and design
Max Bruinsma

163 A Call for a New Relationship Between Art and Place

Miwon Kwon, *One Place after Another. Site Specific Art and Locational Identity*
Dees Linders and Mariska van den Berg

166 Personalia

167 Credits

Editorial

JORINDE SEIJDEL

(IN)SECURITY

This is the first issue of _open_ to come out in _cahier_ form and to be published by NAi Publishers. The new _open_, redesigned by Thomas Buxó, is published twice a year in a Dutch-language as well as an English-language edition. The _cahiers_ are thematically arranged, with art and public space as starting points — not as an isolated phenomenon, however, but as a component of the cultural and social developments that define the dynamics of the current public domain, and in relation to relevant areas such as architecture/urban planning, landscape architecture, spatial planning and digital media. The new _open_ strives more than in the past to achieve a balance between theory and direct contributions from actual practice. It is intended for all with an interest in the function and organization of the public space and/or the role of art within it.

open 6 is devoted to art, public space and security. Within today's public domain, the call for more protection, supervision and care dominates on all fronts. The individual and the community are demanding maximum security for the public space and for themselves, and ever more control over the other. There seems to be a veritable obsession with security. A fearful culture is being postulated, in which, however, little is clear about the nature or the provenance of the threat. Is there really danger out there, socially, politically or economically speaking, or is the new fear coming out of a collective sense of being powerless to exert any influence on everyday reality, for instance? Are there perhaps so many new structures and associations emerging in the pluriform, multicultural and global network communities as to engender a universal perception of being uprooted and alienated, with all the feelings of unease that this entails? Has the gap between citizens and government perhaps grown too wide as well? Or have the media, with their over-exposure of danger and their barrage of shocking images, become the primary authors of our fear?

The issue of security seems to consist of a steadily condensing constellation of disparate as well as related socio-cultural, political and economic factors, which is increasingly coming to dominate the culture. At all events, it is questionable whether the solution lies in the implementation of a society of control, or in a capsular society in which everything and everyone is suspect and we move from one protected enclave to the other: the rhetoric of security is not far removed from the rhetoric of danger. In any case, thorough and critical analyses of the current propositions on security seem to be in order. For the implications of thinking in terms of security for the public domain, for its organization, experience and use, are considerable. Neither the perception of nor the relationship to the public as audience and the public as sphere, in the role they play in the theory and practice of art and public space, can remain untouched.

open 6 examines what lies at the root of the public yearning for security, of the cumulation of fear, and what new questions are being asked of and by artists, designers, theorists, clients and policy makers. Theoretical considerations and scenarios from art, architecture, philosophy and politics are reviewed, in an attempt to uncover something of the current security paradigm, or to propose alternative (conceptual) models.

Legal philosopher Gijs van Oenen analyses the transformation of the public sphere into 'the new securityscape', and art historian and philosopher Lieven De Cauter develops an initial 'short archaeology of the new fear'. Art critic Sven Lütticken considers fictitious and genuine models of the enclosed space in philosophy, art, architecture and media, while the essay by art and culture theorist Thomas Y. Levin examines how artists working in the public space relate to the panoptic surveillance society. In the articles by architecture theorists Harm Tilman and Mark Wigley, security and architecture take centre stage – in the former primarily in a Dutch context and in the latter in direct connection with the World Trade Center buildings in New York. There is also an autonomous visual contribution by artist/photographer Sean Snyder in the context of his Temporary Occupation project.

This open also includes a polemical column by Hans Boutellier, author of De Veiligheidsutopie, offering a personal view from his specific expertise on the possibility of art torpedoing the vacuous order of the Security Utopia. In addition there are contributions more directly connected to concrete events, places or (art) projects, providing insight into the current aesthetics and ethics of security. open 6 also includes the debut of a book section, which will be expanded in the following issue with more reviews and reports.

Gijs van Oenen

Languishing in Securityscape

The Interpassive Transformation of the Public Sphere

The issue of security in the public domain is not so much pre-cipitated by increased danger as primarily a problem of 'inter-passive citizenship', according to legal philosopher Gijs van Oenen. In the follow-ing piece he examines the conditions for the transformation of the public sphere into an obsessive medium of security concerns.

Safety first: on this demand for the public domain, modern citizens and their government agree, however much they may disagree in other respects. Safety requires action: tough measures, clear targets. Such targets include: suspicious immigrants, assinine behaviour in public, highway speeding, financial swindling, unlit cycling, hooliganism, urinating in public places, organized crime, terrorism, smoking, urban decay, unrepentant criminals, permissive culture. In short, everything and everyone can become a target of 'security concerns'.

One consequence of this obsession with security seems clear. We can forget about the ideal of a civilized public sphere. That was the optimistic idea that public confrontation makes for better citizens – a classic republican ideal that, in the second half of the twentieth century, was advocated by people like Hannah Arendt, Jürgen Habermas and Richard Sennett. Let us call this an ideal of *interactive citizenship*, situated in what we might call an ideoscape: a field of human relations shaped through the incessant exchange of opinions and viewpoints. According to this ideal, people self-actualize not simply as private persons, but also and especially through interaction as citizens. In this interaction nothing is 'produced', other than a more sophisticated understanding of what can serve as collective aims.

This interactive ideoscape of the public sphere, however, is undergoing a structural transformation, to use Habermas' classical terminology. I propose that it is turning into an *interpassive securityscape*. In this medium, the primary quest is not for encounter or confrontation, but for security. The public sphere is turning into a security sanctum, which can be briefly defined as a space in which the concern for civilized behaviour

has been *outsourced*. Modern citizens no longer believe that they can control themselves sufficiently to bear the responsibility for civilized public interaction. They prefer to turn this responsibility and accountability over to others: the government, the police, supervisors, providers, security guards.

These old and new managers of public space are responding with a new kind of 'civilitarianism', re-educating the citizen in a way that reflects present-day political anxieties; in other words, in a rather authoritarian and moralizing way. In my view, this exercise is doomed to fail. The attempt to rehabilitate 'public man' collides with a phenomenon that I refer to as *interpassivity*, following cultural philosophers Robert Pfaller and Slavoj Žižek. Involvement or engagement is delegated, outsourced. We would like to get involved, but we no longer believe that we can; therefore we ask others to get involved, on our behalf.

This does not result, however, in obedience or docility toward such others, as promoters of the new civilitarianism hope. Two characteristics of interpassivity stand in the way here. To begin with, delegating engagement does not cause interpassive citizens to forgo their self-will. On the contrary, they persist in an indifferent denial of their public responsibility, even and in fact precisely when called to account for it by those to whom they have delegated it. This is why we see so many manifestations of *autistic* behaviour in present-day securityscapes.

But in addition we are witnessing a less easily explained phenomenon. Interpassivity also leads to an intense, almost compulsive *fascination* for those who have been entrusted with the care and responsibility for public affairs. An obsessive interest develops in the mechanisms of the system to which the bearers of the delegated responsibility are connected. This meta-involvement, an involvement in the involvement of others, explains the current rise of fascination with ('new') *politics*.

What is the condition of the interpassive securityscape? How does it apply in the sphere of labour and that of politics? How has the public sphere turned into an interpassive securityscape? There is a direct relationship between interpassivity, in essence nothing more than a radicalization of the modern ideal of interactivity, and the transformation of the public sphere into an object of 'security concerns'.

The Principle of the *Dromenon*

Robert Pfaller and Slavoj Žižek constructed the concept of interpassivity to explain how some artworks and media endeavour to take care of their own reception. In *interactive* arrangements, the artwork delegates a portion of its actualization to the viewer. In contrast, *interpassive* arrangements adopt the very role normally fulfilled by the viewer, namely the enjoyment or the 'consumption' of the artwork. The spectator or consumer is made redundant; or rather, his or her involvement in the realization of the work has become superfluous. Apparently, the artwork aims to consume itself, actively disinteresting the spectator in its realization.

The archetypal domestic example of interpassivity that Pfaller and Žižek cite is the video recorder. The VCR does more than record broadcasts when we are absent. It watches television, in our place, and more importantly, *on our behalf.* It delivers us from the need of watching TV ourselves. We feel secure in the knowledge that someone or something is watching on our behalf.

This was illustrated by an installation by Eija-Liisa Ahtila in 2002 at Tate Modern. Video recorders and monitors sat on chairs, while visitors were required to stand. The monitors, facing different directions, were broadcasting their content oblivious to human attention. Sometimes they simply just faced each other, explicitly declaring all space in between mediated. The spectator is either shut out, or caught in between, 'interpassively'. The media enjoyed through the spectators, the spectators through the media, albeit indifferently.

The fact that media can enjoy themselves, and each other, does not fully explain why we should delegate *our* enjoyment to them. Why not just be content that media now seem capable of enjoyment? Why project our enjoyment onto their gratification? Pfaller explains this through the principle of the *dromenon*. This concept generalizes mechanisms such as the video recorder, or the Tibetan prayer wheel, another favourite example of Pfaller's and Žižek's. This prayer wheel, which 'prays on our behalf', serves to illustrate the *perpetuum mobile* quality intrinsic to interpassive media, or perhaps to all media. Aimless and vacuous as they are, their motion exerts a strong fascination on those in whose service they operate. This fascination does not affect the content, the broadcast or prayer for example, of what is televised, recorded, or otherwise 'processed'. Rather it is the sensation of permanent connection to a running medium that has a satisfying effect, even obsessively so.

According to Pfaller we in fact delegate our subjectivity to the aimlessly running medium (a pleonasm?). Consider, he writes, how people watching a live football match

Eija-Liisa Ahtila, <u>The Present</u>, 2001 / 5 x 70″-120″+ 5 x 30″, DVD installation for five monitors and five TV spots with sound, 3 x 90″ Courtesy Klemens Gasser @ Tanja Grunert Inc, New York / © Crystal Eye Ltd, Helsinki

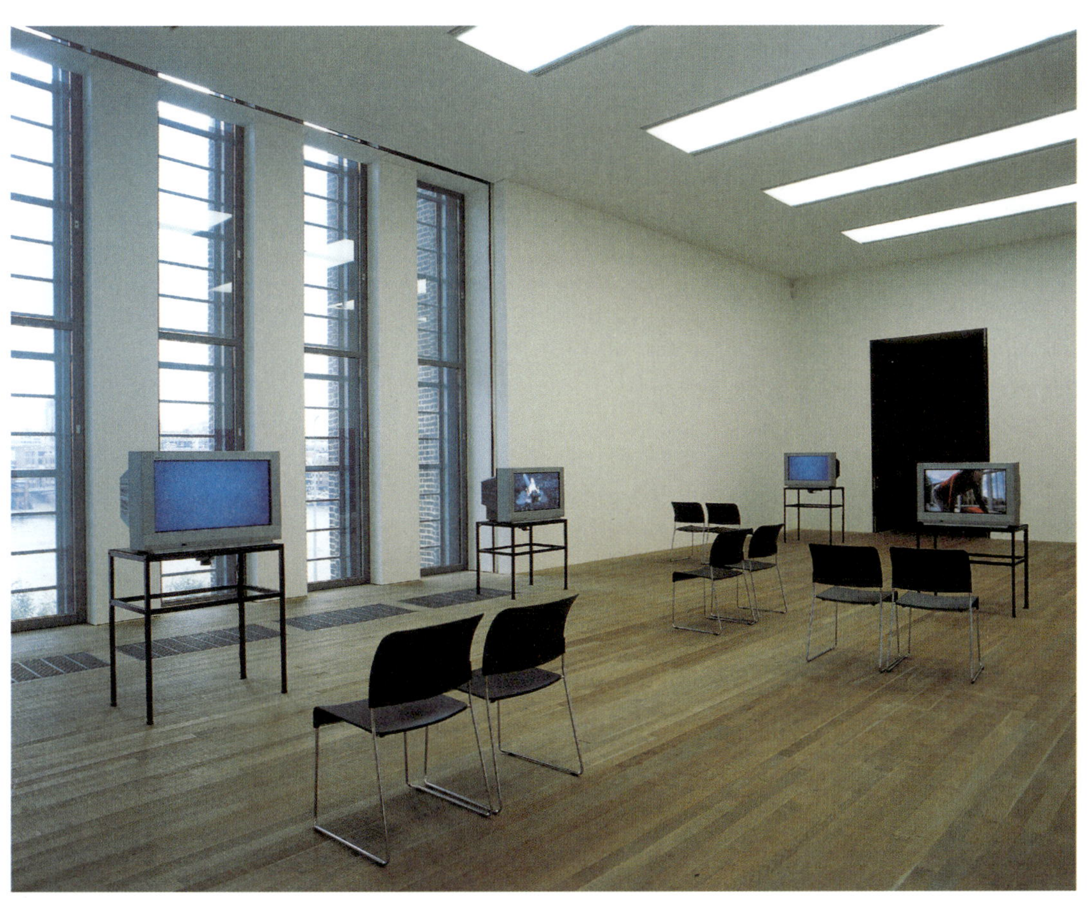

Eija-Liisa Ahtila, <u>Me/We; Okay, Gray</u>, 1993 / 35 mm-film and DVD installation for three monitors with sound, 3 x 90″ / Courtesy Klemens Gasser
@ Tanja Grunert Inc, New York / © Crystal Eye Ltd, Helsinki

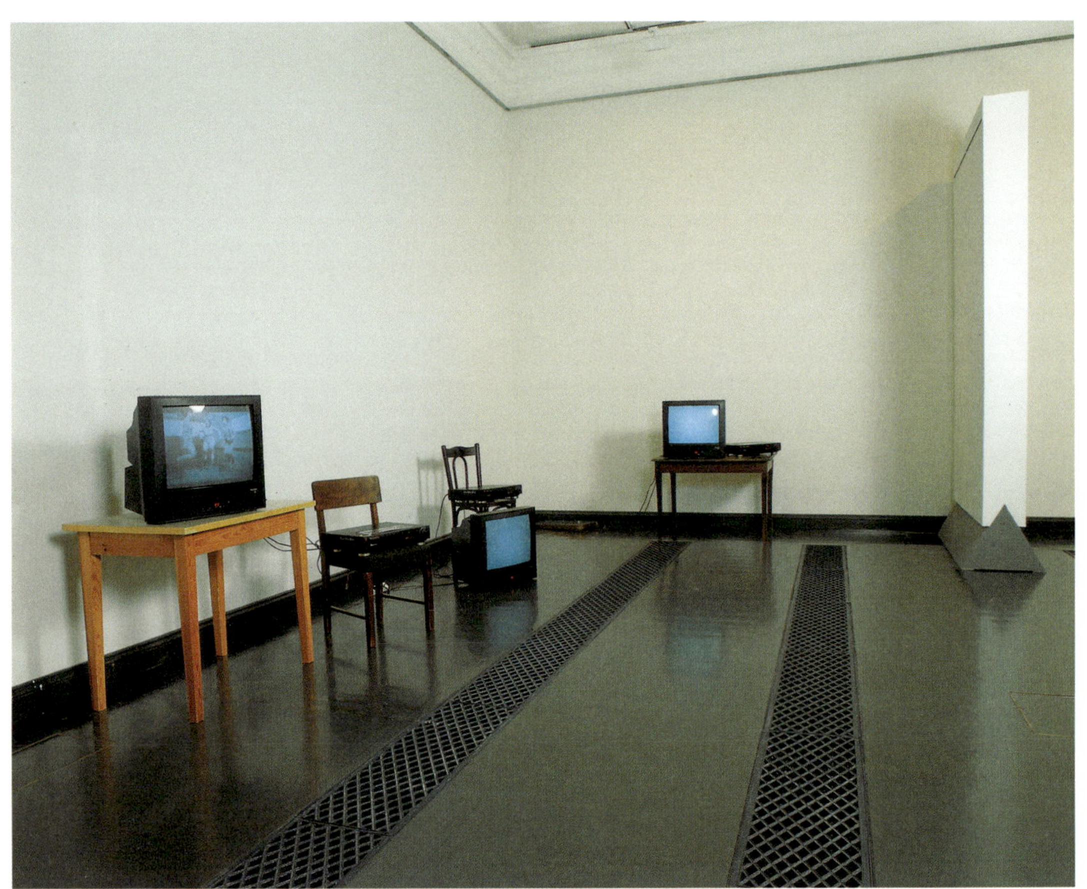

on television often react awkwardly and irritably if we speak to them or otherwise disturb them. This is not primarily because they are anxious they might miss a crucial moment in the match. More pertinent is their desire to 'languish' in front of the television. They want to 'enjoy' not in the sense of having fun and being delighted, but in the sense of 'enjoying' the protection from the machine they have attached themselves to. This is the machine of the dromenon, 'a machine that runs of itself', a pure medium without a message, that 'stands in' for one's own subjectivity. The function of the dromenon is thus to provide 'cover' for the spectator's retreat into oblivion, or self-forgetfulness ('Selbstvergessenheit').

The Flexible Human Subject

Interpassivity affects many domains of contemporary society and its institutions. One prominent example is labour. There we see trends like flexibilization, outsourcement and networking. Invariably, this involves a relationship between the structure of labour and the experience of subjectivity of those who perform this labour. The substance of the work, or of the product, is less and less important. For instance, large media conglomerates unashamedly refer to this substance as 'content': something, *anything*, they can profitably haul through their expensive infrastructure. By contrast, monitoring, process control and supervision are becoming ever more important. Hands-on has been replaced by, or is becoming the equivalent of, *interfaced* operation. In this way, a single person can perform the most diverse tasks. Or conversely, a particular task can be performed by anyone.

Sociologist Richard Sennett has perceptively analysed this process in his book *The Corrosion of Character*. The modern organization of labour requires a 'flexible human subject', that is, a human being that can adapt ever faster to the demands of the constantly reconfigured production process. Flexibility has been turned from a functional requirement into a new *virtue*. Well-functioning institutions are being reorganized incessantly, transforming flexibility from a means to an end. Employees are expected to eagerly anticipate a change of function or location, even when there is no genuine reason for such a change.

The inevitable result is a high level of detachment. Every product imaginable can now be manufactured, but employees have lost their affinity with any particular product. This is the process of interpassivity *pur sang*: a continual reinforcement of 'interactivity', meaning an optimal interaction between the functions of human and machine in the production process, is matched by a loss of involvement and interest in the objective and the product of the process. At the same time, many employees seek compensation for the loss of meaning in their work precisely in such intensified interaction. They have internalized flexibility as a virtue, as an expression of their own motives and goals. They thus suffer from the experience of an inner 'flaw', which they frantically attempt to fill with the very activities that have elicited this experience.

Sennett illustrates this point with a telling anecdote about a bakery in Boston, which he visited during his field research. There was a Jamaican man working there who had come to Boston at the age of 10, and in more than 25 years had worked himself up from assistant to master baker and foreman. The bakery had done well throughout those years, although it had changed significantly: everything used to be baked the old-fashioned way, by hand, and now the entire baking process was computer-controlled. Instead of handling dough and operating ovens, employees now pressed buttons on computerized interfaces. Despite the bakery's economic prosperity, new employees often quit after a short time. As the foreman told Sennett, 'When somebody tells me there's no future here, I ask what they want. They don't know; they tell me you shouldn't be stuck in one place.'

The Outsourcement of Politics

A comparable form of implicit, interpassive frustration can be identified in modern politics. Here too, a loss of interest in the final 'product' prevails. Involvement shifts to the process of – interactive – 'policy making'. Again, the focus is not on the substance of any particular policy. What matters more is the reassuring sense of dwelling in the protective proximity of the ceaselessly running process of policy production (PPP). This is the ultimate place where 'third way' politics and new forms of populism meet. Both promise citizens ever-greater proximity to the political process, and both are essentially uninterested in its content or results. Both are caught in an interpassive fascination with political power.

Interpassivity in politics is the result of a number of recent developments in politics and society, including outsourcing, as already mentioned. In line with current commercial fashion, governments are busily sourcing out everything but their 'core activities'. Former state agencies and services are transformed into semi-public or even private bodies. Supposedly the relevant activities can be better, more efficiently, more cheaply or more reliably performed by private, or privatized, actors. Whether this is true or not, the oursourcing trend has caused great damage to the authority of government. For it has created the impression that almost everything government does can be done better elsewhere. Worse still, that hardly anything need be considered an essential government or state task. Just about every government function can be delegated. Therefore there is no longer anything intrinsically political that requires our commitment, as citizens. And conversely, nothing to which we commit is intrinsically political.

This outsourcement of politics is fully in sync with the liberal credo of the autonomous, self-assured citizen who takes care of his own affairs and should not be bothered by government. This citizen considers himself a capable market operator, to be facilitated, not regulated, by government. More importantly, government agrees with this view. In its increasingly 'interactive' form, it is continually engaged in opinion polls and other forms of monitoring citizen's preferences, rather than developing and implementing substantive views on the interests of nation or society. The citizen, in turn, has unprecedented access to the policy process, yet he has scarce interest in political substance. Expectations and demands in regard to government are rising dramatically – as dramatic as the decline in membership of political parties.

Such is the interpassivity of contemporary politics. A radicalization of interactivity is matched by a loss of substantive interest. Like labour, politics these days is mainly about process control. The system is up and running; all it needs from people is 'monitoring'. Yet at the same time there is an intense sense of connection with the political process, an interest that can almost be called obsessive. The odd thing is that this interest is particularly present in those who have developed distaste for the political system. True, they are prone to complain about the inconclusiveness of actual politicians, but this merely reflects their virtually limitless faith in politics' potential.

At the same time they envy politicians their privileged position. Not because of their privilege of power or status, for politicians no longer enjoy such privileges – as citizens know full well. No, it is about the privilege of interpassivity: the protection that they presume one enjoys in the vicinity of PPP, the constantly spinning policy production process. Politicians are plugged in to this process, and the angry citizens suspect that this is the secret reason why politicians enjoy their profession. The envious citizens want to be 'plugged in' as well. Not in order to participate in deciding the content of politics, or – any more than with the football match on television – because they might otherwise miss vital moments. What they do want is simply the protection of politics as dromenon. As political subjects, as citizens, they would prefer to experience oblivion, and any intervention from the outside is perceived as a painful reminder of their existence as concrete citizens, with concrete social duties. They yearn for the experience of interpassive politics, not because of its practical policy effects, but because of the (temporary) release that it seems to offer from their practical social responsibilities.

Interpassivity & the Public Domain

What about interpassivity in relation with security, and the public domain? Indeed I think the same mechanisms can be observed here. A recent minicontroversy, aptly analysed by Henk Hofland, the *eminence grise* of Dutch journalism, can serve to illustrate this. Around Christmas 2003, 200,000 Amsterdam households received a questionnaire from the 'Registratie Orgaan Nederland' ('Netherlands Registration Organ'). People were instructed to tick off a box, stating whether they knew any illegal immigrants, and if so, whether they were willing to turn them in? This 'organ', however, was not a government agency, but a pseudonym for a project by artist Martijn Engelbregt, working in association with the well-known political-cultural centre De Balie. This caused widespread outrage: partly because of possible associations with the deportation of Dutch Jews during World War II, this issue was widely considered too sensitive to exploit for an art project.

But Hofland realized that an entirely different sensibility is being injured here. As he wrote, 'Holland may be on a crazy individualization course, out-of-control drivers may fire machine-guns at radar devices, bus drivers may well fear that they won't make it home alive today (...) – but send a printed questionnaire by mail, and things change altogether. Authority still exists, you might say, but what authority.' In my terms: Engelbregt offended interpassive sensibilities. Citizens have no problem with excessive, emotional behaviour in the public sphere. They actually enjoy it. However, the questionnaire touches on the even more excessive but secret enjoyment they experience through their proximity to PPP. Filling out the questionnaire makes this proximity explicit and unveils the enjoyment it entails. Thus Engelbregt's interrogation in fact *mocks* the citizen. The questionnaire causes him the embarrassment of being caught indulging in this interpassive enjoyment, his most treasured but most secret excess. As a Lacanian like Žižek would say, more 'common' public excesses exist only to cover up this one most secret excess.

As discussed above, the modern public sphere originated through the principle of 'interactivity'. Citizens used to confront each other publicly, in the press as well as in the street. They not only let their opinions be known, they also created a new domain, the domain of public opinion formation. Here opinions were not simply 'aired', but discussed, defended, reviewed, and further developed. The rise of the public sphere thus bolstered not just individual but also collective opinion formation.

Obviously, the public sphere has been prey to many 'colonizing' tendencies and interests, especially in the last century. These have modified and restricted, but in a certain sense also radicalized it. For instance, it has long been under the powerful influence of financial interests, especially in the United States. In addition, it has been significantly 'mediated'. Such mediation created distortions and misrepresentations, but more importantly, it fostered interpassive developments. The media – and particularly the mass media, such as television – after all function in ways comparable to those described above for labour and politics. They radicalize the interactive nature of opinion formation, while simultaneously 'formatting' it in specific ways (think only of the term 'infotainment'). The spellbound tv-citizen is bombarded with an ever faster spinning circus of opinions, which quickly lose their substance yet retain their fascination, as something 'new' is always being produced. The culmination point is 'breaking news', which rarely contains real live action, but which does create a sense of being intensely connected to the 'news production system'. Like the PPP, this system runs at full tilt, without however creating much interest in its aim or result.

The 'interpassivization' of the public sphere also means a reduction in the interactive capacities of citizens, threatening the communicative quality of this sphere. The problem is not so much that citizens cannot recognize what standards and what behaviour are necessary to maintain a civilized public space. They can. But they increasingly declare themselves incapable of acting accordingly. They simply no longer see themselves as having the required capacities of self-control and self-limitation. This is what the Netherlands Scientific Council for Government Policy, in its recent report on 'social norms and values,' called 'the burden of behaviour', thereby referring to the fact that 'a large and growing number of people, in their behaviour, no longer live by the values they claim to strive for'.

The prototype of this citizen is the guy who, when asked in court to account for his aggressive behaviour in public space, says: 'I just happen to have a short fuse.' Rather than reminding himself how to act in a civilized way, such a short-fused citizen prefers to cruise interpassively in public space. This attitude can manifest itself in many different ways, which have 'experiencing emotion' as their common denominator. Increasingly, contemporary society is seen as a kind of 'experience machine'.

Which nowadays deals with interpassive experience: citizens literally let experience 'get to them'. This can be at a football match, a royal wedding, a mafia funeral, a commemoration, a demonstration. The ultimate form of such collective emotional experiencing is probably the 'flash mob': people who respond to SMS instructions to gather, *en masse*, at some urban hotspot, to languish there interpassively for a few minutes, demonstratively and pointlessly.

The Emotion Machine

The public sphere increasingly becomes a stage upon which interpassive roles and sentiments are played out. Emotions are experienced, reputations flaunted and frustrations vented, de-subjectified and without aim. The mood can be joyful or grieving, a silent march or a loud display of aggression, and one can instantly change into the other. Someone who happens to be 'interactively' present in this space has no way of knowing whether he will be perceived as a supporter or as an opponent.

A good example is provided by my own experience on the late afternoon of 8 May 2002, on the Coolsingel boulevard in Rotterdam. Two days earlier the 'revolutionary' would-be politician Pim Fortuyn had been assassinated, and many people were lining up in front of city hall to sign the condolence books. From the shopping area of the Lijnbaan, on the opposite side of the Coolsingel, a vast legion of Feyenoord supporters flowed across the street at the same time, in festive anticipation of the UEFA Cup soccer final later that evening. The two groups with their very different emotions went together surprisingly well; they encountered each other effortlessly and without conflicts. The nature of the emotion was less important than the yearning to experience it along with others in public space.

For the modern citizen, participation in public sphere means collectively experiencing emotions. He wishes, as it were, to be plugged into the emotion machine that is deployed in the public sphere. It is the public equivalent of plugging into a Discman, mobile phone or video recorder. People continually seek out the protection of the *dromenon*: the spinning object or process that simply through its proximity manages to provide us with the sensation of protection and oblivion – the ontological core of what René Boomkens as far back as eight years ago called the 'security machine', 'all those practices which in the absence of a lively public domain (...) take care of the protection and supervision of our daily lives'.

This does not imply that we are indeed protected from aggression or violence – far from it. It means we feel liberated from the necessity of taking responsibility for it. The modern citizen feels both enthralled and carried away by the collective experiencing process. Yet, that is too interactive a way of putting it. The experience of such a citizen more closely resembles a 'testimony'. Like an interpassive artwork, experiencing emotion in the public sphere can do without the subjective input of the modern citizen. On the contrary, it relieves him of his subjectivity. The citizen becomes purely a stand-in in this process, a 'fellow traveller', so to speak. The *dromenon* runs, and the citizen follows suit. Think of what the movie business calls a *sequel*: 'coming soon!', fascinating already, a must-see, 'out-violencing' any previous experience...

This is the paradox of the *dromenon*: it is

an 'attachment machine', the most important product of which is, ironically, detachment. Citizens feel ever more deeply
'involved', but their commitment is in fact
ever decreasing. Public demonstration
becomes a medium for oblivion. Once facil-
itating self-formation, the public sphere now
promotes self-forgetfulness. It enables us to
delegate our subjectivity to the interpassive
emotion machine.

The 'security issue' in the public sphere
is thus to a large extent an issue of interpassive citizenship. The modern citizen no
longer feels capable of operating subject-
ively, or interactively, in public space. If
required he can easily 'plug in' to PPP, the
always spinning public policy process, but
simultaneously he feels unable to intervene
in that process. What the modern citizen
wants is not to commit, but merely to 'join'.
He does not want to act, but merely to
appear. Whatever happens, he is neither for
nor against, but simply 'present'. The
contemporary citizen is, in short, a one-
person flash mob. He seeks protection and
security, but in doing so only makes the
public domain more unstable and more
insecure. The enjoyment of the *dromenon* is
simultaneously the enjoyment of the loss of
one's own resilience, and that of the
communicative quality of the public sphere.
This explosive interpassivity is the real
security issue of our society.

Sources

Eija-Liisa Ahtila, 'Real characters,
invented worlds'. Exhibition at Tate
Modern, London, 30 April–28 July
2002
Arjun Appadurai, *Modernity at
Large: Cultural Dimensions of
Globalization*. University of
Minnesota Press, Minneapolis 1996
René Boomkens, *De angstmachine*,
De Balie, Amsterdam 1996
Jürgen Habermas, *Strukturwandel
der Öffentlichkeit*, Luchterhand,
Darmstadt 1962
H.J.A. Hofland, 'Formuleren', *NRC
Handelsblad*, 9 January 2004
Gijs van Oenen, *Surplus van ille-
galiteit*, De Balie, Amsterdam 2002
Gijs van Oenen, *Ongeschikt recht*,
Boom Juridische uitgevers, The
Hague 2004
Henk Oosterling, *Radicale middel-
matigheid*, Boom, Amsterdam 2000
Robert Pfaller, *Interpassivität.
Studien über delegiertes Genießen*,
Springer Verlag, Wenen/New York
2000
Robert Pfaller, *Die Illusionen der
anderen. Über das Lustprinzip in der
Kultur*, Suhrkamp, Frankfurt 2002
Gerhard Schulze, *Die Erlebnis-
gesellschaft. Kultursoziologie der
Gegenwart*, Campus, Frankfurt/
New York 1992 (1997)
Richard Sennett, *The Corrosion of
Character*, W.W. Norton, New York
1998
Netherlands Scientific Council for
Government Policy, *Waarden, normen
en de last van het gedrag*, Amsterdam
University Press, Amsterdam 2003
Slavoj Žižek, *The Puppet and the
Dwarf*, MIT Press, Cambridge
(Mass.) 2003

Lieven De Cauter

A Short Archaeology of the New Fear

The Belgian cultural philosopher Lieven De Cauter has written extensively on the emergence of the capsular civilisation, in which public space is divided into monitored and enclosed, secure enclaves (gated communities, shopping malls, theme parks, camps, ghettos). In this article he makes an initial attempt at analysing the new fear upon which this capsularization is based. Is it a frightening but fleeting hallucination, or does collective fear suggest a genuine danger?

'Freedom and fear are at war, and there will be no quick and easy end to this conflict.'

(The National Security Strategy of the United States of America, September 2002)

Collective fear is a large, partly invisible continent that manifests itself throughout entire epochs. In other words, fear is a historical constellation, often to a large extent subconscious or repressed, that defines the consciousness of groups and entire societies, yet it is also to a significant degree in its turn defined by facts, rumours, moods, cultural expressions, religious tenets or practices, customs, social rituals, and of course political manipulations.

But first: what is fear? Fear is a signal that communicates to a living organism that it may be in danger. Fear is one of the most important instruments to guarantee the survival of an individual member of a species, and therefore of the species itself. For this reason, fear is catalogued as an affect that is closely linked to the survival instinct. Fear, perhaps along with aggression and the mating drive, is one of the most instinctive impulses in any living being. Therefore fear is primarily a biological rather than a psychological phenomenon. But that is not the whole story, of course. Fear moves inwards. One might even say that fear is the basis for the human capacity to think. That is perhaps going a bit far, yet 'if not strong then be smart' is a basic motto for a timorous species (just as antelopes and rabbits scrupulously live by the maxim 'if not strong then be fast'). Humans are fearful animals. And who could blame them? Fear is a survival instinct, in humans as well, although they are a species without instinct and therefore compelled to be free and unfettered. In this sense, the hypothesis could be turned on its head: humans are a fearful species precisely because of their intelligence. When one is constantly able to perceive all the possibilities and impossibilities, all the dangers and risks, one is quite likely to become nervous, timorous or just plain afraid.

All fear is, ultimately, the fear of death. Yet only humans feel death to be unnatural and conduct their lives in a negation of death. The huge numbers of traces we leave behind and which we collectively call products of culture are all, in their focus on durability (bronze, marble, parchment), rebellions against finitude. The entire culture consists in the incessant establishment, re-establishment and handing down of traces, of monuments that 'are more eternal than bronze'. Culture, in this sense, is a negation of or symbolic victory over death. One might call it 'immortality drive': a drive that manifests itself at the level of the individual as a quest for fame (in order to become 'immortal') and at the level of the species as the need to maintain and pass on the meanings, the world of signs that define the uniqueness of the human race as a species.

Allthough fear originates in the survival instinct, it is a poor counsellor – certainly in its more intense form, which we call panic. The more intense the fear, the poorer counsel fear provides. And once the suspicion has been aroused in the fearful that he has fallen prey to a poor counsellor, that is precisely the point at which fear risks turning into panic: a fearful person loses control, because he is afraid of his own fear. In that sense, we should indeed be afraid of our fear.[1] Panic attacks are horrible. 'It's really a bad trip, you know.' A 'bad trip' is slang for a hallucination. A hallucination is being awake and yet dreaming (this can be pleasant in a state of intoxication, even blissful – the artificial paradises of Baudelaire and the like), but a waking dream usually turns sooner or later into a nightmare, as is the case in schizophrenia, paranoia, et cetera. And that might well be the case: humanity is 'having a bad trip'.

1. *Wij moeten bang zijn van onze angst* ('We should be afraid of our fear') is the title of a manuscript by Frank Vande Veire, an opinion piece inspired by 9-11.

We awake in a hallucinatory world, and however much we rub our eyes, we cannot drive away the bad dream: the twenty-first century looks bleak – somewhat spine-chilling, in fact. This is why we can speak of a new fear[2]. Texts and books are being published about it. Let us attempt to chart the continent of the new fear and produce a brief, rough sketch of it, more as a 'geology of fear' than as a genealogy of it. Or as a short archaeology, in the sense of the science of strata. Let us begin with the lowest stratum in this continental drift.

2. A few examples: René Boomkens, *De angstmachine* (1996), and very recently Alain de Botton, *Status Anxiety* (2004) and Benjamin Barber, *Fear's Empire* (2003).

1 Demographic or Ecological Fear

My hypothesis is that the deepest layer of our new collective fear, barely detectable at the surface, is the almost bio-sociological awareness, at the level of the species, that the world is getting so overpopulated that we are as a species reaching the limits of our biotope, the Earth. A fact of the twenty-first century is that nine billion people will have to survive on this planet by 2050. This awareness results more in a sort of unease than in a knowledge. Sometimes it is banal: the morning rush-hour traffic jams. But the extraordinary succession of problems is not at all banal: shortages in drinking water, threats to bio-diversity, global warming, rising sea levels, growing aggression, waves of migration, growing poverty, et cetera. Although warnings were issued as far back as 30 years ago (especially the report of the Club of Rome in 1972) about the demographic explosion, it is still not an issue of everyday discussion nor, sadly, a top priority for the world's political leaders. The ecological, social, economic and political consequences of overpopulation are incalculable, because of the many interactions among the various factors. I have dubbed this constellation 'the permanent catastrophe'.[3]

As a poor counsellor, fear might very well come to play a significant role in the approach to global problems. At the same time, ecological

3. 'Die permanente Katastrophe. Thesen zur Globalisierung/ The Permanent Catastrophe. Theories on Globalisation', in *48th International Short Film Festival Oberhausen*, cat. Oberhausen 2002. Longer version in Dutch: 'De permanente catastrofe', *De Witte Raaf*, no. 97, May-June 2002, p. 9-12.

or demographic fear might also push through the signal that humanity is in genuine danger and that we must therefore take action. For the moment, it seems unlikely that sufficient energy will be devoted to this. The Kyoto accords getting torpedoed is a bad sign.

One important consequence of the on-going demographic explosion is migration. And here we might just touch on the most volcanic aspect of the new fear. From the deepest strata of the demographic/ecological fear, migrants represent, within the constellation of the new fear, an all-too-visible bone of contention, personifying unease about an all-too-rapidly changing world.

2 Dromophobia

Just as invisible as demographic fear is the pressure exerted by the third Industrial Revolution (a term no longer in use, because the information-technology revolution seems to have acquired a semi-permanent character). Technological changes are so swift and so drastic, the acceleration they generate is so infernal, that people are kept in a constant state of subliminal fear, a state we identify as stress. The acceleration of our lives is, from first to last, a by-product of our technological extensions, of our media. Yet are we afraid of technology? At first glance, it seems the era of technophobia is over. Unfortunately, perhaps: there is hardly any resistance to technology anymore, or even criticism. An almost unquestioned sympathy predominates, a slavish adoration of technology, expressed in the thousands of consumer goods we purchase compulsively. We are dependent on information technology: anyone unplugged cannot function in our new, much-vaunted information society. Yet perhaps this new 'technophilia' is nothing more than a latent fear of falling behind on the acceleration. One might call it the fear of acceleration: *dromophobia*.

3 Economic Fear

Neoliberal capitalism has produced a society of winners and losers. The dismantling of the welfare state has generated an unprecedented dualization of society, a division between haves and have-nots. The fear of losing prosperity is enormous. Nothing is certain anymore: job security, social security, health insurance, pension schemes are all in jeopardy. The celebrated flexibilization not only forces us to be flexible, it makes us fragile. One might call this stratum of our new collective fear economic fear – the fear of a loss of security. We miss the family affection of the welfare state, and our house, our household (*oikos*), is no longer secure. This fear can be seen as a problem of luxury, but that does not make it any less real. 'Privilege engenders fear': our privileged position and our unprecedented standard of living turns us into fearful bourgeois. The dualization of our society is made most visible by and is projected onto the large groups of migrants who are increasingly populating our cities. This brings us, as mentioned earlier, to the most volcanic stratum of our new fear.

4 Xenophobia

Xenophobia is, literally, fear of foreigners. I make no pretensions of presenting here an instant solution to the issue of racism and xenophobia, but the frictions associated with migrations are a historic and sociological, or even anthropological, phenomenon, just as, conversely, all complex cultures are products of mixing and not of purity – from philosophy, which had Egyptian astrology as one of its ingredients, to the oh-so-native potato, which comes from South America. However, the pace at which the West, and especially Western cities, are having to cope with increasingly large groups of migrants is causing a sense of alienation and fear. For many people, it is very difficult to live with the fact that the street or the school that was once 'theirs' has become 'foreign'. I believe an entirely new kind of education is required to learn to live with this; political correctness, which immediately dismisses any expression of unease as racism and xenophobia, makes any therapy for this deep alienation impossible. This alienation is of course dangerous, because it can indeed lead to xenophobic movements and parties such as the Front National in France, the Vlaams Blok in Flanders and the Lijst Pim Fortuyn (LPF) in the Netherlands. Yet a problem does exist. All the more because the migrants are alienated as well – what is the identity of a second- or third-generation migrant? – and have great difficulty in establishing an image of their own, with the result that sections of the migrant population, primarily young people, are poorly socialized, create trouble, make neighbourhoods unsafe, et cetera. Although the time is definitely past when such problems could be dismissed as racist fabrications, one cannot deny that our fear of migrants is the fear of our own migration or mutation, of the changing of our own street, our own city, our own culture into a multicultural, eclectic, chaotic culture. The call for 'integration', which is sounding increasingly hollow (or, as with the ban on veils in schools, could even be counterproductive) is based on a fear of disintegration. I suspect that we shall have to learn to live with this disintegration; the era of the homogeneous civil society (symbolized by the uniform custom-made suit) is definitely over. We have arrived at a post-civil situation. And that brings us to the fifth stratum of the new fear.

5 Agoraphobia or Political Fear

The disintegration of the state is perceptible not just at the macro level, where individual states are losing importance because of the globalization of the economy and the formation of supranational entities, but also at the micro level: on the street, the monopoly on violence of the police is increasingly being challenged by an often diffuse aggression or simply acute violence. Add litter, vandalism and decay and you have all the ingredients for a new agoraphobia, a fear of the *agora* (the public space). Violence reaches into our sitting rooms through the evidently unstoppable tide of ever more violent action movies. Fear and aggression are increasingly exploited as commercially profitable forms of stimulation and enjoyment. Perhaps this oft-lamented explosion of violence in our media and visual culture is nothing more than a practice exercise for our new fear.

It cannot be denied: our world is

becoming more chaotic. This tendency toward chaos can partly be ascribed to the increasingly complex structure of our society. The network society – just think of the World Wide Web – is absolutely not hierarchical and ordered, but rather fickle, 'rhizomatic'. The new imperial world order conceived by the American think tank Project for the New American Century (PNAC) and being implemented by the Bush administration plays upon this increasingly chaotic world and the disintegration of states.[4] And this brings us to the very latest fear: the fear of terrorism.

4. See http://www.newamerican-century.org. See also http://www.brusselstribunal.org.

6 Fear of Terrorism

On the one hand, disillusionment with a globalization that has for the most part passed them by and bitterness within Islamic communities about the Middle East policy of the United States have created fertile ground for terrorism. On the other hand, the hegemonic claims of the United States in general and the American war industry in particular require a strong perceived enemy. Following the collapse of the Soviet Union, Bush Sr. gave the 'war on drugs' a try, but now the time is ripe for the real coup. Bush Jr.'s 'war on terrorism' is intended to bring about nothing less than a state of emergency, within America as well as on a planetary scale – within America through the curtailment of civil rights (Patriot Act), media manipulations, outright lies or censorship, outside America through the obliteration of the whole post-war system of international law, symbolized by the United Nations. This state of emergency is further demonstrated by refusing to recognize the International Court of Justice in The Hague, pulling out of the Kyoto accords and installing camps all over the world that are outside any legal jurisdiction, of which Camp Delta at Guantanamo Bay is but the most well-known. In their famous report *Rebuilding America's Defenses* in 2000, the PNAC, whose members include American administration officials Donald Rumsfeld, Paul Wolfowitz and Dick Cheney, wrote that their plans could not be implemented without, and I quote, 'a catalysing catastrophic event – a sort of new Pearl Harbor'. After 9-11, which must have been a godsend to them, they were finally able to implement their plans. What were these plans? The PNAC's objectives are unequivocal: achieving a ubiquitous military presence through a technologically revolutionized military; preventing the emergence of a competing superpower and waging preventive wars against any power that might threaten American interests. The best catalyst for the PNAC programme is fear. The American political scientist Benjamin Barber has since given the new America and the new imperial world order a particularly apt name: 'fear's empire'.[5]

Yet the state of emergency is sadly not a spectre that will vanish after the nightmare of the neo-conservative Bush administration; martial law is being imposed everywhere. The measures contemplated by the city authorities in Rotterdam to make the city 'liveable' again, namely by

5. Benjamin Barber, *Fear's Empire: War, Terrorism, and Democracy*, New York/London 2003.

barring any new migrants and poor people (people under a certain income), because the city already has too many migrants and too few well-to-do citizens, are a sign of the times. The proposal is of course to a certain extent a consequence of the Pim Fortuyn effect and was in fact put forward by his party, Leefbaar Rotterdam ('Liveable Rotterdam') but it was approved by the entire city council – and knowing the Netherlands, this is surely not composed only of racists or extremists. Although it is a direct violation of the right of any citizen to choose his or her place of residence within a certain country, it cannot therefore simply be swept off the table as absurd. It shows that people, in this case a city administration, for the most part democrats wary of offending voters, feel compelled, correctly or not – that can be debated at length – to opt for drastic measures and are evidently prepared to carry them out as well. Such emergency measures are a sign that we find ourselves in a sort of state of emergency – or at least that we are moving in that direction faster than we had anticipated.

The world is becoming more inhospitable all the time, and thus we shall have to learn to live with our new collective fear. And we must take care not to use this as a poor counsellor, but rather as a signal to carefully examine the causes of the fear and to draw careful but resolute conclusions – not become paralyzed or panicked, for that, as everyone knows, is the most dangerous of all reactions in a situation of genuine danger. And there is, unfortunately, genuine danger.

Postscript: Futurology of an Ancient Anger

To be angry is to no longer be afraid. I can only hope that humanity will become angry and say 'no' to exploitation, to illegal wars, to crimes against international law, to limitations on free expression of opinion through the monopolization of the media (Murdoch, Berlusconi) or through outright lies and censorship (the Bush administration), to the curtailment of fundamental civil rights (the Patriot Act), to the ecological catastrophe we are headed for with open eyes, to poverty around the world, to the cynicism with which the New Imperial World Order is outfitting global neo-capitalism with its attendant political structure, in short to the state of emergency. We must stand up against 'the empire of fear'. Otherwise the battle between freedom and fear will indeed be long and difficult.

In October 2004 NAi Publishers will publish Lieven De Cauter's *The Capsular Civilization. The City in the Era of Transcendental Capitalism.*

Sean Snyder

Temporary Occupation, 2003

A Visual Essay by
Sean Snyder

In 2003, Sean Snyder (USA, 1972)
showed his project <u>Temporary
Occupation</u> (DVD, 4′ 33″, colour, sound)
as part of the 'Territories' exhibition at the Witte de With centre for
contemporary art in Rotterdam. The
military bases shown are temporary and
scattered all over the world. They are
enclaves offering all necessary facilities and services. They are
constructed and outfitted in such a
way that military personnel never need
to leave the base, creating an
illusion of security. For this

project, Snyder made a video using
images made available by the US
Department of Defense and its imagery
services. He mixed these images with
photographs by (former) residents and
with photographs he took himself of
decommissioned bases redeveloped by
local authorities. Snyder compiled
a selection of photographs and video
stills from this project especially
for <u>open</u>.

The term 'military installation' means a base, camp, post, station, yard, centre, homeport facility, ship, or any other activity under the jurisdiction of the Department of Defense.

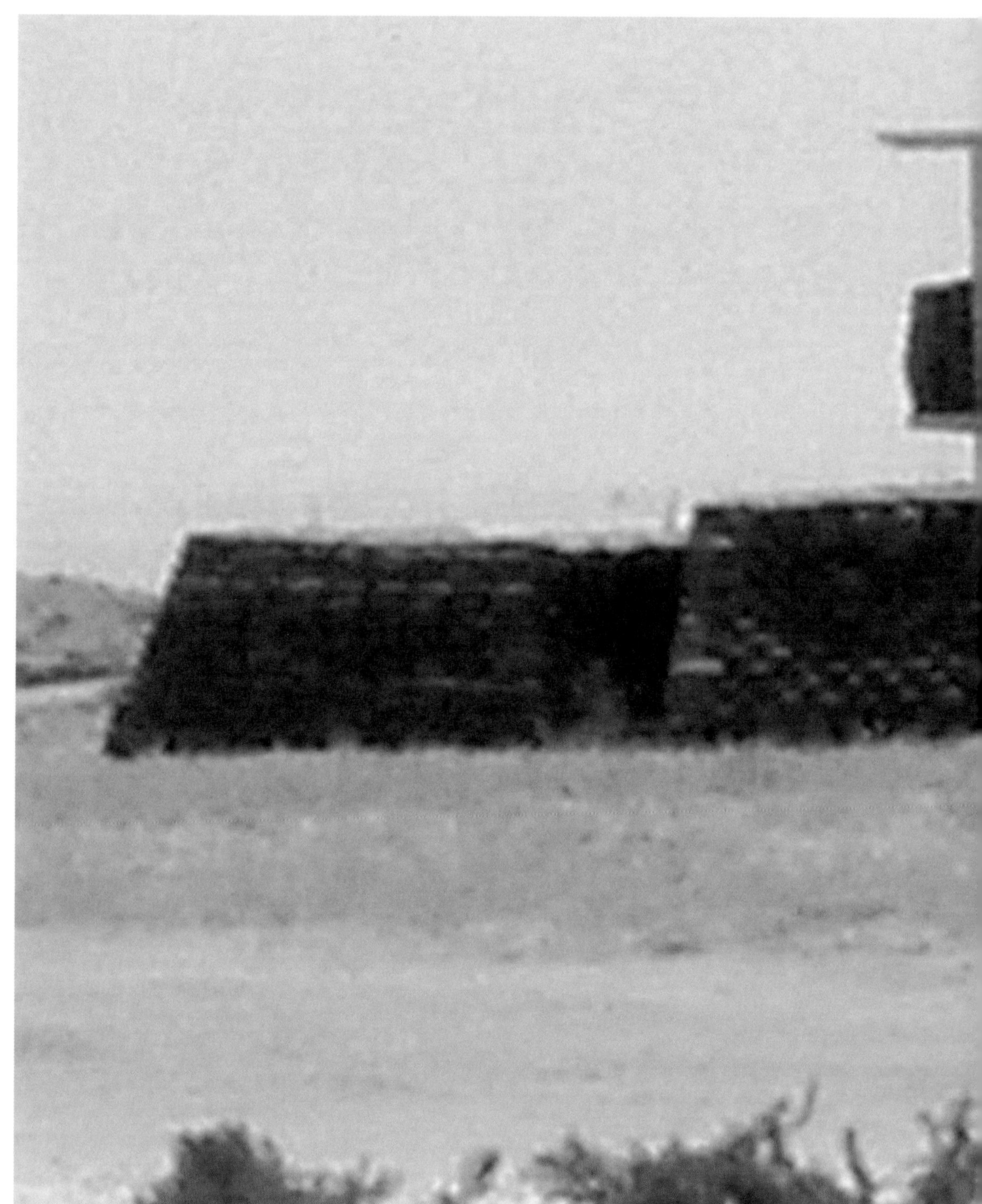

According to the Pentagon, the United States military currently maintains a presence overseas in 93 countries, forming a network of American dependencies. The existence of some bases is only speculated. Photo globalsecurity.org

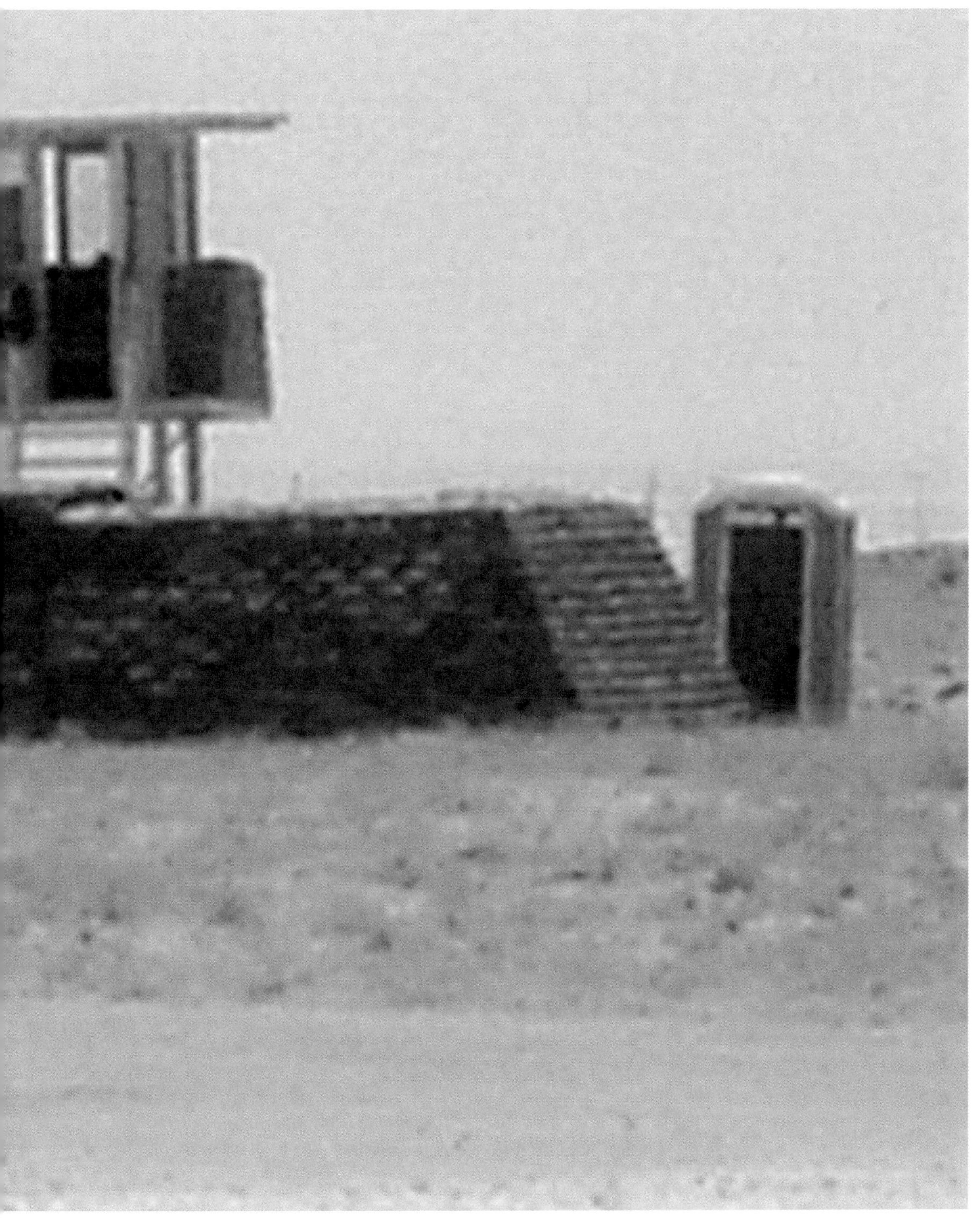

Private commercial intelligence companies that analyse geo-political
currents are contracted by the US government to scope out prospective
base locations in Eastern Europe, the former Soviet Republics in Central

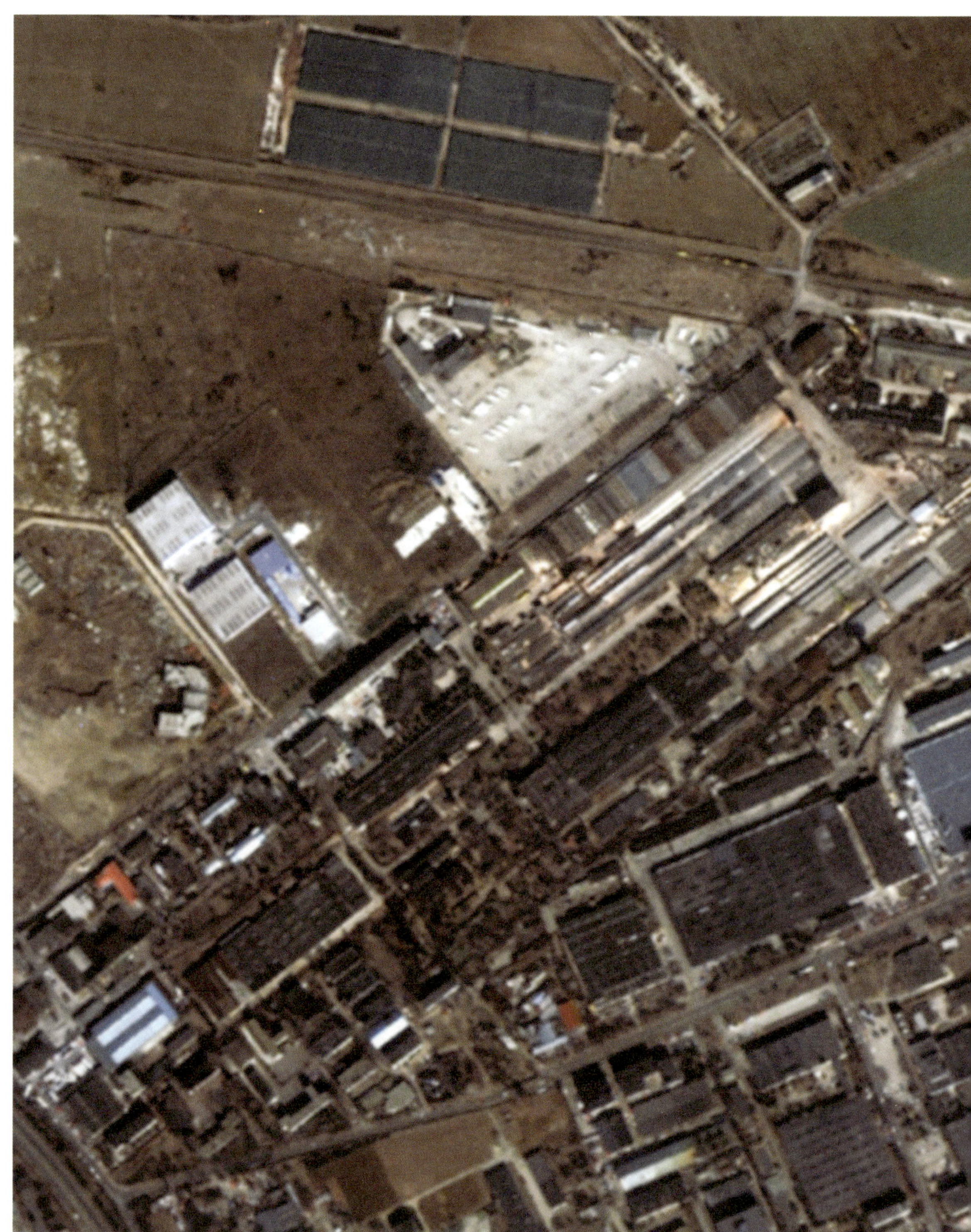

Asia and elsewhere. America subsidizes and invests in local resources
and products in exchange for space and infrastructure.
Photo Ikonos/Space imaging Inc.

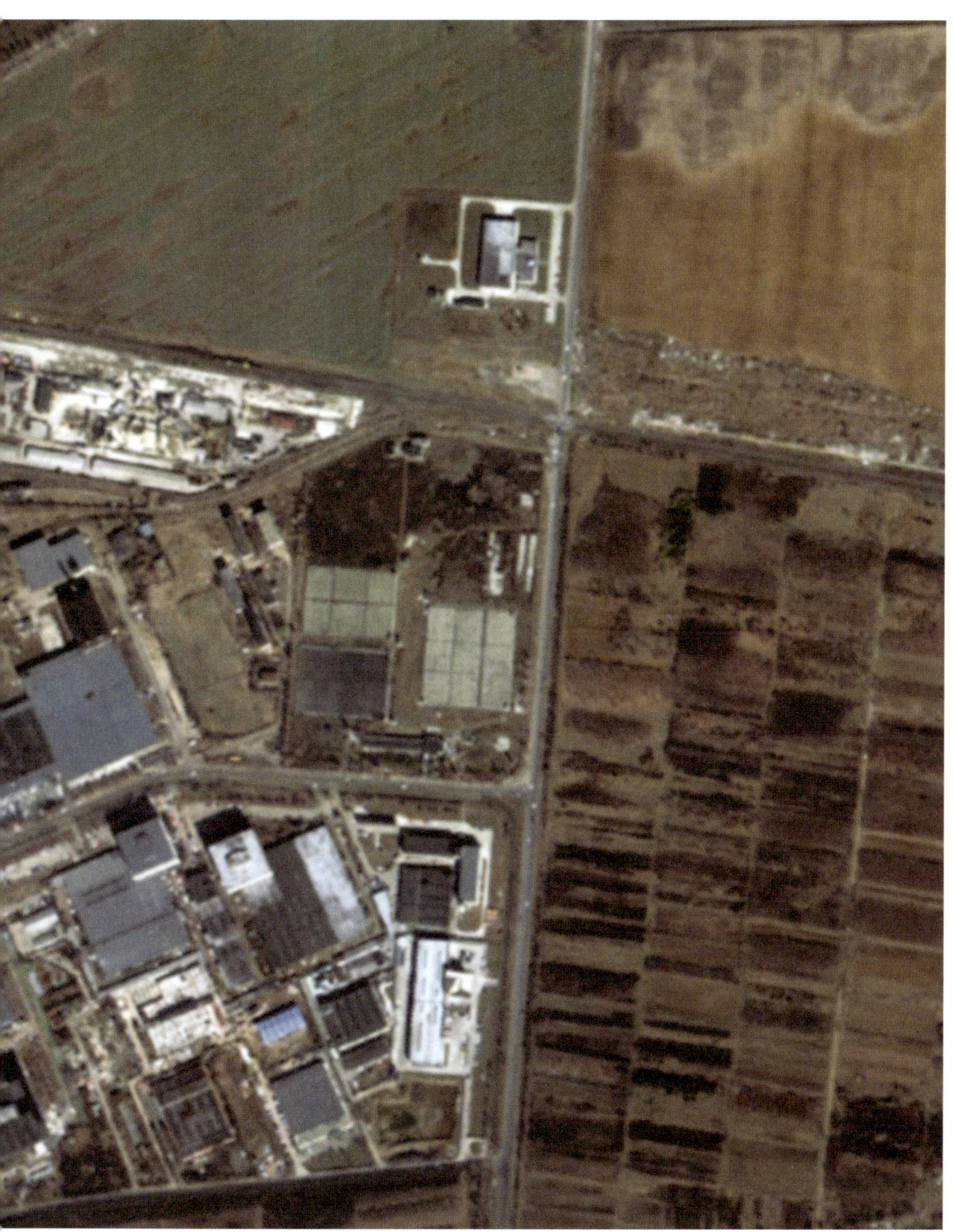

Detailed satellite imagery charts the processes of military worldwide.
In US government circles, there is open concern about military security

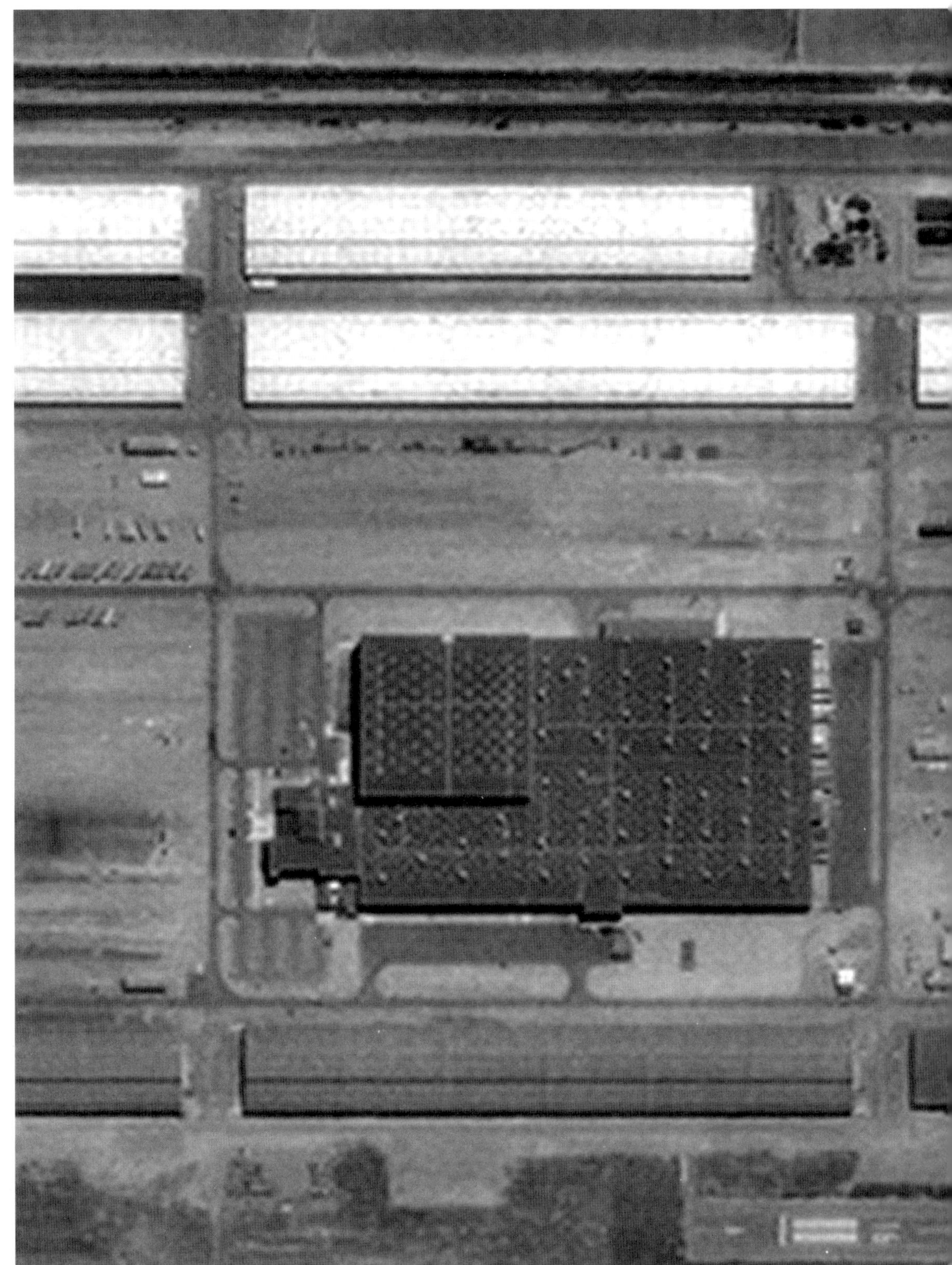

because of the democratization of imagery. Photo Ikonos/Space imaging Inc.

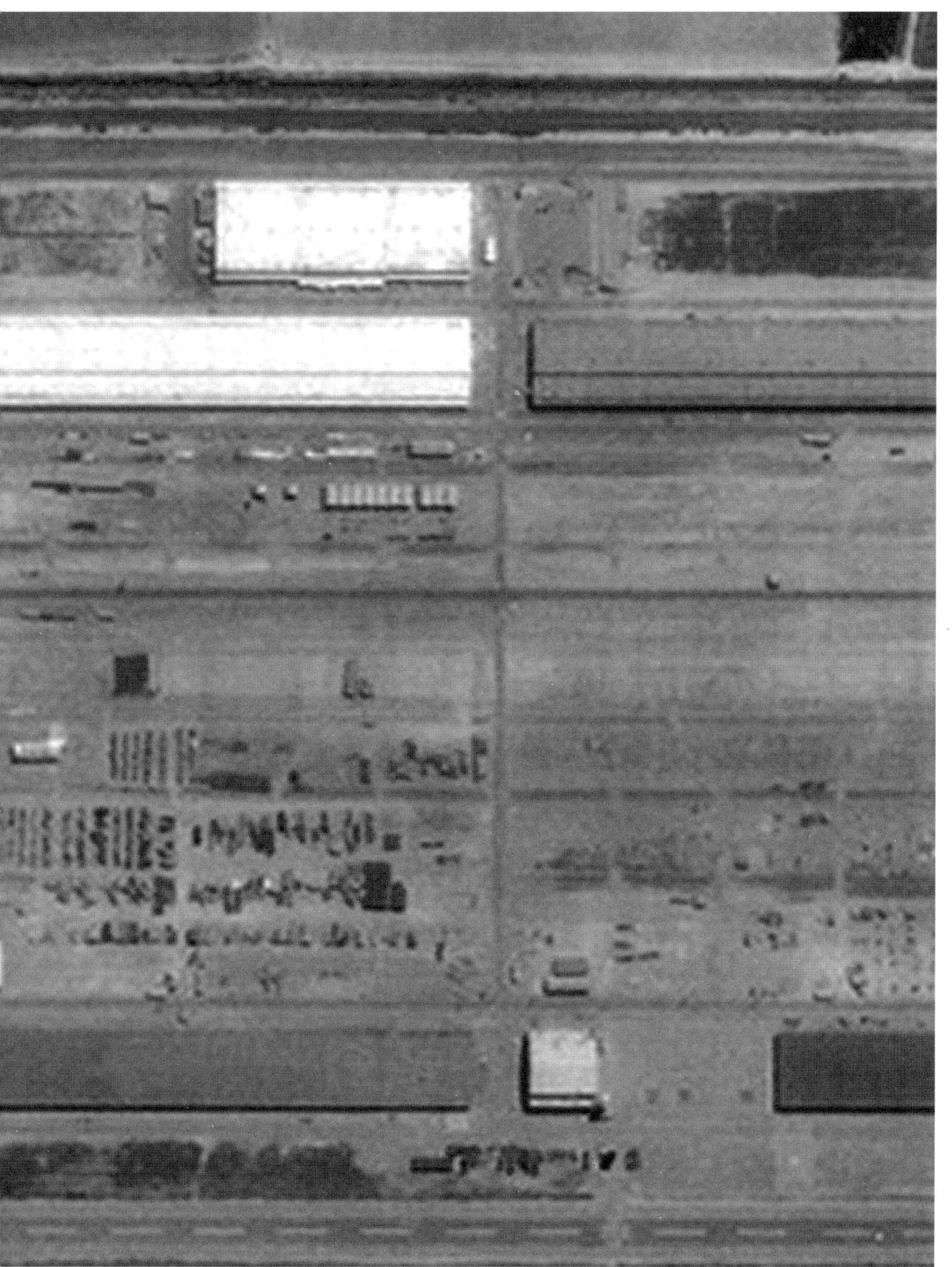

Highly edited documentation of what goes on inside of the bases are made
public through official agencies responsible for the diffusion of
imagery, like CENTCOM, the Defense Visual Information Center, and

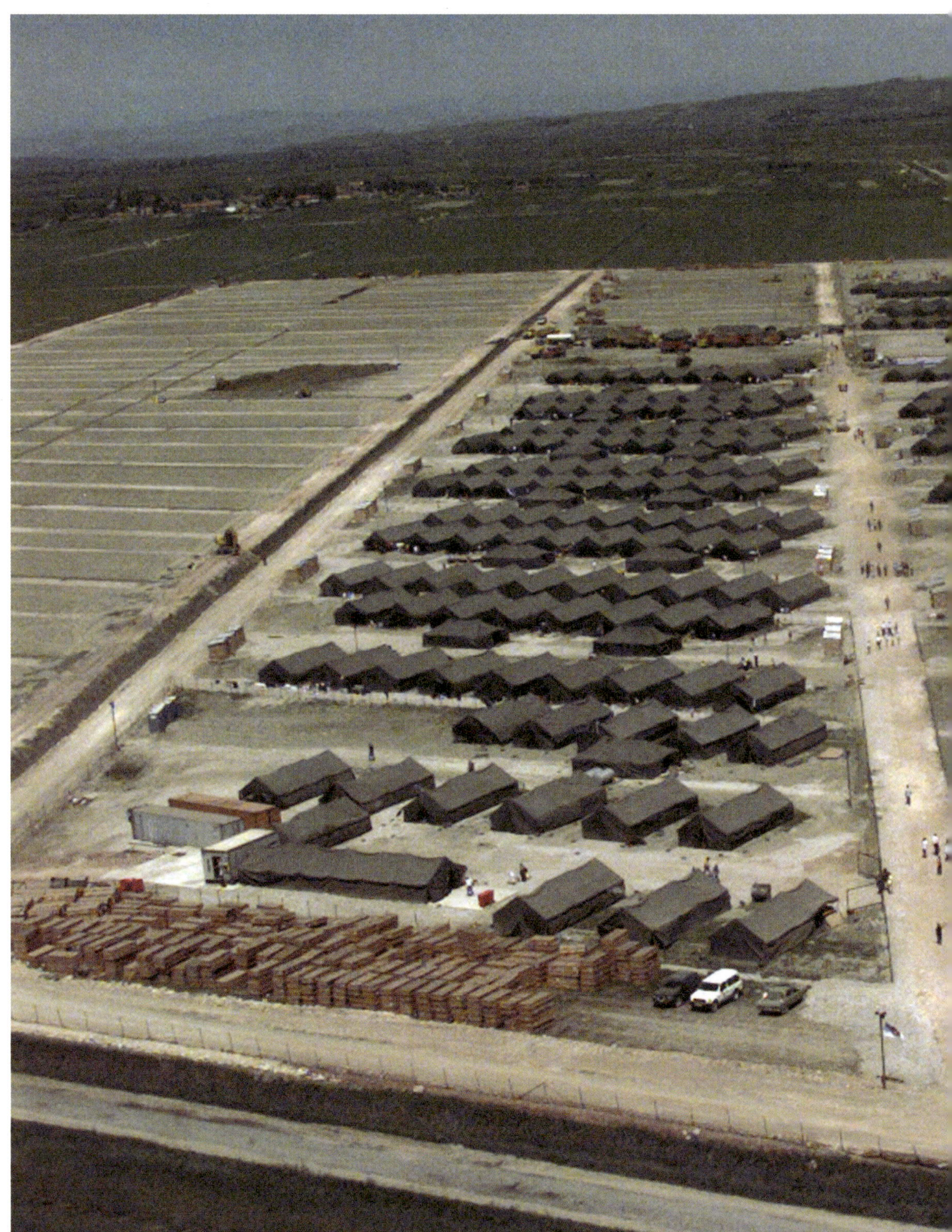

various branches of the armed services. Photo Department of Defense
Visual Information Directorate

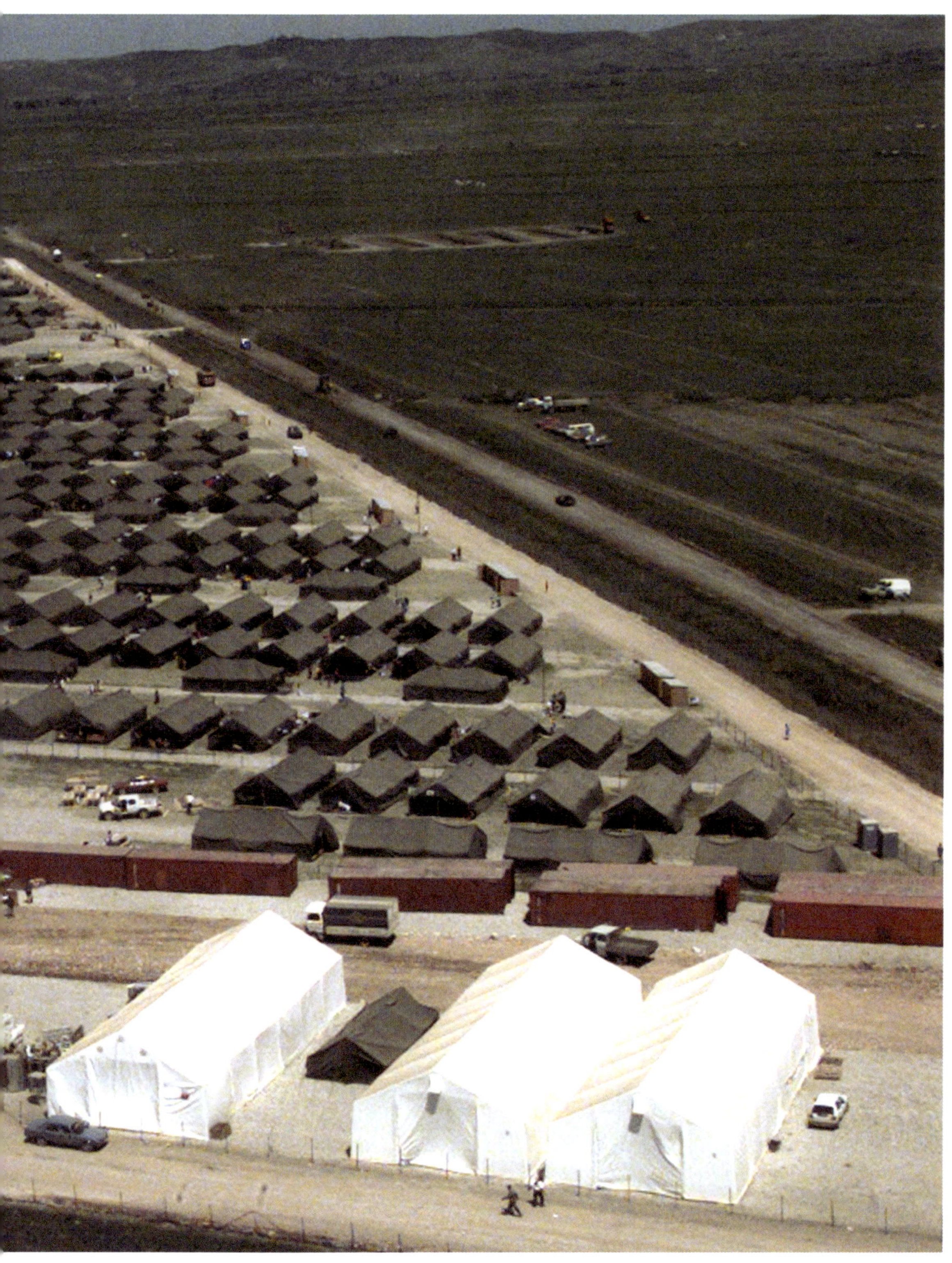

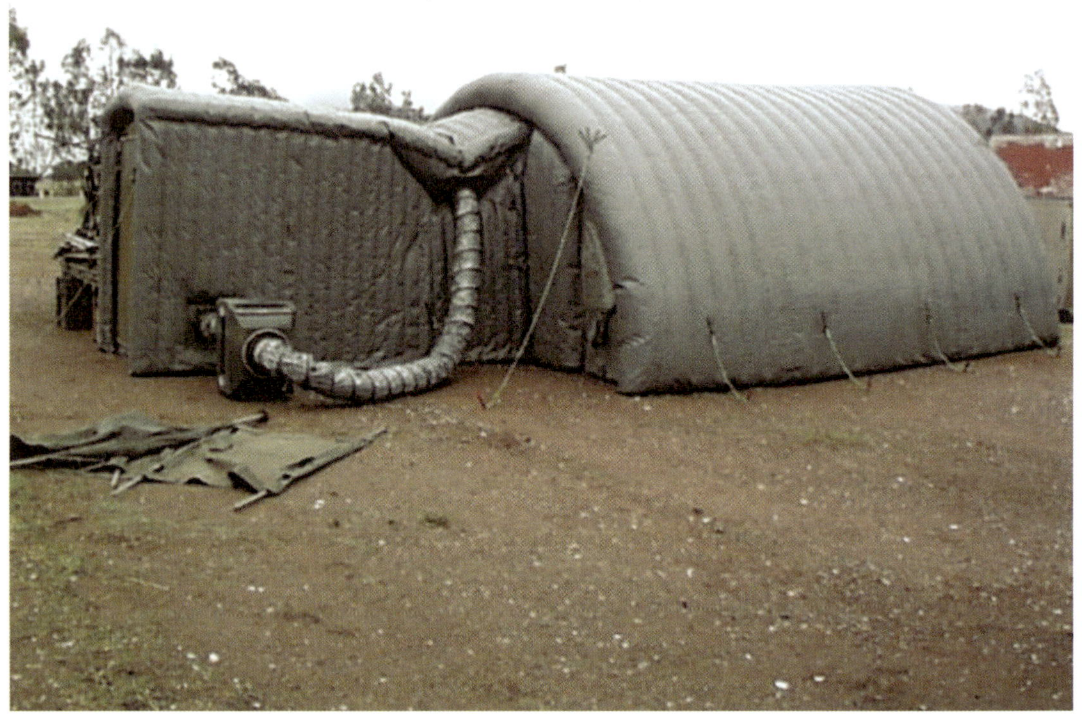

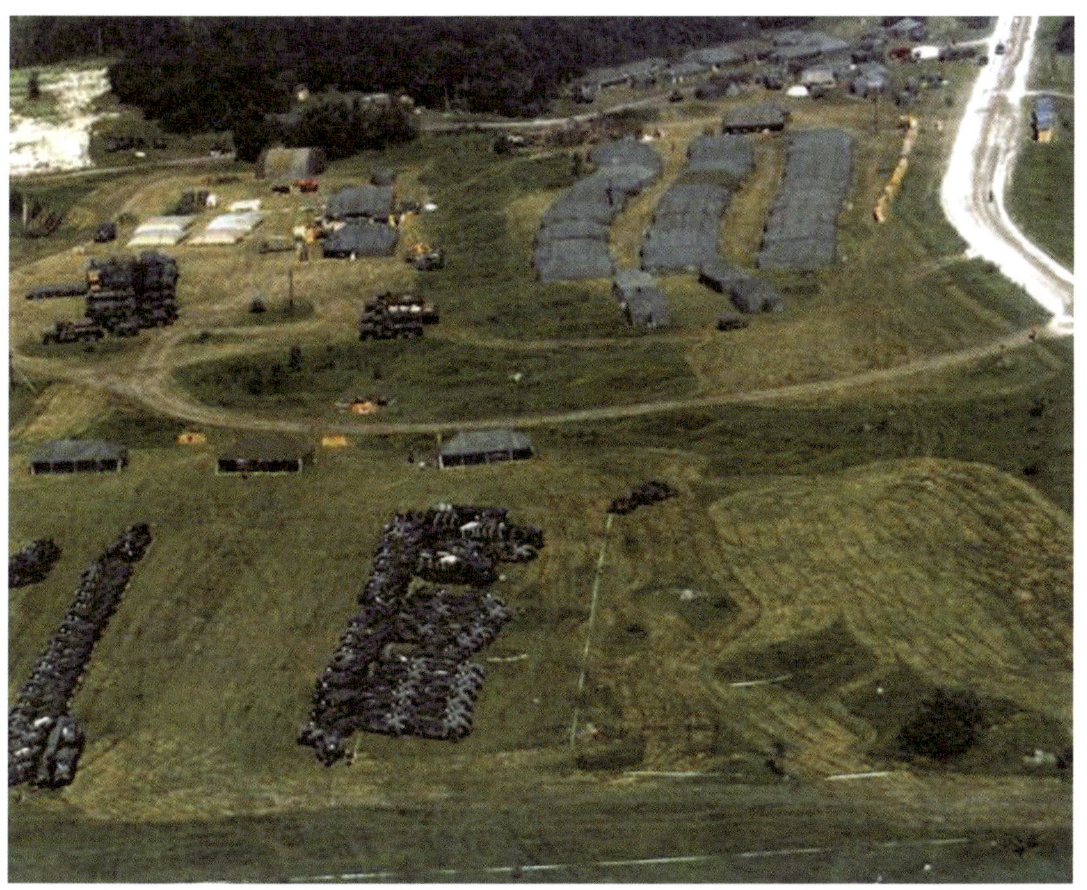

The Army and Air Force Exchange Service operates a number of service industries that make it unnecessary for a soldier to ever leave the base. The vast majority of money paid to American soldiers and civilians is spent in the on-base shopping and social facilities. Before the end

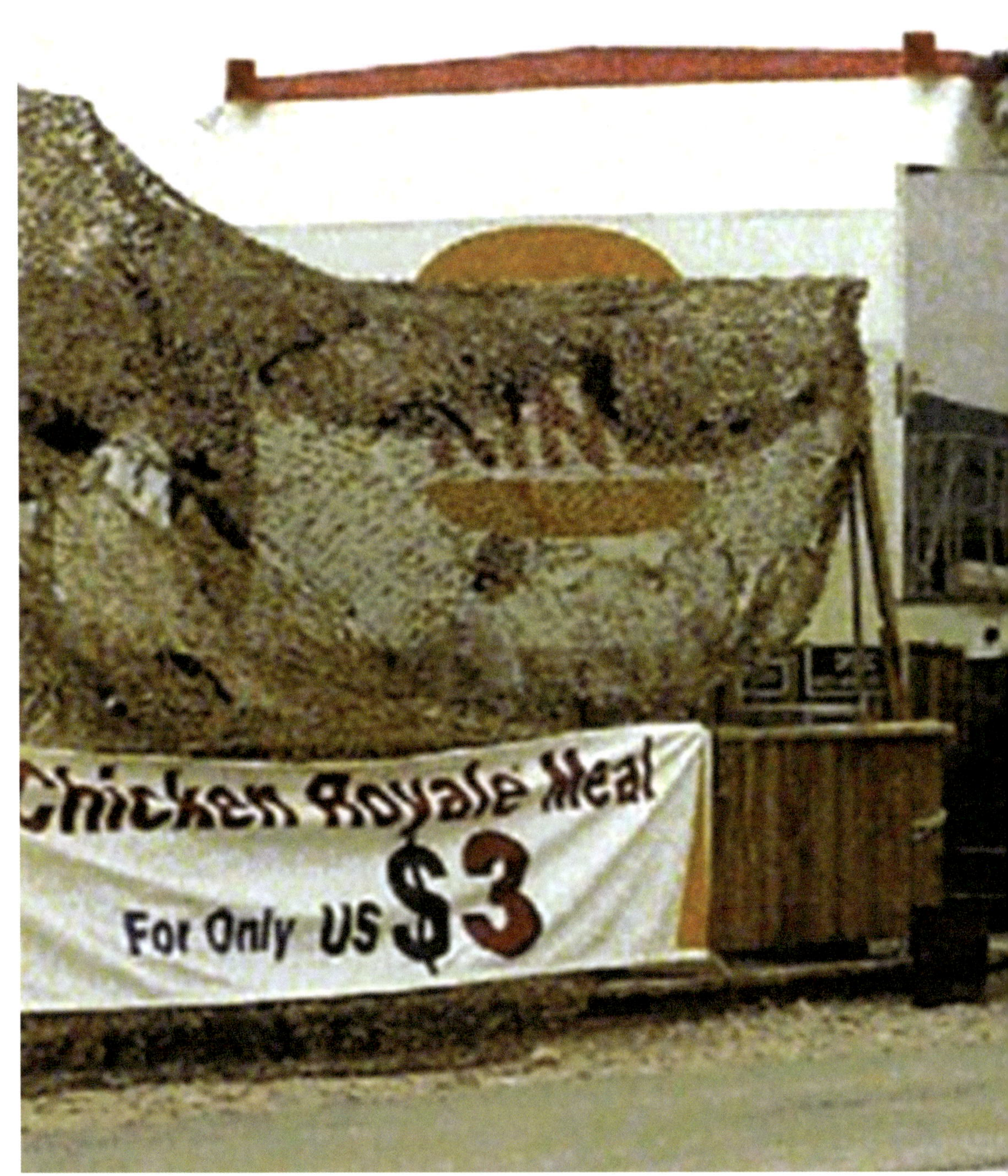

of the Cold War, US forces started using American contractors rather than local suppliers. Tax money spent inside the military facilities is meant to return to the US economy. Photo globalsecurity.org

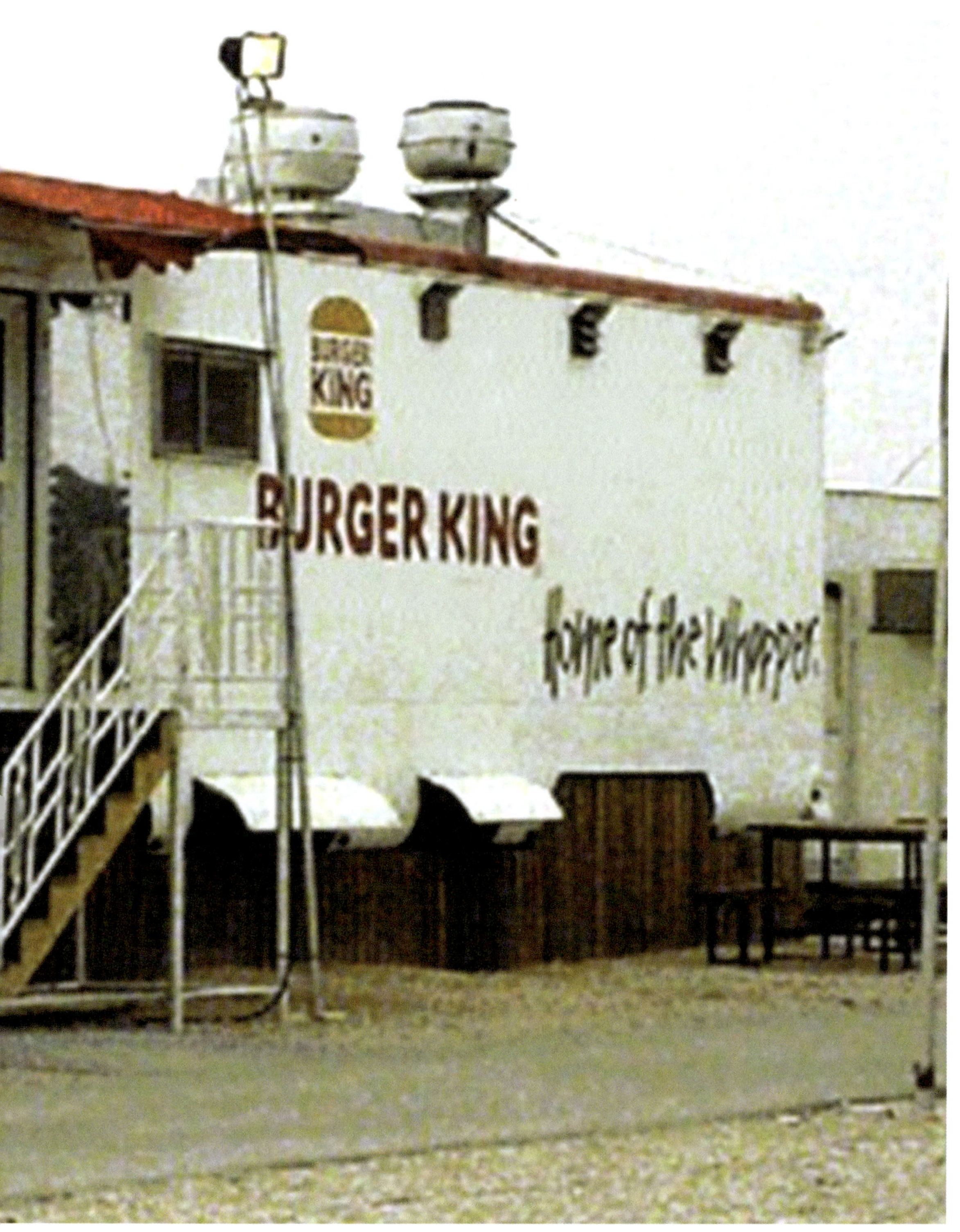

Many US military bases, containing enclaves of housing, commercial and recreational facilities, are temporary oases for military personnel within secure boundaries. To insulate personnel from the potential

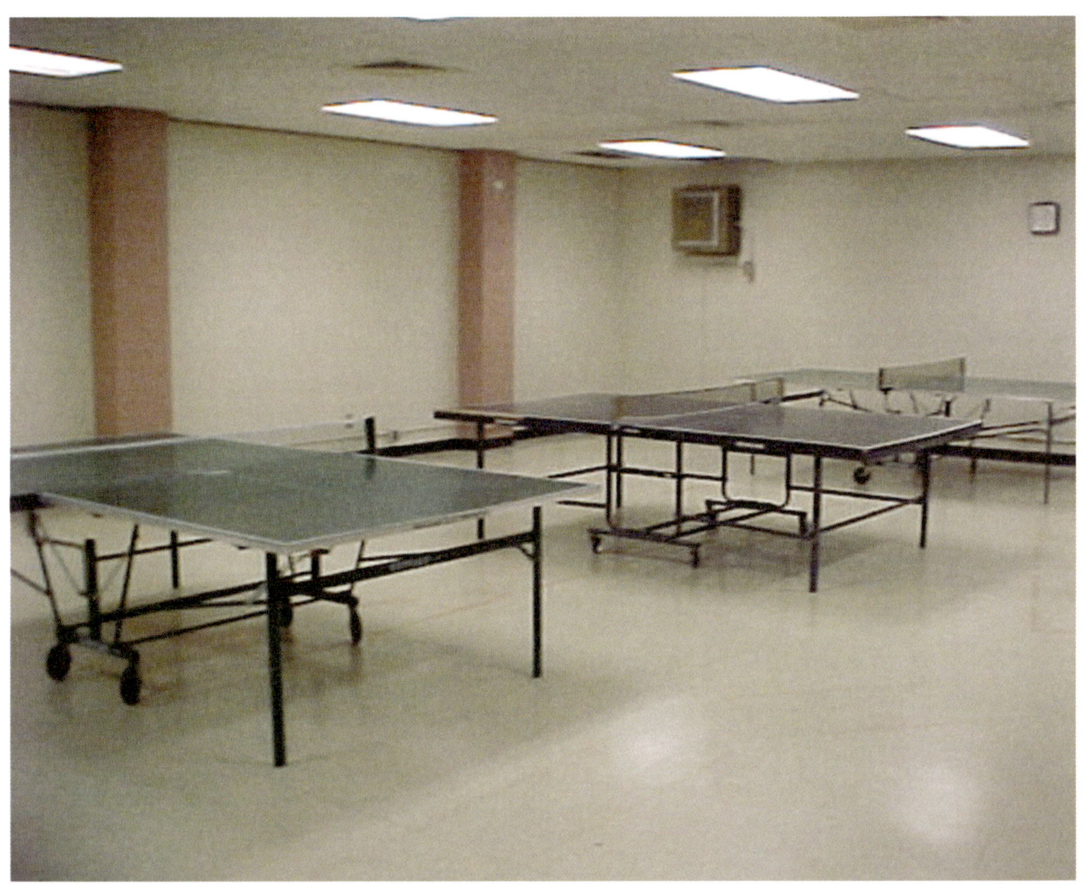

culture shock of overseas duty, the physical structure of the bases as well as the amenities and services are built in a way that is familiar to them. Photos globalsecurity.org

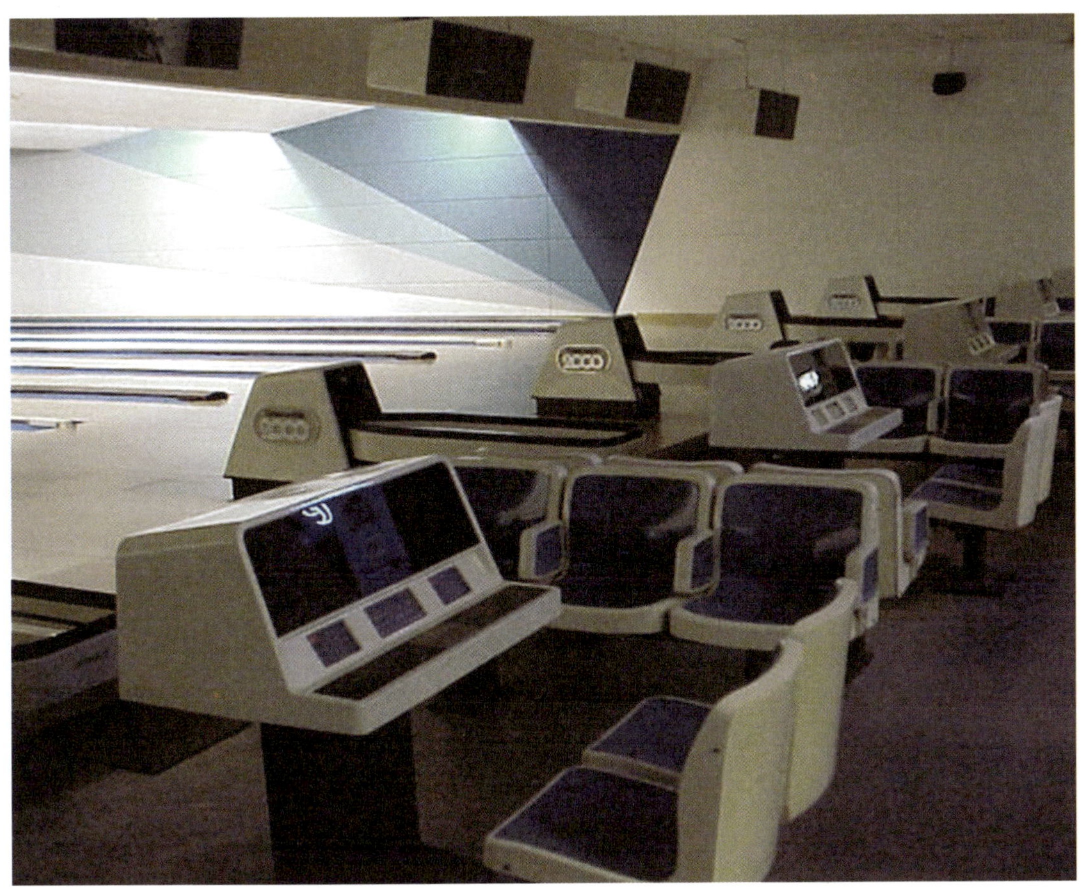

Media run by the military, such as AFN (American Forces Network),
broadcast television and radio programming wherever they go. The same

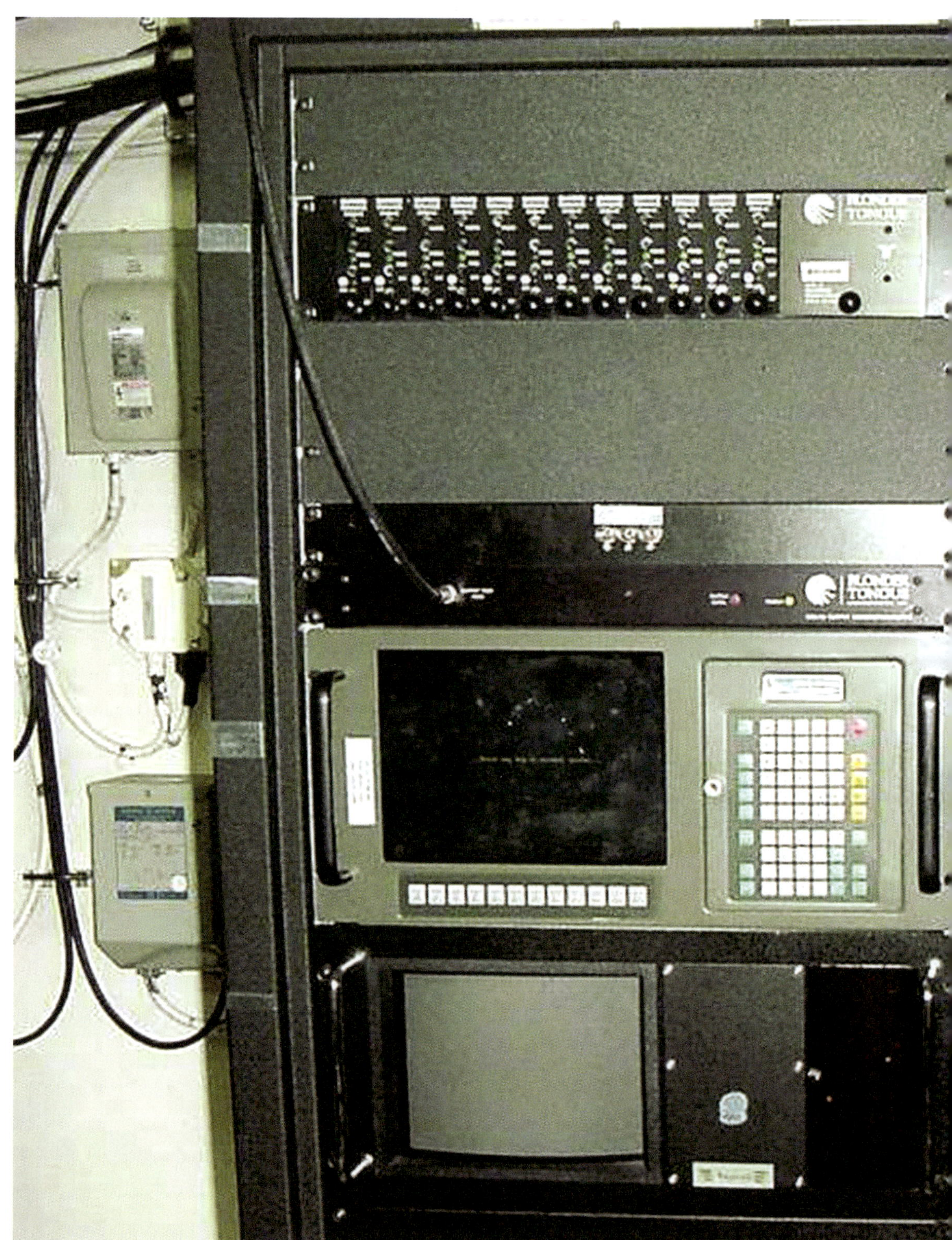

mobile/aerial broadcasting equipment used to entertain the forces can be used for psychological operations. Photo globalsecurity.org

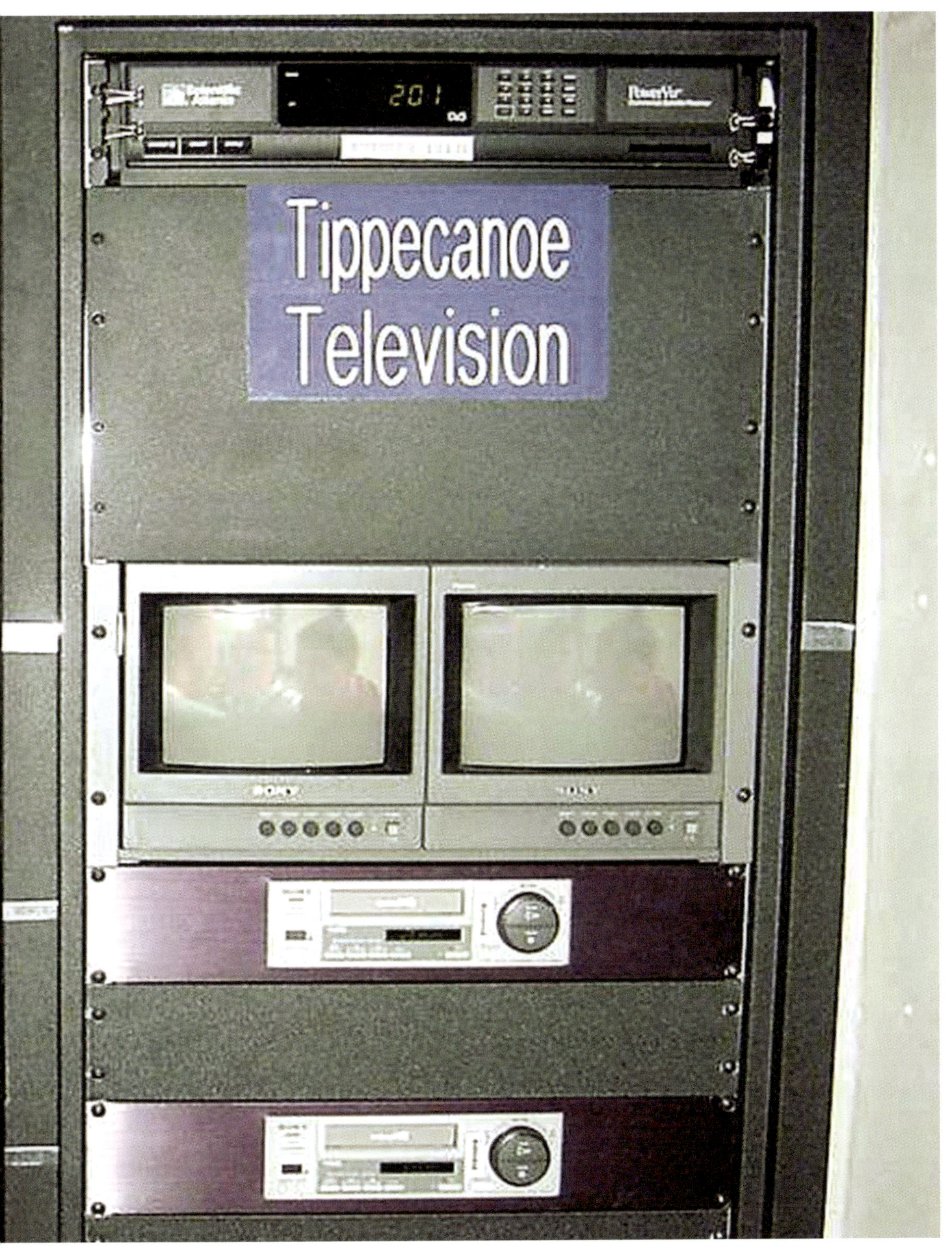

The post-usage restructuring of military bases poses a difficult problem as well as a secondary base industry. Bases that are returned to local authorities are redeveloped to new uses; an old officer's club might be used as a discotheque, fuel reserves might be used by a petroleum

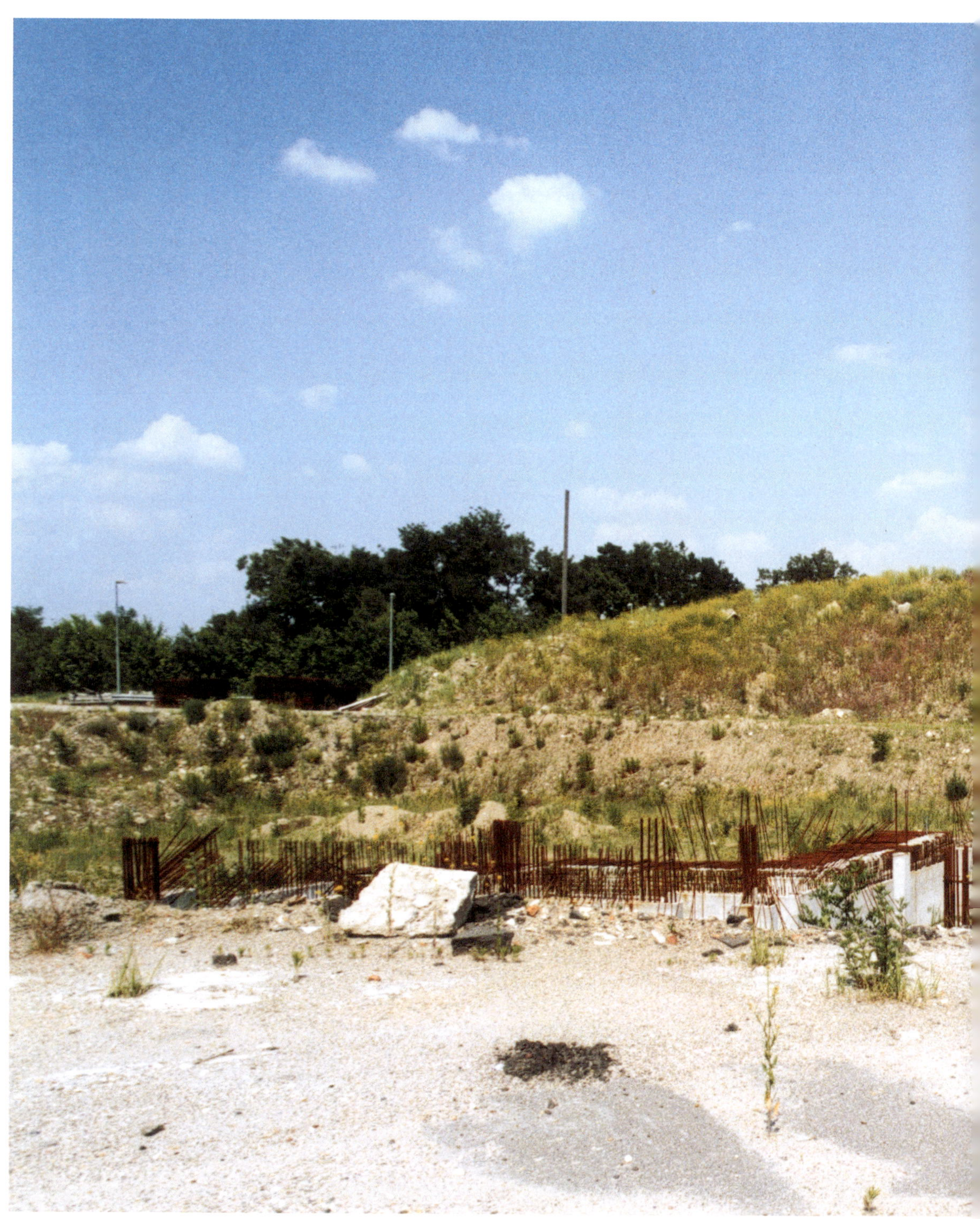

company, an airfield might be turned into a budget airline hub. Many facilities such as housing, administrative offices and storage areas may be reused immediately, while facilities like helicopter airfields and ammunition dumps lack realistic conversion options. Photo Sean Snyder

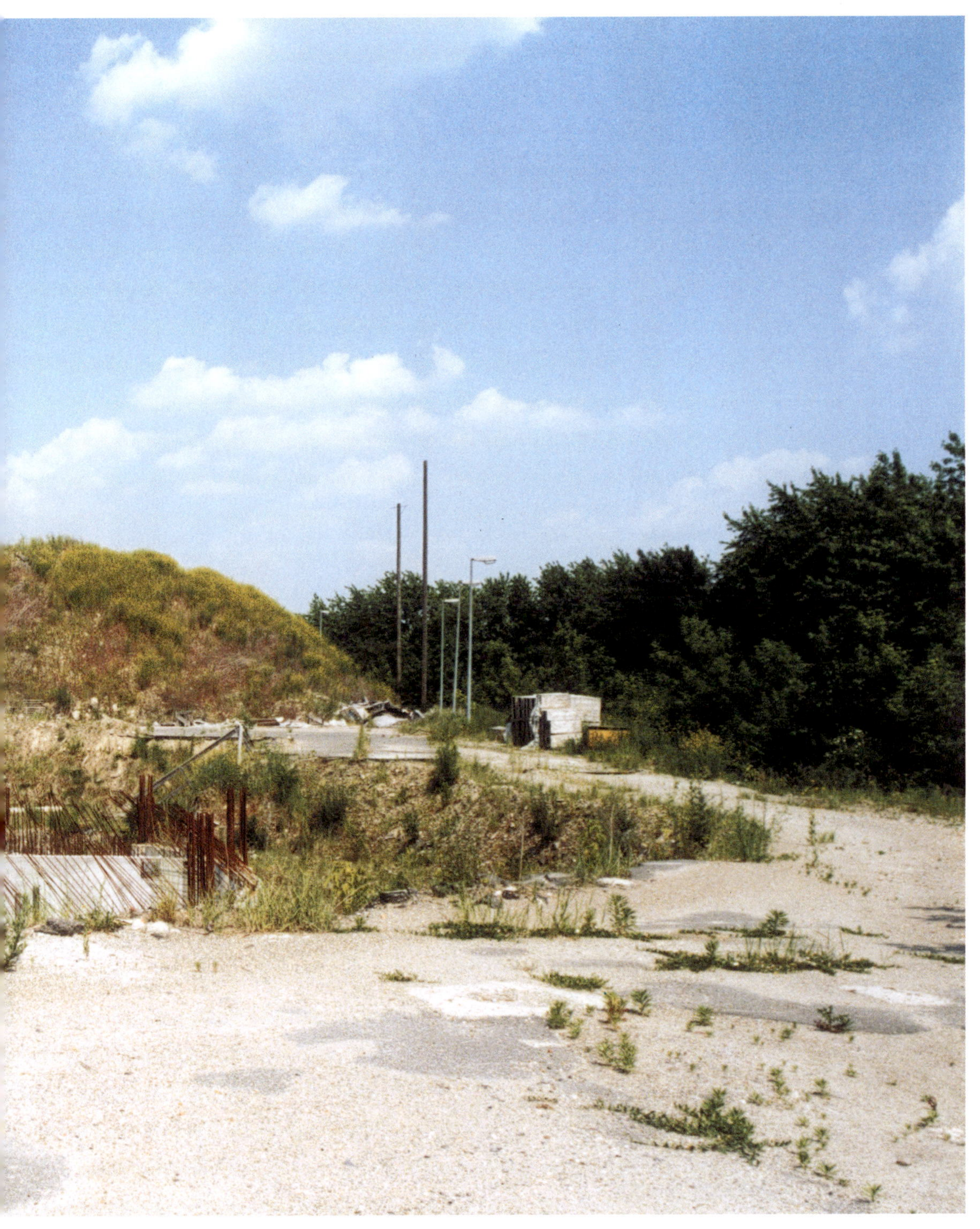

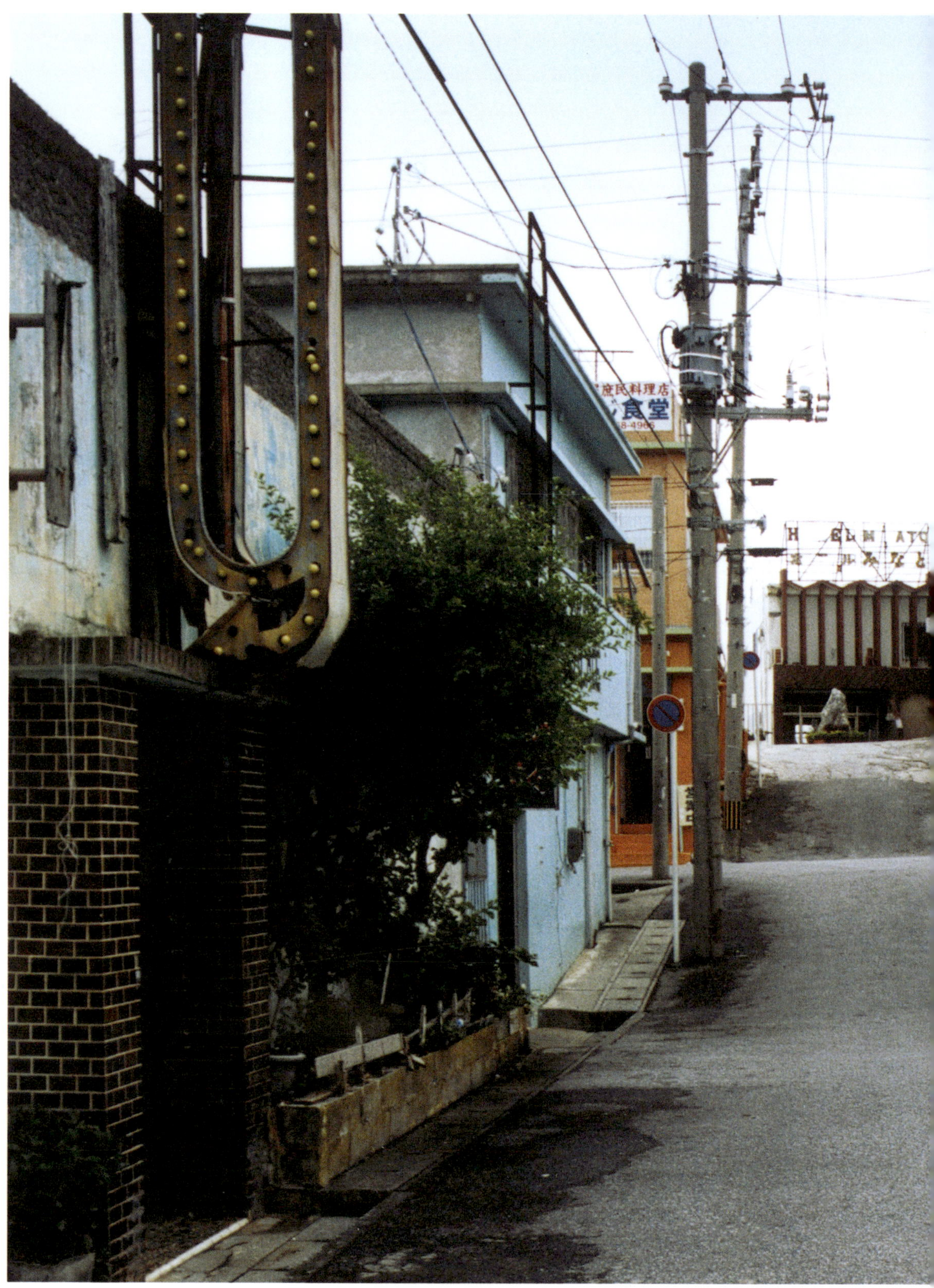

Photo Sean Snyder

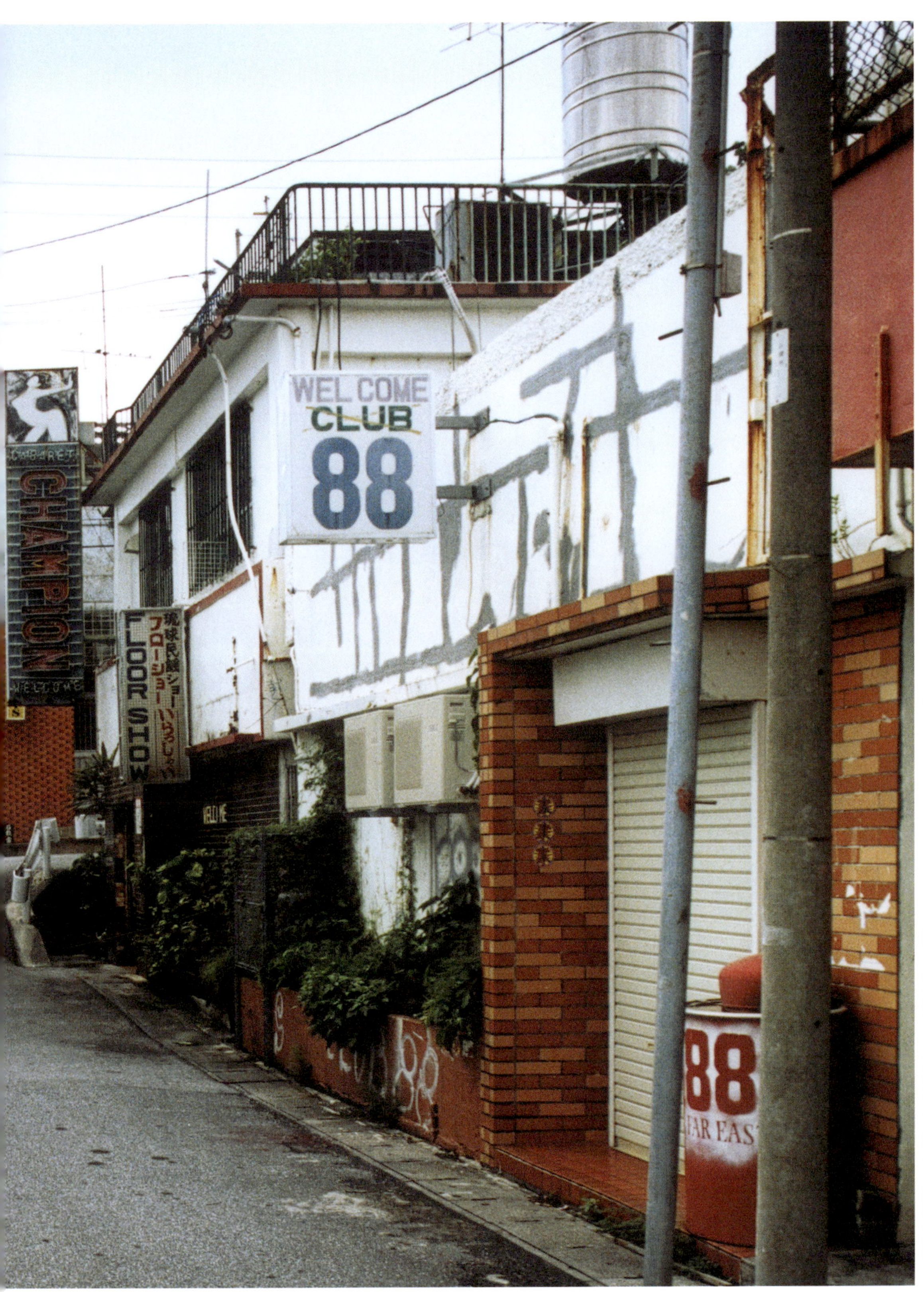

WEL COME
CLUB
88
CHAMPION
CABARET
WELCOME
FLOOR SHOW
琉球民謡ショー
フロージョー いらっしゃい
WELCOME
88
FAR EAST

- housing area
- library
- 24-hour gas station
- post office
- medical and dental clinic
- optical shop
- military clothing store
- clothing store
- sports store
- gift shop with local items
- theatre
- 24-hour cinema
- chapel
- off-base travel and entertainment
- hunting and fishing office
- safari park
- officers' club
- banquet and special event hall
- Armoured Division Museum
- commissary
- base exchange
- bakery
- deli
- Pizza Inn
- Taco Bell
- Burger King
- shwarma bar
- Popeyes Chicken & Biscuits
- Baskin Robbins
- pub
- service club
- shopette

**** SAMPLE LIST OF FACILITIES ON ****
***** AMERICAN MILITARY BASES *****

- laundry service
- bookstore
- Box Office video rental
- Toyland
- furniture store
- shoe department
- jewelry store
- Power Zone audio/video equipment
- entertainment and gaming equipment
- garage and auto accessories
- hobby shop
- flower shop
- garden centre
- basketball court
- volleyball courts
- men's sauna
- women's sauna
- swimming pool
- whirlpool
- aerobics centre
- fitness centre
- gym
- community arts & crafts
- games tent
- miniature golf course
- pool tables
- bowling centre
- shooting range
- golf course
- camp ground
- outdoor barbecue area

Thomas Y. Levin

Surveillance and the Ludic Reappropriation of Public Space

Based on the work of artists such as the Australian Denis Beaubois (1970), Thomas Y. Levin analyses the significance and the effect of the ever-expanding system of surveillance cameras in the public space. Through performances in the public space, Beaubois plays a game with security devices. In this way he has developed a strategy for turning the panoptic effect of security and surveillance by means of cameras and facial recognition software back upon itself.

Sometime in 1996 the Australian artist Denis Beaubois embarked on a series of performances which took place throughout the city of Sidney in public spaces marked by the more or less visible presence of the increasingly ubiquitous surveillance camera. Arriving on the scene three days in a row unannounced and without having solicited or received permission to do so, Beaubois simply positioned himself in direct view of the camera whose impassive gaze he returned in kind. Armed with an unusual capacity for willed immobility (thanks to training in Butoh performance technique), his ostentatious stasis and ocular fixity sooner or later provoked some sort of response. Sometimes it was so swift that Beaubois was 'escorted' off the 'public' premises only minutes after his arrival, the 'explanation' being that he was disturbing the peace, or lacked a permit, or some equally inconsequential – and symptomatic – bureaucratic banality. On other occasions, where his stoic performances were graciously (even if often uncomprehendingly) tolerated by the authorities, it was the passers-by who became engaged by his presence, interrupting their purposive passage to stare and inquire in an attempt to establish what exactly was going on.

What exactly *was* going on here? According to Beaubois, these performances – entitled *In the event of Amnesia, the city will recall…* – posed a series of questions to the site which explored the dynamic between what he calls the 'primary' and the 'secondary' audience. The primary audience, as in the classical performance situation, is the 'targeted' collective which is both willing and eager to watch and interpret. In the context of the *Amnesia* performances, this primary audience was, as Beaubois put it, 'the surveillance camera (or those who monitor them)'. The character of the spectatorship of this particular 'audience' – which will be dealt with at greater length below – is highly teleological: scanning the scene with a 'watchdog consciousness', it measures all behaviours against a template of norms and responds pre-emptively against any violations. For someone in its field of vision this means that by 'citing' any of the profiles in its database (by means of one's appearance – race, fashion, etc. – or behaviour) one can readily 'become' a suspect and provoke the system to focus its attention on oneself. In so doing, however, the apparatus could also be said to become part of the performance. For Beaubois the consequence of this proleptic character of surveillant observation (i.e. the fact that it already knows what it is going to see) is a mutually ideal condition: from the perspective of the camera, it effectively ensures that he will be read and attended to as suspicious; and from the point of view of the performer/suspect, it guarantees that he will be accorded an attentive and vigilant audience.

But if the camera and/or camera-operator and the 'suspect' are both part of a collaborative performance, for whom is this event taking place? Enter the notion of the secondary audience: this largely contingent and spectatorially uncommitted group is a function of the deeply transitory locales (malls, passageways, etc.) which were chosen as the performance sites. It consists of the chance community, passing by en route to various places and tasks, who find themselves fascinated by

Denis Beaubois, _Amnesia_ performance, Sydney, 1996 © DV Rogers

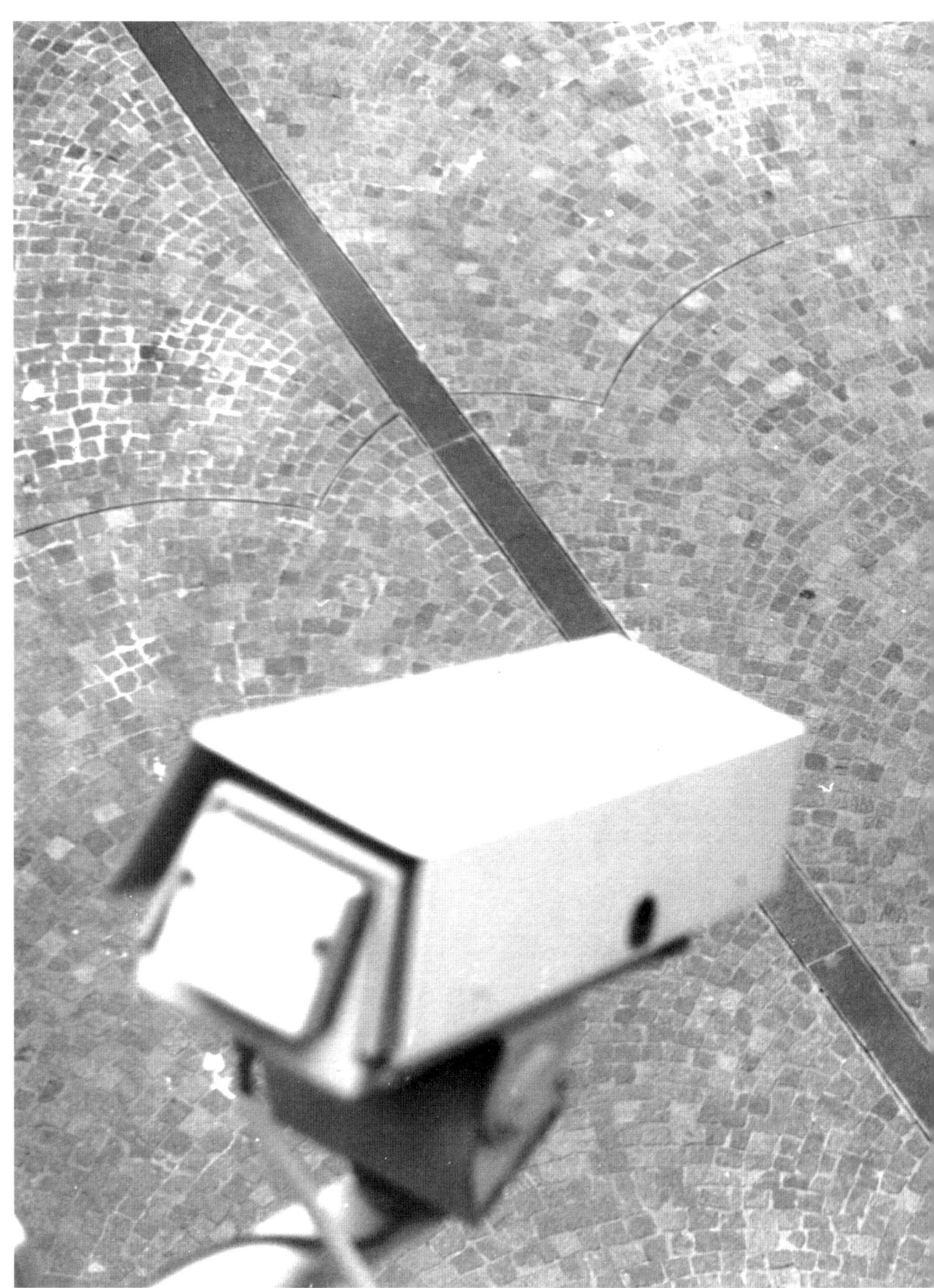

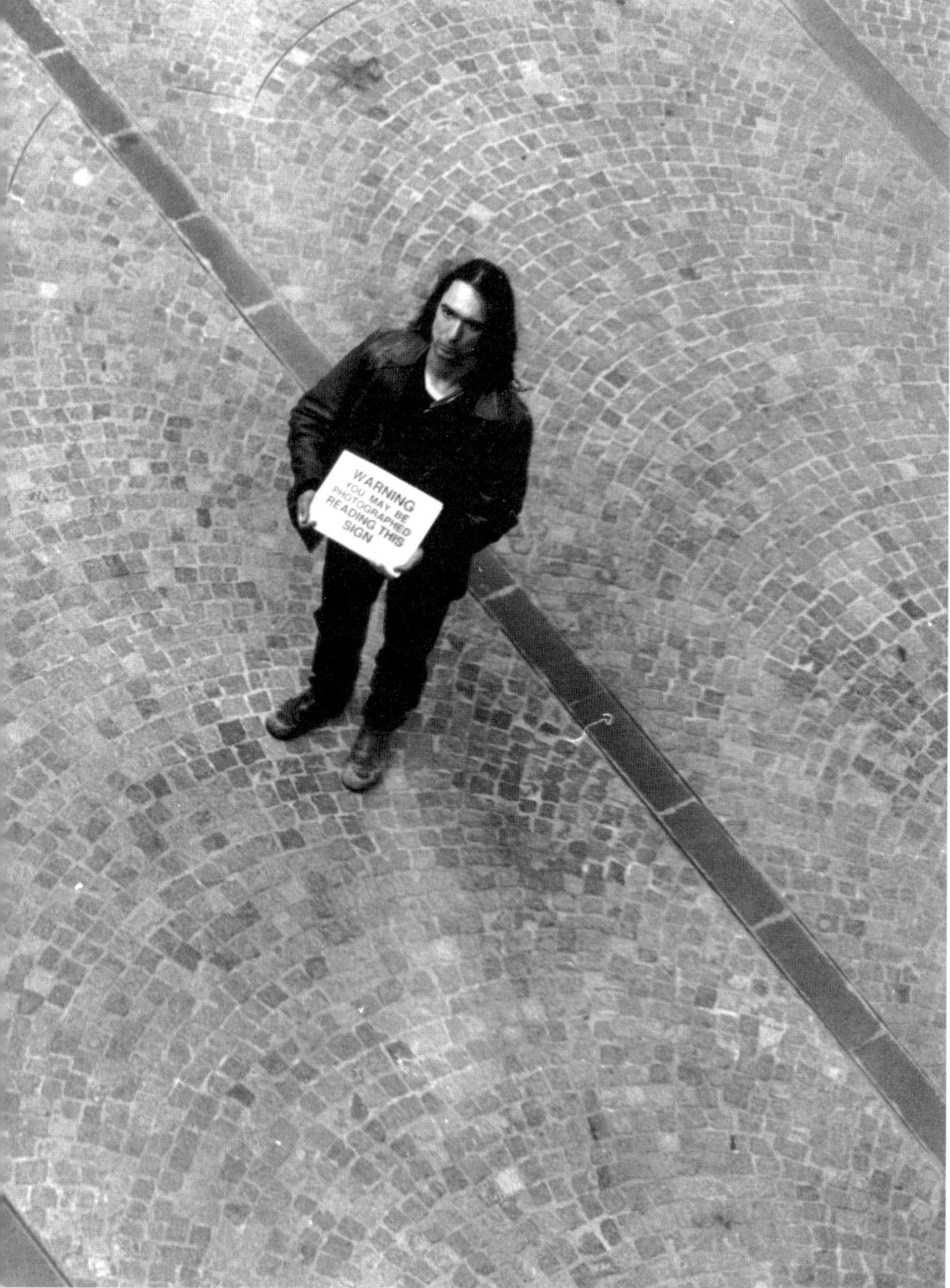

WARNING
YOU MAY BE
PHOTOGRAPHED
READING THIS
SIGN

Denis Beaubois, <u>Amnesia</u> performance, Sydney, 1996 © DV Rogers

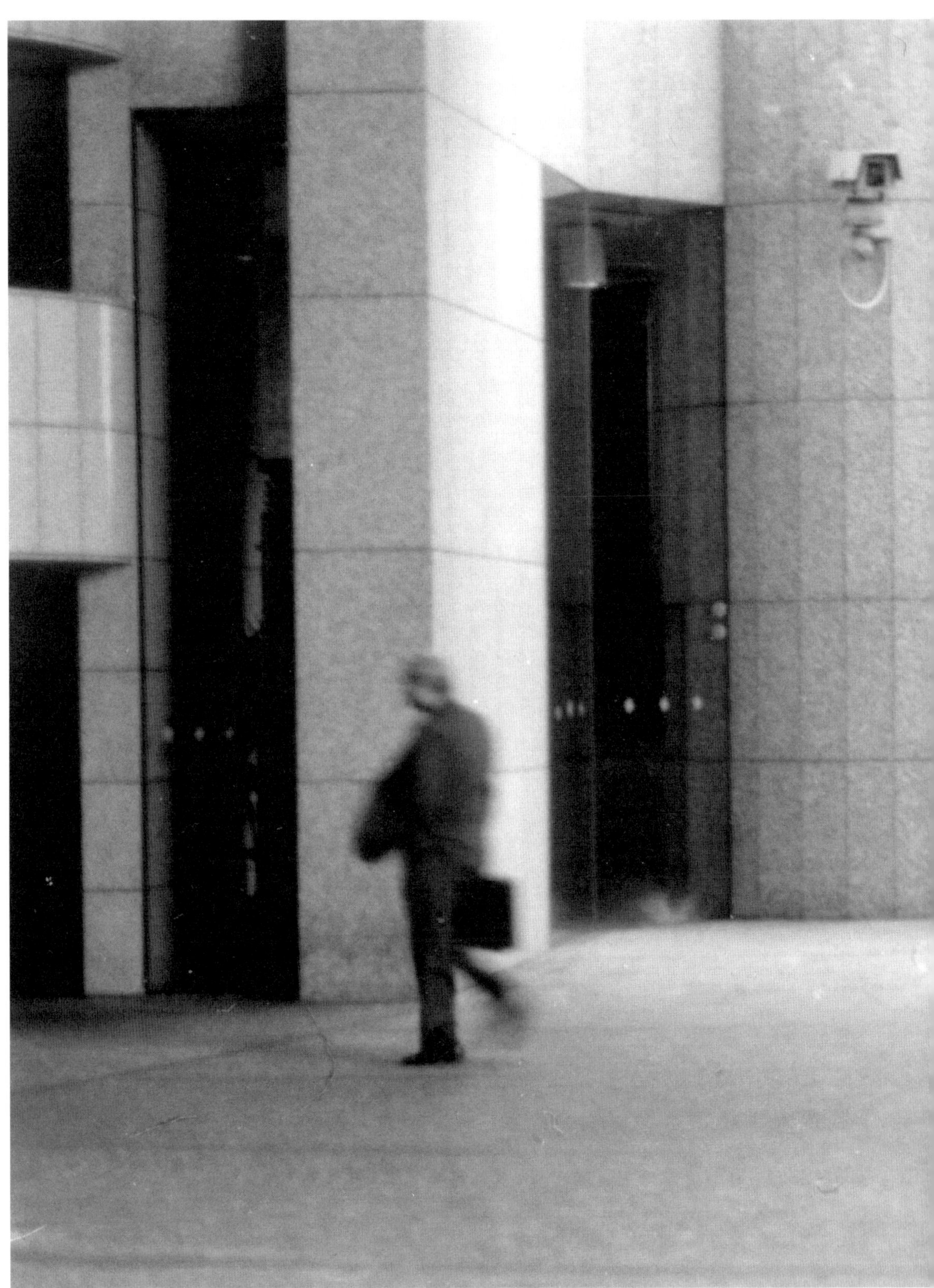

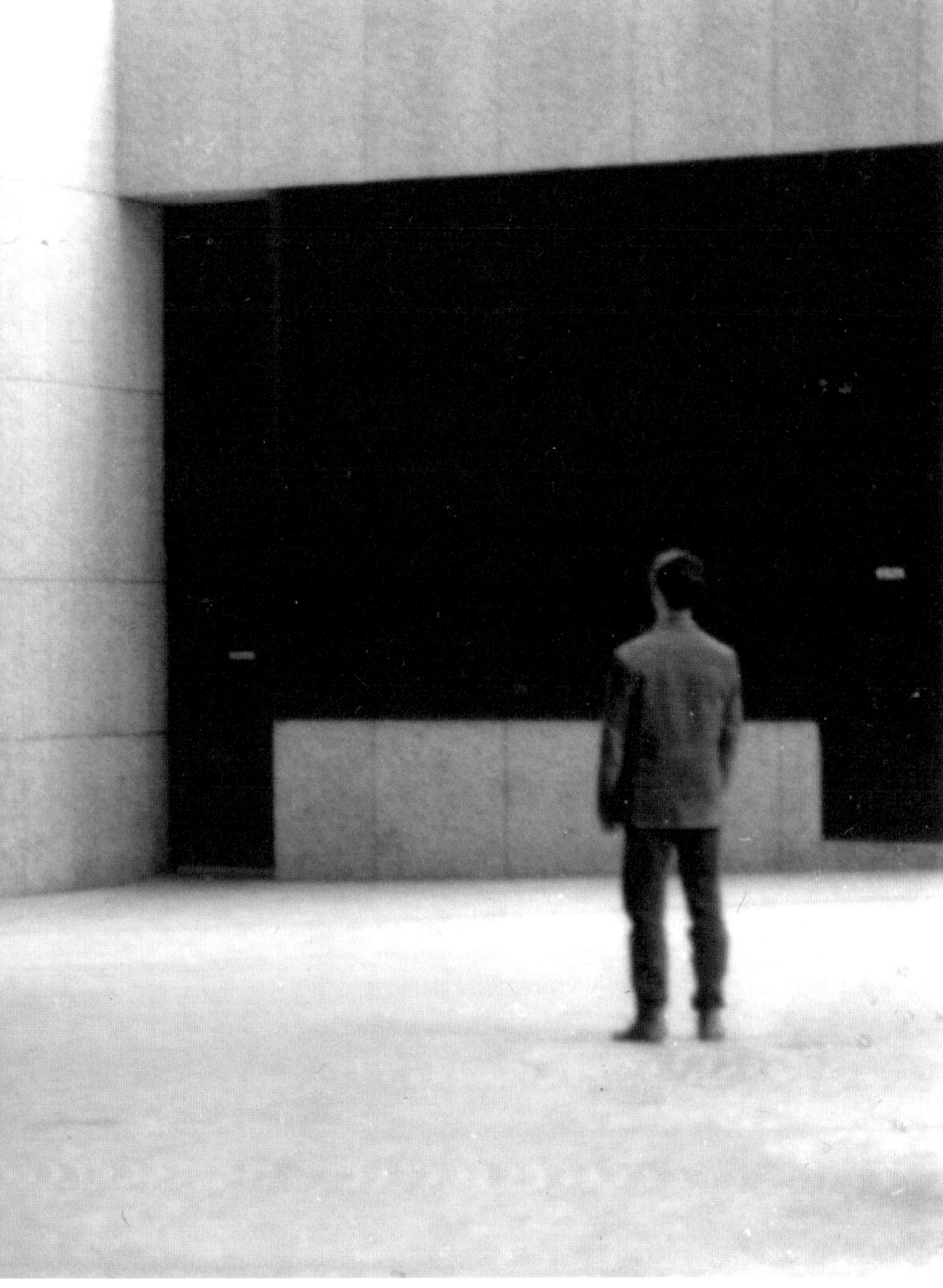

Stills from video of the <u>Amnesia</u> performance in Sydney, 1996, by Denis Beaubois

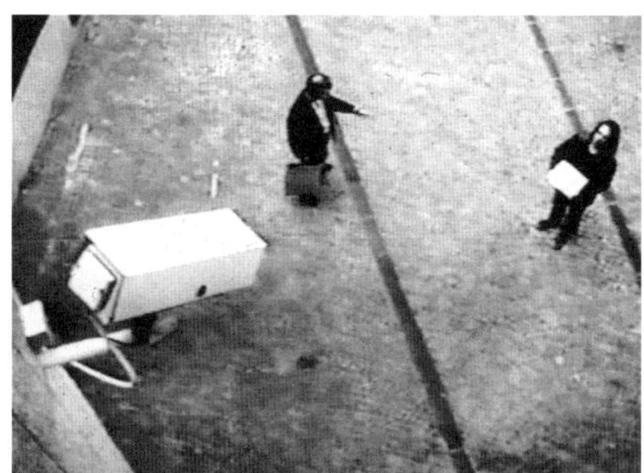

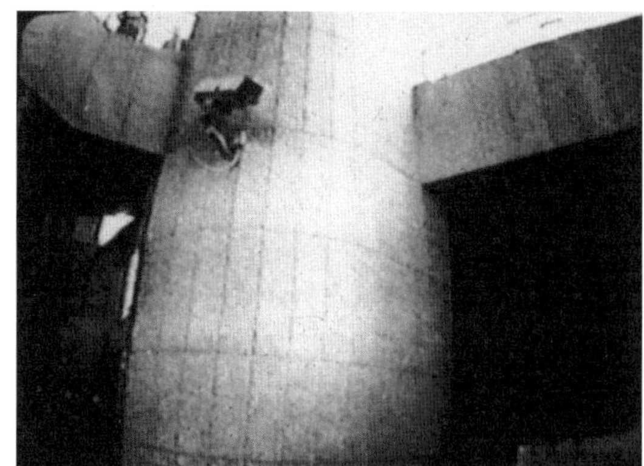

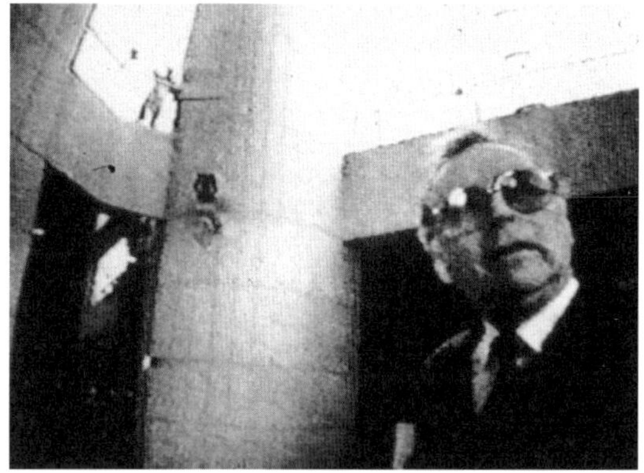

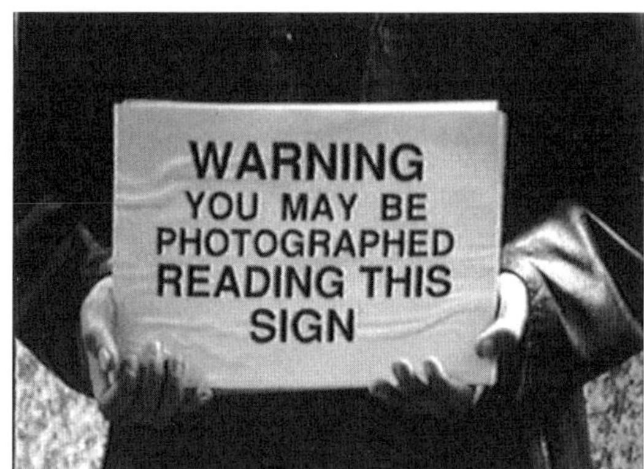

the curious spectacle and stop, if only for a moment. Perplexed by the inscrutability of Beaubois's encounter with 'his' primary audience, they suddenly become aware not only of the presence of the (previously unseen even if not hidden) camera but also, possibly, of the 'other actor' in this collaborative performance, i.e. the surveillant agency exposed by the readable dynamic between the frozen Beaubois and the seemingly 'active' observation apparatus. It is, as Beaubois suggests, an economy of the glance encountering the spectacle of the gaze – as is rendered strikingly evident in a later staging of the *Amnesia* performance in Cleveland, Ohio (1997), where Beaubois's static stance at the entrance to the wonderfully panoptically named 'Tower City' shopping complex catches the attention and then opens the eyes, as it were, of two inner-city youths to the surveillance system they had never noticed despite their extensive familiarity with the mall.

Exposure
___

But just how is this spectacle staged? First and foremost simply by standing with intensely focused attention, in an ironic inversion of Walker Evans's famous admonition to the potential surreptitious photographer: 'Stare. It is the way to educate your eye and more. Stare, pry, listen, eavesdrop. Die knowing something. You are not here long.'[1] Beaubois is indeed staring, but in a way that serves to 'expose the apparatus' in the tradition of the ideologically critical and technologically involuted left-wing film practice of the post-May '68 Dziga-Vertov Group, (itself a

1. Walker Evans, *Walker Evans at Work*, Harper & Row, New York 1982, p. 160.

recasting of the Russian formalist notion of the 'laying bare of the device'). This gesture is equally evident in other more or less contemporary works by Beaubois which also pointedly refunction (and thereby also expose) different sorts of surveillant devices imbedded in the texture of daily life: typical in this regard is the *ATM Family Portrait* (1996), in which Beaubois exploited the hidden transaction-recording camera in an automatic bank teller machine located in the Kings Cross section of Sidney as a means to produce a group photograph of the artist and his parents. In another similar project called *Red Light Camera Portraits* (1996) Beaubois carefully positioned himself at an intersection known for its photographic 'infraction'-recording device and had a colleague drive through on red to trigger the apparatus, the 'proof' of the 'transgression' here being recast as an urban portrait generated by the state for a fee (i.e. the cost of the fine for the traffic violation).

Both the *ATM* and the *Red Light* are very much in the tradition of a still largely unknown body of work that has engaged questions of surveillance from a variety of perspectives for many years. Most immediately, the playful ingenuity of Beaubois's projects recall the brilliant *Fonce Alphonse* (1993) by the Paris-based photographer Jeff Guess, in which the American artist and his partner raced down a Lyon street known to have a radar speed trap en route to their marriage ceremony and then waited for home delivery of the police image (complete with date and time stamp) that would constitute their sole wedding photograph.

Similarly, at its most basic level,

Stills from video of the <u>Amnesia</u> performance in Cleveland, Ohio, 1997, by Denis Beaubois

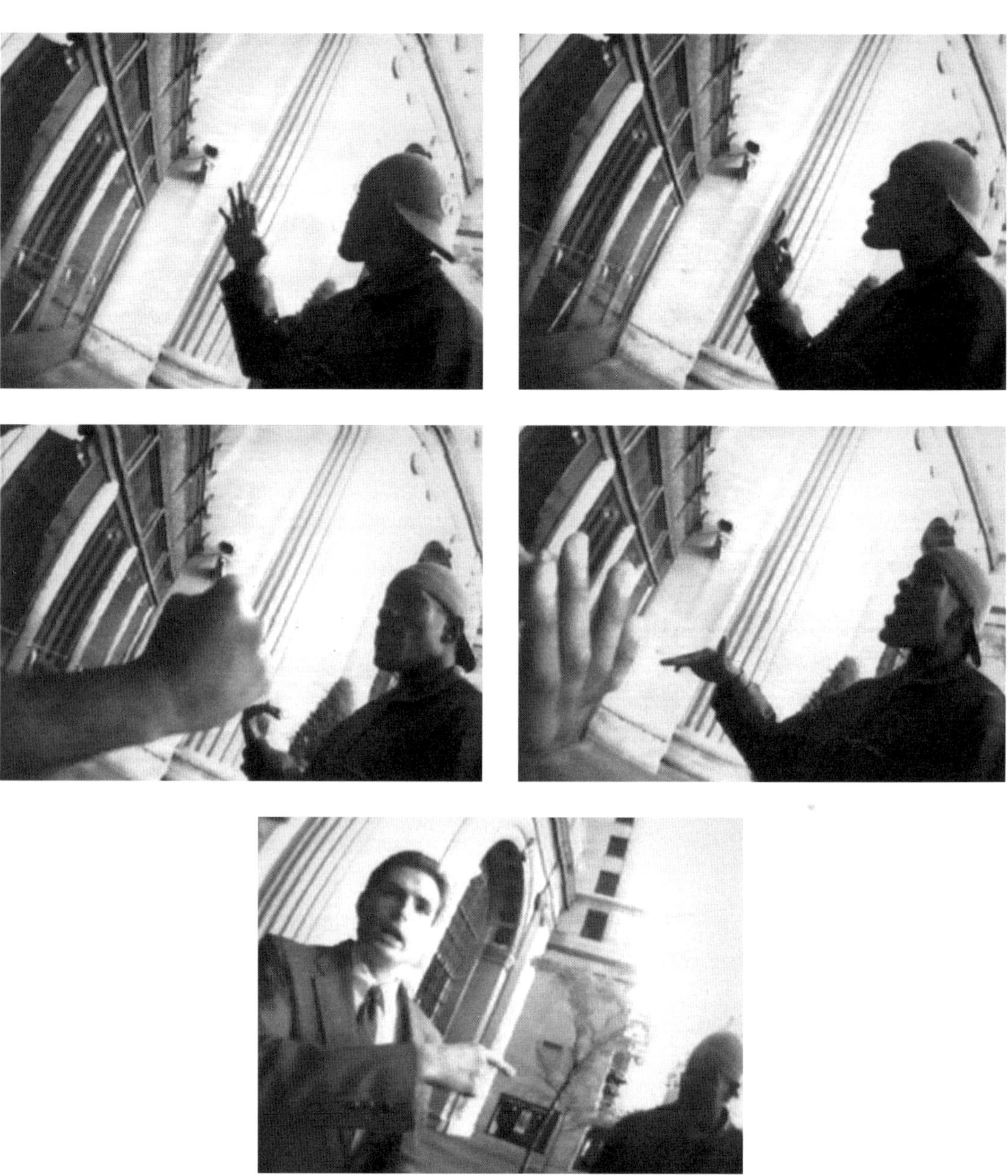

Stills from <u>Red light camera portraits</u>, Sydney, 1996, by Denis Beaubois

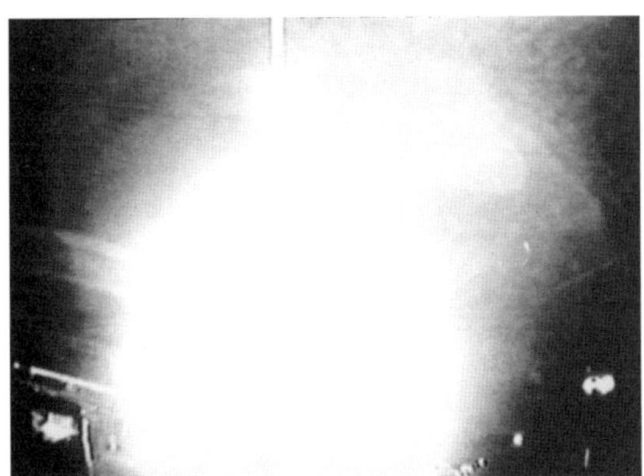 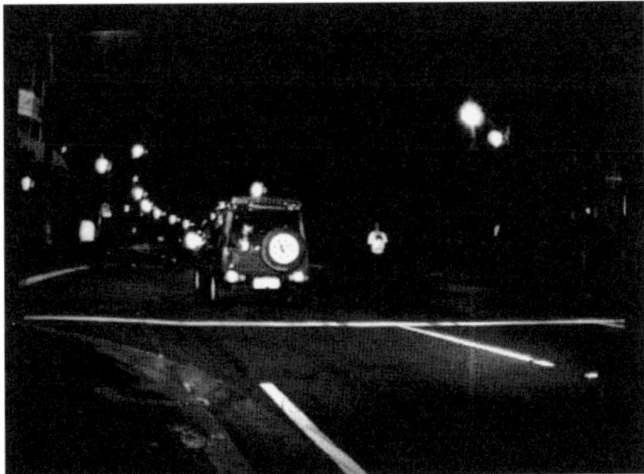

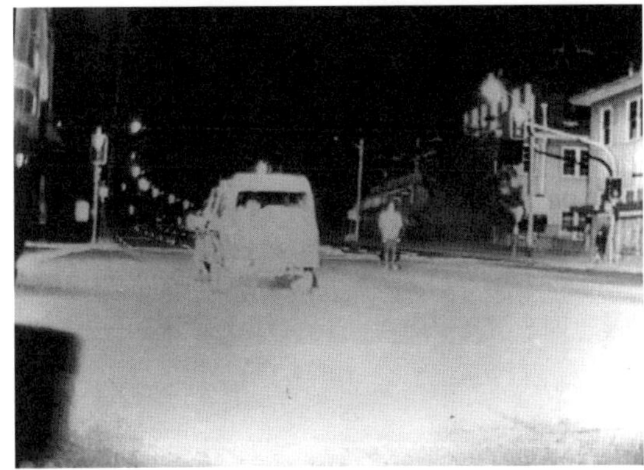

Jeff Guess, <u>Fonce Alphonse</u>, 1993

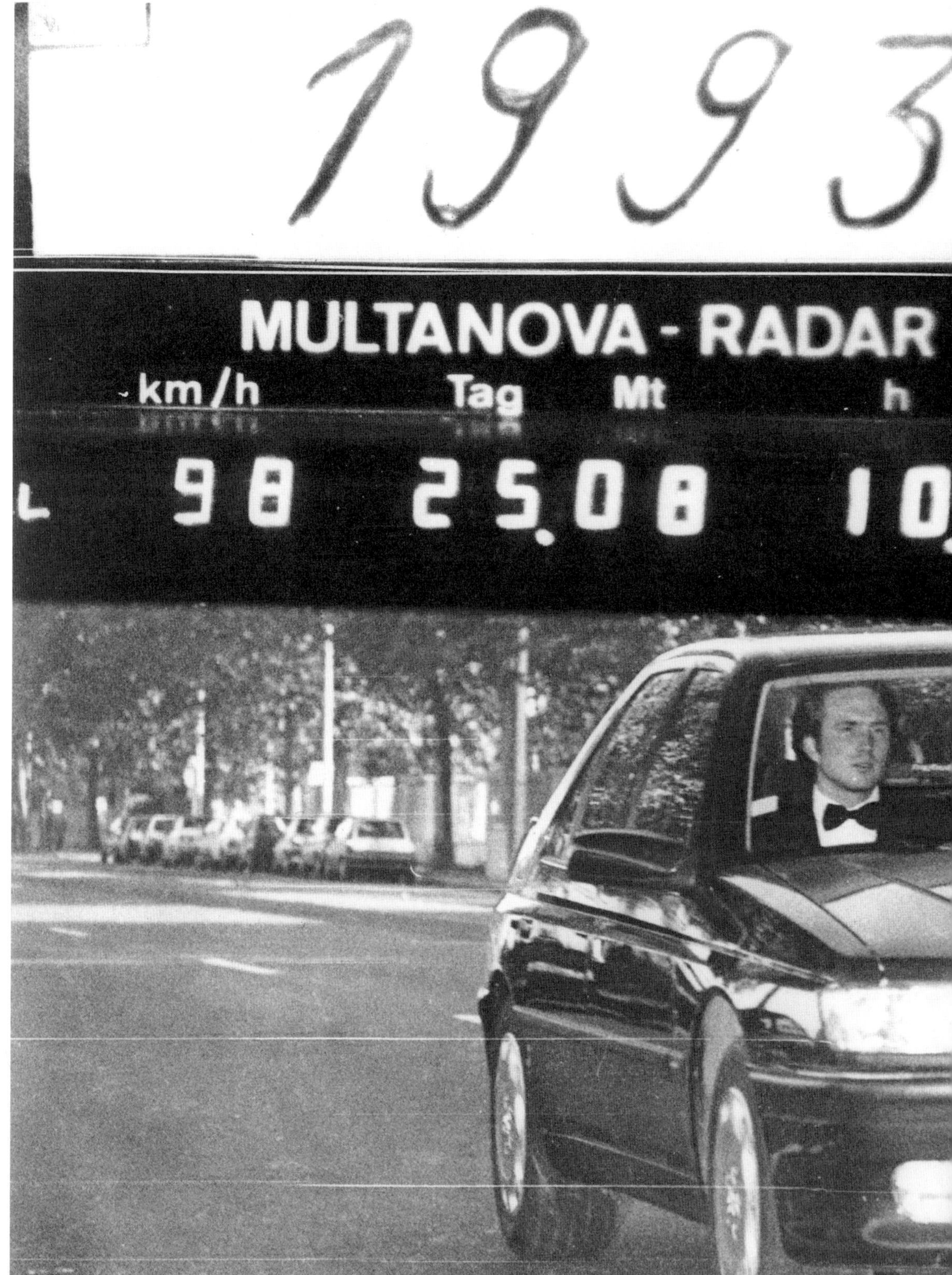

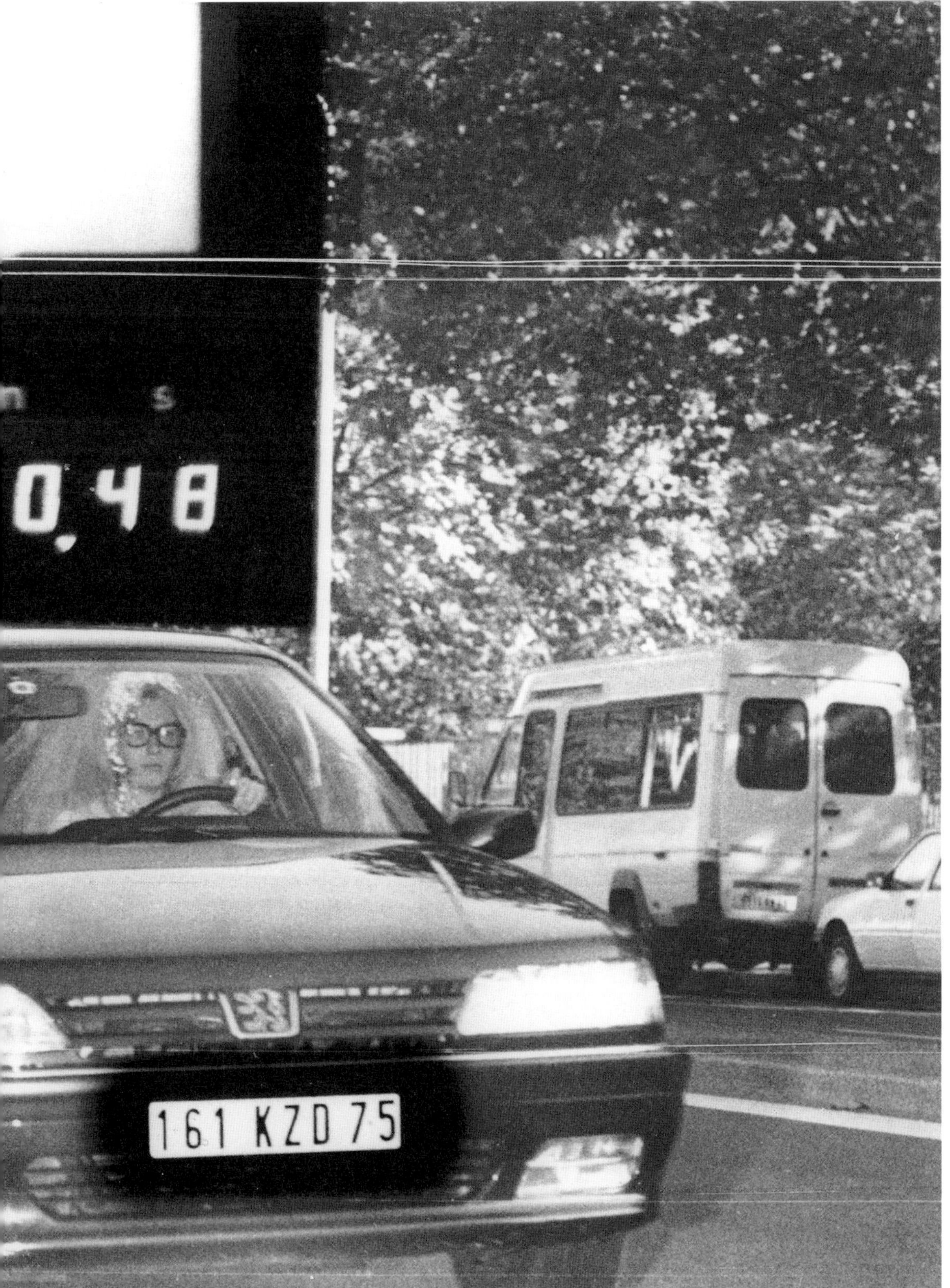
048
161 KZD 75

Beaubois's Medusian gaze in the *Amnesia* project also invokes a number of earlier works in the history of critical artistic encounters with surveillance. It renders explicit, for example, what was already *implicit* in Michael Klier's important film *Der Riese*, the almost feature-length compilation of footage taken entirely from an encyclopaedic catalogue of public and private surveillance cameras, whose sheer range itself already indicated the extent to which such visual tracking technology was already fully in use by the time the calendar actually made it to the allegorical year of 1984 in which the film was released. Klier's brilliantly simple move – to gain access to and just quote (i.e. reproduce) the output of various operational surveillance systems – is then echoed almost a decade later in the work of the British artist duo Pat Naldi and Wendy Kirkup, albeit inflected through a somewhat different strategy of appropriation. Making effective use of what one could call the strategics of aesthetic drag (i.e. using the pretence of an 'art project' to undertake a political action that would, if recognized as such, most likely be impossible or much more difficult to do), Naldi & Kirkup gained access in 1993 to the 16-camera system installed by the Northumbria Police in the city centre of Newcastle-upon-Tyne in order to stage a 'synchronized walk'. Like Beaubois's catatonia, the very triviality and aesthetic formalism of this flaneurial gesture, which may have enabled them to undertake the project in the first place, also serves to shift attention away from the artists as the 'subjects' of the work and onto the very means of production – i.e. the CCTV system – itself. In a country such as England, where the absence of almost any legislative constraint had already then made possible an unparalleled proliferation of CCTV systems in 'public' spaces, this gesture was hardly inconsequential. A similar impulse is also readable in the manner in which the footage that Naldi & Kirkup 'harvested' from the police surveillance system was then presented – not as some sort of fascinatingly ominous montage but rather as a series of punctual TV spots, brief 10-second silent black-and-white interruptions on the local Tynes TV network, a strategy that they employed again when they re-staged the project at the 1996 Adelaide Telstra Arts Festival in Australia and then broadcast their (now full-colour) footage as a series of 15 10-second sequences on Festival Television's Channel 7.[2] This intermittent rupturing of the normal televisual flow – a strategy which Beaubois also employed to disseminate some of the *Amnesia* performances – almost seemed to suggest the continuous presence of this economy of visual tracking 'behind' or 'beneath' the seemingly harmless continuum of daily programming. As such, it performatively invoked the constant lurking omnipresence of the surveillance system which was both the project's condition of possibility and the then still largely invisible fact that it served to expose.

Guerrilla Strategy

Considered in terms of classic panoptical dialectics, such 'exposing' of the surveil-

2. See Helen Caldwallader, 'Pat Naldi & Wendy Kirkup, "Search"', in: *Locus+ 1993–1996*, Newcastle upon Tyne: Locus+, 1996, p. 12-17; rpt. in: Julian Stallabrass, Pauline van Mourik Broekman & Niru Ratnam (eds.), *Locus Solus: Site, Identity, Technology in Contemporary Art*, Black Dog Press, London, 2000.

Still from <u>Der Riese</u> (82′00″) by Michael Klier, 1984
Collection of the Netherlands Media Art Institute, Montevideo/TBA

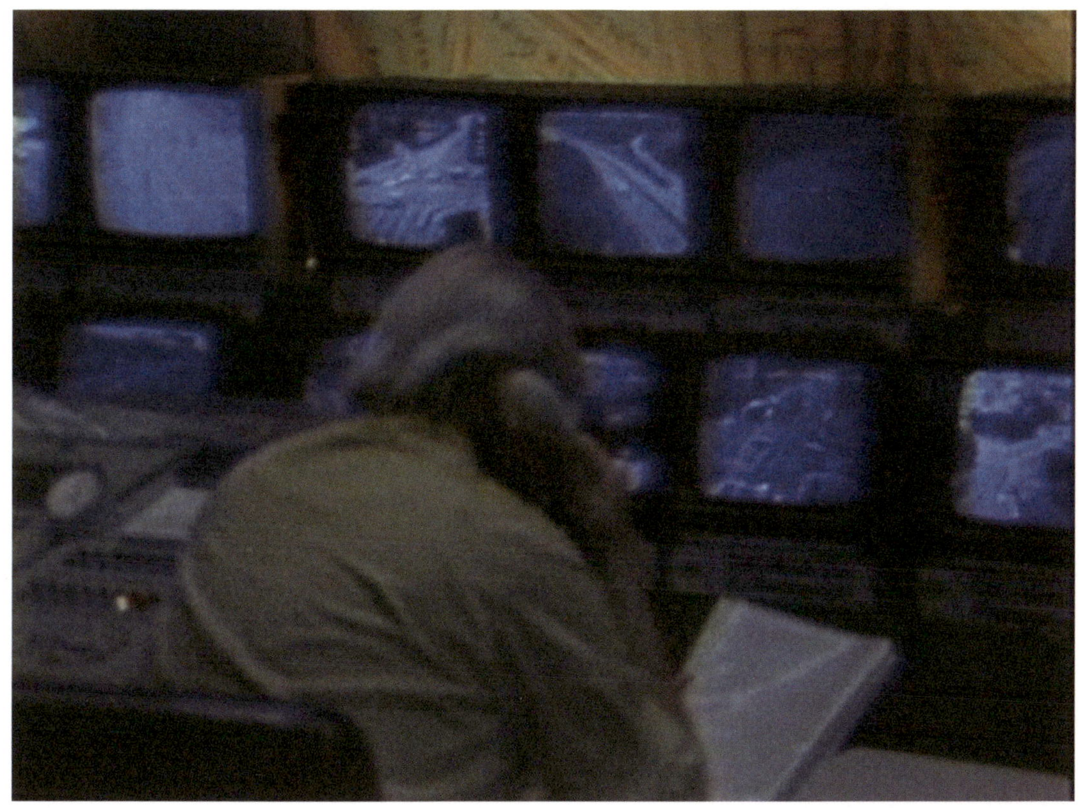

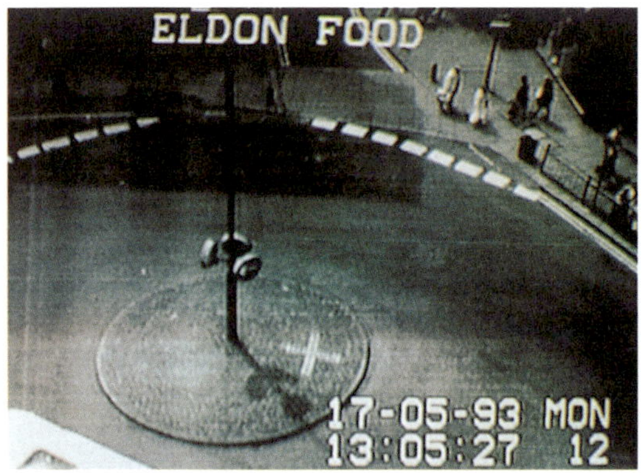
ELDON FOOD
17-05-93 MON
13:05:27   12

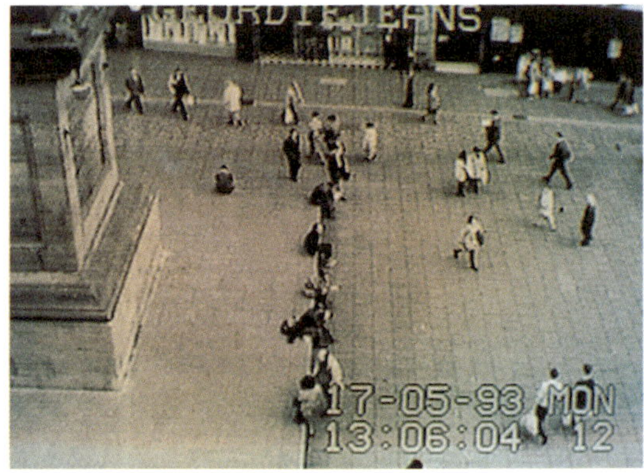
GEORDIE JEANS
17-05-93 MON
13:06:04   12

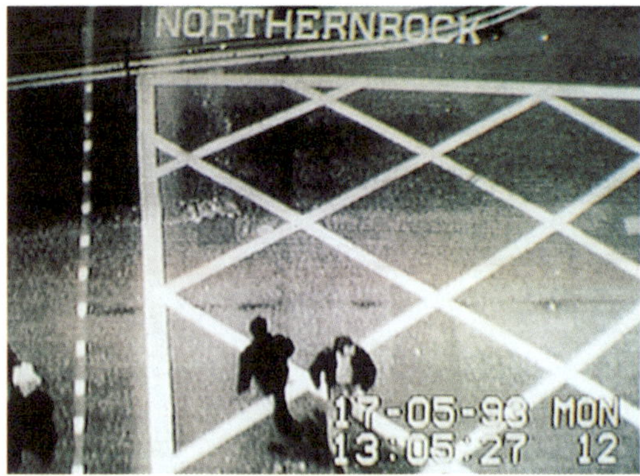
NORTHERNROCK
17-05-93 MON
13:05:27   12

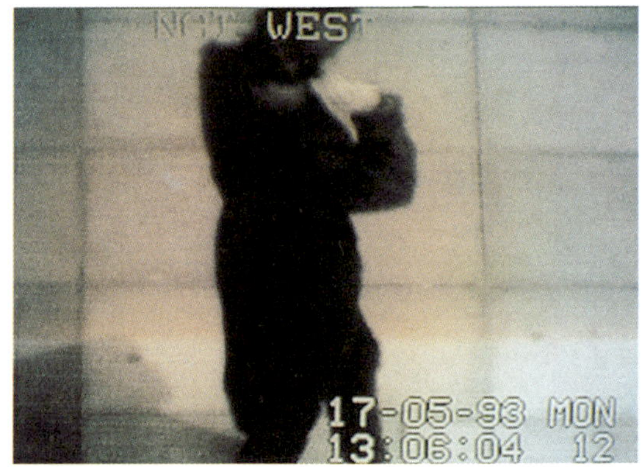
NAT WEST
17-05-93 MON
13:06:04   12

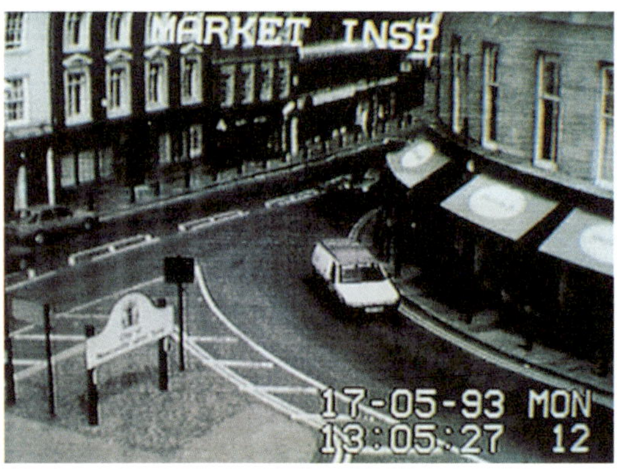
MARKET INSP
17-05-93 MON
13:05:27   12

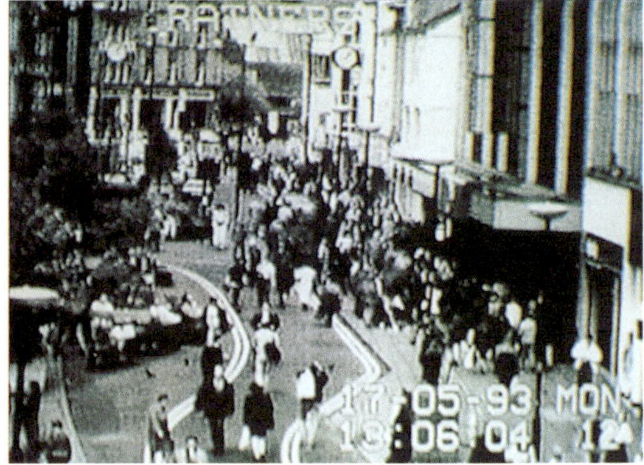
RATNERS
17-05-93 MON
13:06:04   12

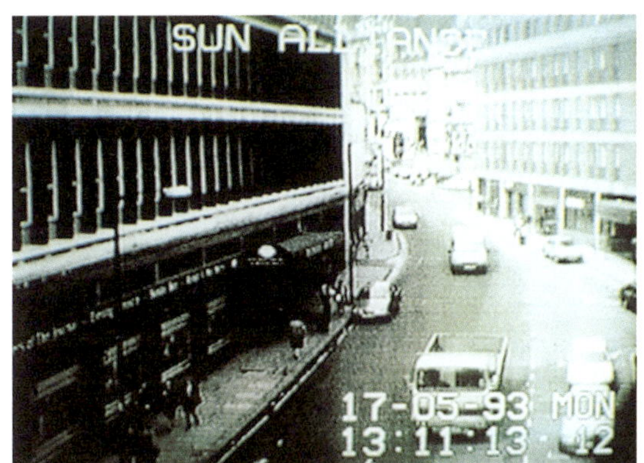
SUN ALLIANCE
17-05-93 MON
13:11:13   12

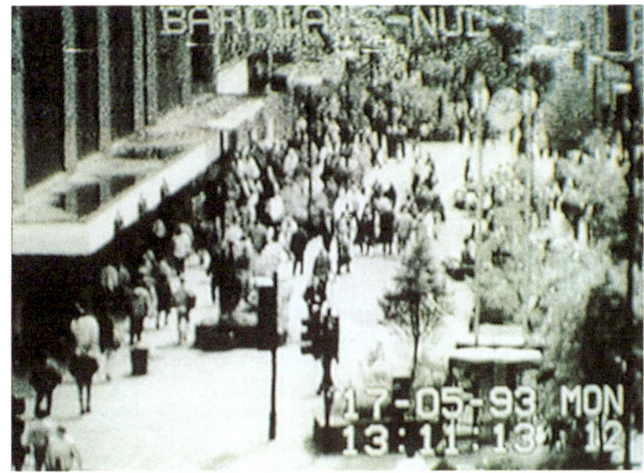
BARCLAYS NU
17-05-93 MON
13:11:13   12

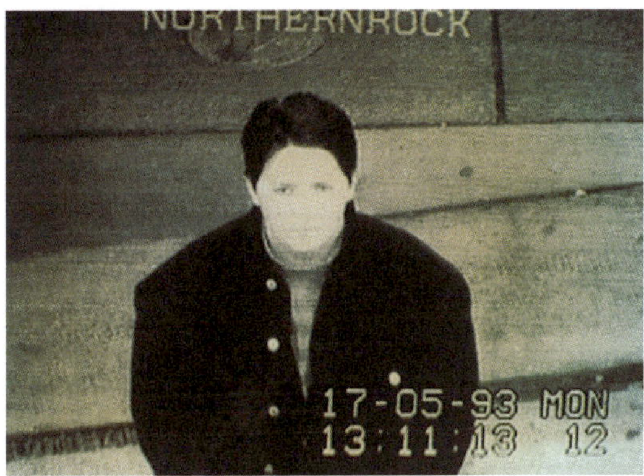
NORTHERNROCK
17-05-93 MON
13:11:13   12

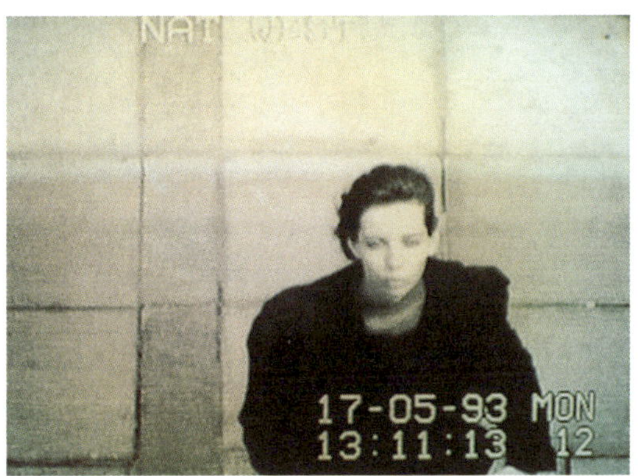
NAT
17-05-93 MON
13:11:13   12

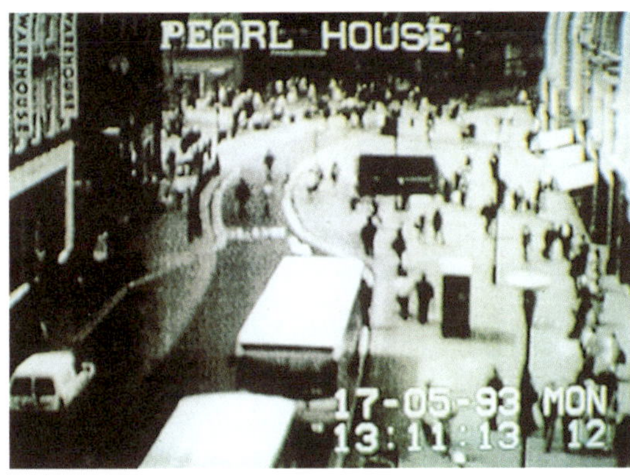
PEARL HOUSE
17-05-93 MON
13:11:13   12

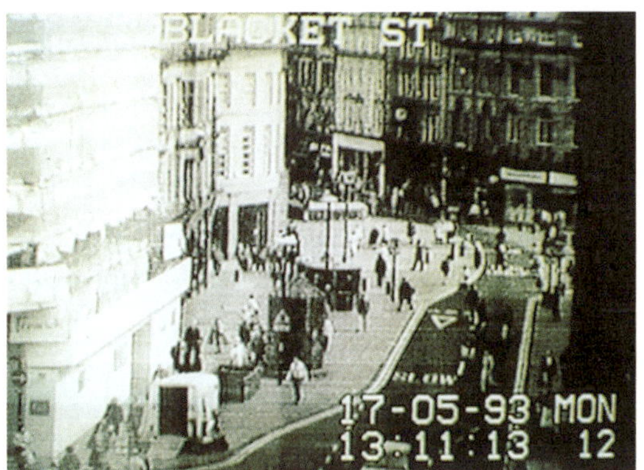
BLACKET ST
17-05-93 MON
13:11:13   12

lant system is at some level, of course, not only compatible with its successful operation but in fact actually promotes it: the more people know of the existence of the surveillance the 'better' it functions as a social technology. Since this is always more or less the case, the question is rather exactly what it is that any intervention exposes. In the case of Naldi & Kirkup what is interesting is that in their performance of the CCTV system, their controlling of the control space, they foreground both the space of the image (they 'become the subject' of the tracking) and the structuring of the images (the site of their production, selection, examination – i.e. the police's surveillant control booth). In so doing they both point to the space of daily life as the site of this new form of urban spectacle, and to the surveillance apparatus as the locus of a new sort of audience. This gesture is subsequently literalized and activated in the late 1990s by the New York-based neo-situationist anarchist performance collective known as the Surveillance Camera Players. Eschewing the guise of aesthetic drag in favour of a guerrilla version of the more classically Brechtian intervention, they stage their telegraphically reduced renderings of literary works such as Orwell's *1984* by simply barging in and appropriating extant public surveillance systems such as those present everywhere in the Manhattan subway system.[3] In their commandeering of the 'live' closed-circuit video transmission loop between a fixed camera and a 'captive' (and usually singular) surveillant viewer in

3. Their rendition of Alfred Jarry's *Ubu Roi* took place in Manhattan's Union Square Station, Edgar Allan Poe's *The Raven* and Samuel Beckett's *Waiting for Godot* at the Astor Place Station, and *1984* at the IRT Station on West 14th St. Further information on the group can be found on their home page at http://www.notbored.org/the-scp.html.

the ticket booth, the Surveillance Camera Players employ the anti-mimetic vocabulary of the protest movement (placards on sticks, masks, and mock-acting) and then simply disappear, if they have not already been 'asked' to leave by the 'forces of order'. Like Naldi & Kirkup, the Surveillance Camera Players also hijack sites of quotidian transience for their surveillant performances, but unlike the former, the colour and synch-sound record of their actions is produced by filming (in continuous time) the monitors to which the signal of the cameras send their output.

Texts also play a role in the *Amnesia* performances, albeit in a slightly different manner. Having captured the attention of both the 'primary' and 'secondary' audiences (i.e. the surveillance apparatus and the bystanders) by means of his interrogative corporeal fixity, on Day Two (indicatively titled 'the introduction') Beaubois begins holding up in front of his stomach a series of white sheets with printed texts, starting with one that contains only his name. Willingly proffering to the system information which it is meant to establish against one's will is, as such, already deeply suspicious, which in turn only makes the performer/suspect of greater 'interest'. Having thereby further riveted the attention of one (if not both) of his audiences, the silent Beaubois then suddenly shifts registers. On day three of this silent performance (entitled 'the dialogue and the response') the text sheets begin to invoke their media-historical antecedents – the intertitles of early cinema – not only *formally* qua text frames that interrupt the 'action' of the performance, but also *functionally* in that, like these, the texts now also begin conveying crucial

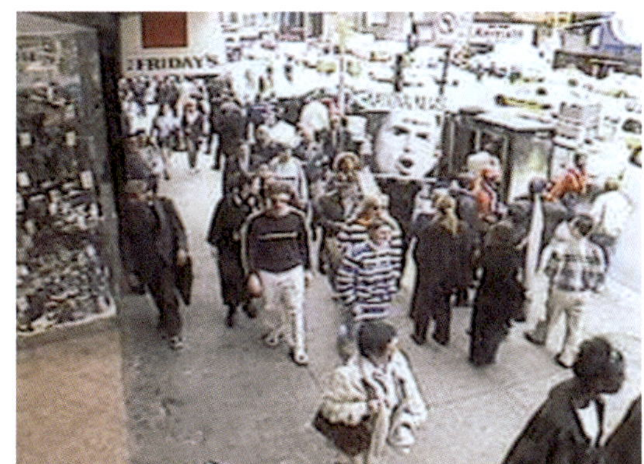

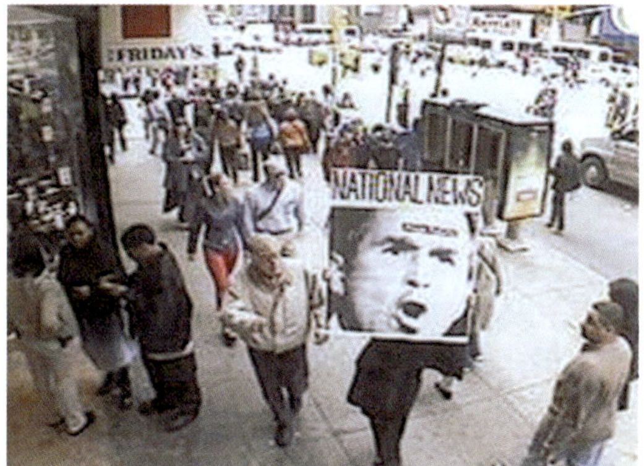
NATIONAL NEWS

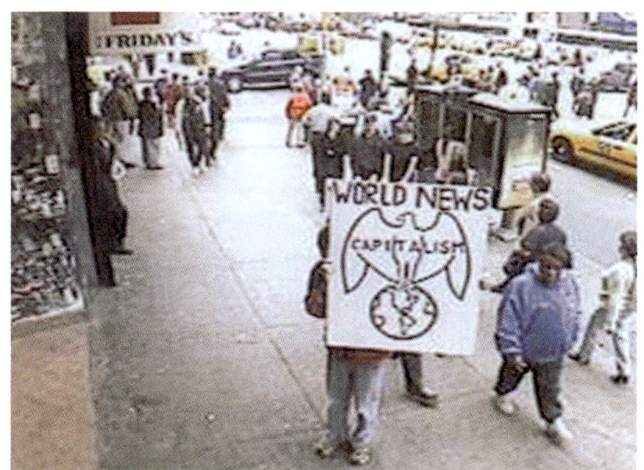
WORLD NEWS
CAPITALISM

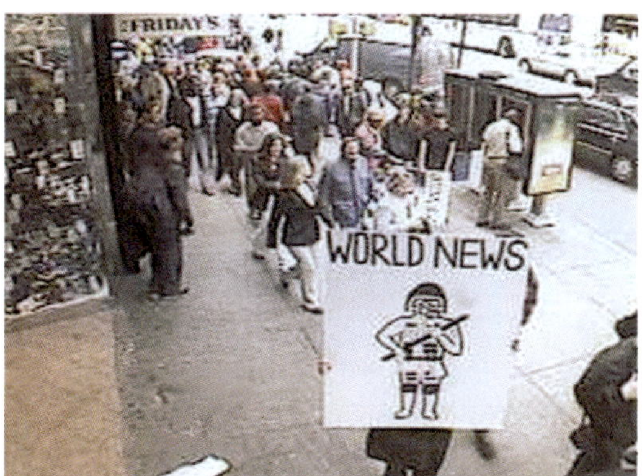
WORLD NEWS

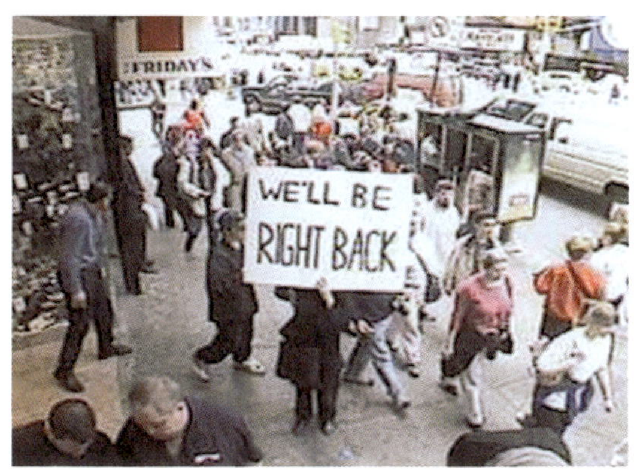
WE'LL BE
RIGHT BACK

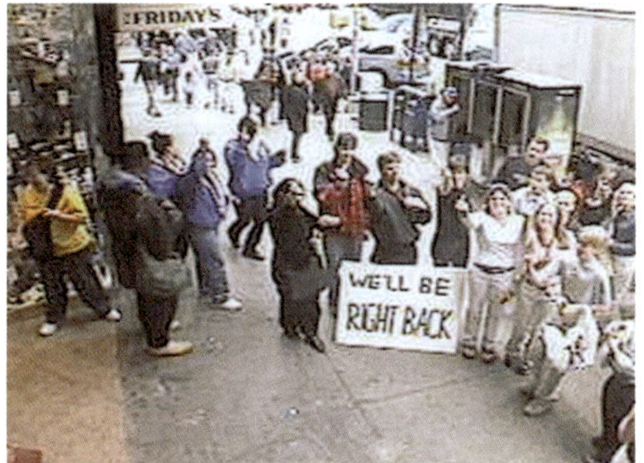
WE'LL BE
RIGHT BACK

narrative information. 'May I have a copy of the video footage?' the next card inquires, indicating, through instructions spelled out on the two that follow, that a positive answer is to be indicated by moving the camera up and down, while a negative response is to be conveyed by moving the camera side to side.

Panoptic Anxiety

This hilarious *interpellative* moment – which is then literally performed in the Cleveland *Amnesia* when one of the youths turns to the surveillance camera and repeatedly asks 'where my tape, man?' – also expresses a classically panoptic anxiety: when staring into that unblinking surveillant lens, who has not wondered whether there is somebody actually out there observing him right now? As Orwell's Winston Smith understood all too well, there was, of course, no way of knowing whether you were being watched at any given moment. How often, or on what system, the Thought Police plugged in on any individual wire was guesswork. It was even conceivable that they watched everybody all the time. But at any rate they could plug in your wire whenever they wanted to. You had to live – did live, from habit that became instinct – in the assumption that every sound you made was overheard, and, except in darkness, every movement scrutinized.[4]

Indeed, Beaubois's request for a copy of the 'footage' points not only to the fact – and general unavailability – of surveillance *as taped record*, but also to the concomitant and uncomfortable possibility which always haunts surveillance systems based

4. George Orwell, *1984* [1949], Penguin, London 1989, p. 4-5.

on taping: that the camera may not even be manned, i.e. that it simply may be recording without anyone watching in so-called 'real' time. Since we cannot know for sure we must assume there is, but a response to such a query would nevertheless be an ambivalently welcome corroboration that our 'performance' does indeed have an 'audience'. And it is just such a confirmation of his worst panoptical suspicions that Winston gets during the routine morning sessions of the Physical Jerks: 'Smith!' screamed the shrewish voice from the tele-screen. '6079 Smith W! Yes, *you*! Bend lower please! You can do better than that. You're not trying. Lower please! *That's* better, comrade. Now stand at ease, the whole squad and watch me.'[5]

The implicit ocular reciprocity with which this admonition concludes ('watch me') is of course a seductive figure of speech: the one thing that Winston – or anyone else – *cannot* do is return the gaze of the tele-screen. The phantasmatic possibility of a dialogic relation with the surveillant apparatus that it invokes, however, is precisely what is staged in the *Amnesia* performance, through what one could call the *semanticization of the PTZ* [Pan, Tilt and Zoom] camera. Ingeniously recasting the *mechanics* of the apparatus as a *semantics*, i.e. as a meaning-bearing economy, we see the camera pan from side to side 'in response' to Beaubois's request. The hilarious anthropomorphization which is the condition of possibility of reading this 'denial' of his request would seem to quell all panoptical doubts (and in this case also thespian anxiety): if I was concerned before that nobody was actually watching me, I can rest assured, since the discursive

5. Ibid., p. 39.

character of the camera movement, the semantics of the mechanics, clearly confirms that we are dealing with some form of agency. But does it really? Given the irreducible dimension of projection involved in such a dynamic, how can we deny the possibility that the seemingly so expressive PTZ movement was in fact totally random and (in this case) fortuitous? If this were so, then we would still not know *for sure* whether there was someone in the tower, as it were (even as we would have to assume that there was).

Facial Recognition Software

The foregrounding of this undecidability is one of the key elements of Beaubois's *Amnesia* performance, which as such presciently put its finger on a panoptic tendency that, while long in the making, has only very recently begun making its first tentative – and highly controversial – public appearances. On Sunday, 30 January 2001, the 100,000 fans who crammed into Super Bowl XXXV in Tampa all had their faces captured by a video surveillance system which then digitized them in the stadium's 'law enforcement control room' so that – without their knowledge – they could be cross-checked against a biometric database containing the facial data of 1700 known 'criminals, terrorists and con-artists' from the Tampa Police Department and the FBI.[6] While the facial recognition software by Graphco Technologies identified only 19 people with 'insignificant' criminal histories, none of

6. The story, first reported by Robert Trigaux ('Cameras scanned faces for criminals', *St. Petersburg Times*, 31 January 2001) was then picked up by the *Los Angeles Times* on 2 February 2001 ('Criminal Faces in the Crowd still elude Hidden ID Cameras Security'). For a useful introduction to the subject, see the special section on 'Biometrics: The Future of Identification' in the February 2000 issue of *Computer*, esp. 46.

which subsequently could be apprehended, it did mark the first highly public employment of a technology that has long been used by casinos to identify con-artists, by the welfare department to detect 'double-dippers', and by motor vehicle bureau's to nab license forgers. Less than six months later, the city of Tampa Florida installed a similar 'Smart CCTV™' system in conjunction with a network of 36 state-of-the-art surveillance cameras in the Ybor City section of town (a popular but crime-ridden night-life district which regularly enjoys between 75,000 and 150,00 visitors during the evenings and on weekends). Here the images captured are analyzed in real time by a biometric software program called FaceIT™, manufactured by the Visionics Corporation, which breaks down every face into 80 salient data points in order to compare it with a database of 30,000 ostensible 'criminals'.

As Tampa is the first city in the US where such a system has been installed – and it is only on loan from the manufacturer on a trial basis – the national media have been following its employment – and public reaction to it – quite closely. While FaceIT™ so far has yet to produce a single arrest, a few weeks after it was installed, there was a – surprisingly modest – public protest, at which demonstrators, some of them with bar codes on their faces, others wearing gas masks, objected to such public digitization. But by far the most revealing response came in the wake of the city's presentation of the new system to journalists. A random image taken from the system's cameras to demonstrate its capacities – of a man seated at a café in the Centro Ybor entertainment complex – was published widely as an illustration for the reports on this latest biometric development. Upon seeing it in *U.S. News and World Report*, a woman in Tulsa, Oklahoma, 'recognized' her ex-husband, who was wanted on Federal child neglect charges, and called the Tampa police. When they went to arrest the man, however, it turned out that he had never been married and had never been to Oklahoma – in short, they had identified the wrong guy.[7] What is at stake in the dissemination of this story, of course, is the comparative fallibility of human face recognition capacities (the wife who mis-recognized her husband) when compared to that of the newest state-of-the-art biometric software: humans make mistakes, while biometric programs such as these – with a capacity of 15 million searches per minute per CPU and an 'equal error rate of 0.68% on standard databases'[8] –generally, so it is claimed, do not. While all such systems include human monitoring at some point in the chain, they do, however, raise the spectre of the ultimate prosthetic panoptic eye – one that never sleeps and is capable of the most astonishing feats of parallel processing and facial recognition. As described by the manufacturer: 'FaceIT™ can find human faces anywhere in the field of view and at any distance, and it can continuously track them and crop them out of the scene, matching the face against a watch list. Totally hands off, continuous and in real-time.' In short, we may be noticed, followed and even identified by a 'primary audience' which is nevertheless entirely algorithmic.

7. Amy Herdy, '"They made me feel like a criminal": He was just having lunch in Ybor City when a surveillance camera captured his image. Weeks later, the police show up', *St. Petersburg Times*, 8 August 2001.

8. Publicity sheet handed out at the Visonics Stand at the 2001 CEBIT Technology Convention, Hanover, Germany.

Rhetorical Question

The possibility of real-time biometric processing of visual surveillance data has dramatic consequences, of course, for the seemingly 'dialogic' dimension of Beaubois's *Amnesia* performance. In response to the 'refusal' of the request for a copy of the video tape – which at first glance would seem only to confirm the imbalance of power characteristic of the surveillant *dispositif* – the final text frame retrospectively reveals that this was, in fact, a strictly rhetorical question. 'Warning,' it reads, 'you may be photographed reading this sign.'[9] Indeed, Beaubois is not really asking, since he is not according the apparatus the meek acquiescence it assumes (and all too often gets). On the contrary, Beaubois has instead answered the question in advance, and in the affirmative: he has no need to wait to be given a copy of the surveillant video footage because he himself is *taking* that footage *himself*, 'shooting back', as it were, to use the phrase so aptly invoked by the Toronto-based digital media activist Steve Mann to describe his counter-surveillance practices. In fact Beaubois's video records of his *Amnesia* performances in Sidney involve quite a lot of shooting, a three-camera set-up which

9. This sign subsequently reappears in another Beaubois performance entitled *The Accidental Contract*, which took place on Eddie Ave. Central in Sidney in 1996. Here Beaubois again employed the strategy of a signifying stasis in a public space, albeit this time staring directly at a wall only a few inches from his face as a steady stream of pedestrians passed by behind him. Below the warning sign attached to his perfectly still back Beaubois held two imaging devices: one, a still camera, would take random shots of the pedestrian landscape which Beaubois himself could not see. The other, a video camera, provided a continuous record of the street dynamics and was complimented by another (manned) video camera across the street which effectively provided the 'reverse shot'. In gallery installations of the project, the still images would be accompanied by the two video feeds presented on either side of a room, placing the viewer in the force field of the original 'secondary' audience.

includes one behind and on the same plane as Beaubois that provides many of the 'establishing' shots, one located above the surveillance camera (thus able to invoke, even if it cannot exactly reproduce, the latter's high-angle optical vector), and one wide-angle camera attached to the performer's chest. The carefully edited and elegantly structured video that serves as the record of this performative détournement of the panopticon – and circulates in an art-world economy – reveals that *both* Beaubois's primary and secondary audiences must in fact be understood as components of a performance which is staged, one could say, for the tertiary audiences in galleries, museums, and at film- and video-festivals. Here, at least from time to time, there *is* actually somebody watching.

Sven Lütticken

Park Life

The need to keep out the big, bad, unsafe world is growing, as evidenced by the increase in enclosed spaces. Using the concept of the 'human park' introduced by Peter Sloterdijk in 1999, as well as old and new examples from film, architecture, art and television, Sven Lütticken wonders whether the new societal form these places conjure up for us is in fact safer.

Contemporary space is quickly becoming less homogeneous. 'Gated communities' and other closed, fenced-in spaces are proliferating. This is not, of course, unprecedented. We are dealing with a return of something that modernity seemed to eradicate bit by bit, but this return occurs from *within* capitalist modernity (or postmodernity) itself. The modern age held out the promise of a continuous space that does away with old privileges and restrictions (based on class, religion, property or ethnicity). During the French Revolution, a proposal for a new map of France was drawn, with a structure of provinces that had the shape – at least in the first, most 'ideal' drawing – of perfect squares.[1] The whole of France was turned into a perfect grid. This proposal, which was soon diluted until the grid structure was barely recognizable, shows modern, disenchanted, abstract space in a terrifyingly radical manner. In somewhat less spectacular ways, this development of modern space meant the erasure of the old legal and physical boundaries between the town and the countryside, as town walls were torn down and replaced by a less drastic transition. But the current segregationism, which appears to reverse that process, is in fact an effect of capitalist modernity itself. 'Geometry and arithmetic take on the power of the scalpel. Private property implies a space that has been overcoded and gridded by surveying' – and, elaborating on Deleuze and Guattari, if the scalpel cuts deep enough, the homogeneous, gridded space of modernity is cut into pieces.[2] The modern nation state, although it may have seen internal spatial coherence and continuity as an ideal, is itself a fenced-in piece of land that people from other countries cannot enter at will.

Some of the new closed spaces, those intended for recreation or leisurely living, take the form of *parks*. Up to and well into the nineteenth century, access to parks was often restricted to a select elite; not everyone was deemed fit for a taste of Arcadia. But the nineteenth century also saw an increase in public parks, in theory open to all. Before the French Revolution, Marie Antoinette had a little Disney-like village constructed in the park of Versailles, the Hameau, where she could pretend to lead a bucolic life – away from the stifling court, but also free from confrontations with any real peasants or paupers. The age of the Hameau seems to have returned, not so much for individual queens as for a small bourgeois upper class. This tendency is reflected in symptomatic fictions like Peter Weir's film *The Truman Show* (1998), whose protagonist is living in a small town that is in fact a huge, domed TV-studio – a simulation of life. The scenes that show this town, Seahaven, were filmed in a real Florida town, Seaside, a neo-Victorian fantasy for the wealthy. Seaside, built between 1984 and 1991, has also inspired Disney's more recent Celebration development – a town completely controlled by the Walt Disney Corporation, where everything is banned that might be a blemish on this idealized 'small town America'. Celebration, like Seaside, defines the good life in terms of a secession from the rest of society. The big

1. Daniel Nordman, Marie-Vic Ozouf-Marignier, *Atlas de la Révolution Française 4: Le territoire (1): Réalités et représentations*, Éditions de l'École des Hautes Études en Sciences Sociales, Paris 1989, p. 29-30.

2. Gilles Deleuze, Felix Guattari, *A Thousand Plateaus* (1980), transl. by Brian Massumi, The Athlone Press, London 1988, p. 212.

bad world has to be kept at bay. A theme-park town such as this demonstrates that the real and fictional fenced-in spaces cannot be kept neatly apart; Celebration is a phantasmagorical reality. If *The Truman Show* is 'just' fiction, and non-Disneyfied gated communities 'just' a social and political reality, they nonetheless all function in the symbolic register of contemporary culture.

The rationale behind these settlements, with their varying degrees of fictionality, can be elucidated by the term human park, which was introduced by Peter Sloterdijk in his notorious lecture *Rules for the Human Park* (*Regeln für den Menschenpark*). At the end of this lecture, given in 1999, Sloterdijk made some references to genetic engineering that were ambiguous enough for many critics – Jürgen Habermas among them – to assume that he advocated some sort of eugenics in order to 'improve' the human race. Indeed, Sloterdijk seems to take it for granted that genetic engineering might really control such a complex affair as human behaviour; an assumption that might as well be criticized for its scientific naiveté as for its political implications. Sloterdijk's remarks about genetic engineering were triggered by his despair over the state of the 'humanist' tradition. In his view the humanist *Schriftkultur* is threatened by the Dionysian mass media, which appeal to the beast in man. Whereas traditional *Bildung*, with its emphasis on text, has represented a humanizing, civilizing impulse, image-saturated mass media loosen inhibitions.

Imperial Now-Time

Sloterdijk perceives a similar conflict between word and image in ancient Rome, where the theatre (by which he means gladiators and similar brutal entertainments) triumphed over the culture of the classical orators, with well-known consequences. Taking ancient Rome as an example of what happens to a culture when it becomes decadent may be a familiar trope of conservatism, but Sloterdijk is original insofar as he sees the decline of ancient Rome in terms of a clash between *media* – the spectacular medium of gladiatorial fights versus the medium of writing. 'As the book lost the fight against theatre in antiquity, so the school could now lose the fight against indirect forms of violence, in television, in the cinema and other disinhibiting media.'[3] Sloterdijk might have paused to think whether he did not project a post-Gutenbergian view of the central role of 'the book' on ancient culture, and whether it is helpful in the present situation to complain about the decline of writing and accuse image culture as such of being dehumanising; it is however remarkable that the visual culture attacked by Sloterdijk actually seems to mirror itself in ancient Roman spectacles.

One of the biggest blockbuster films of recent times is *Gladiator*, in which the decadence of imperial Rome and its addiction to cruel spectacles are depicted in lavish detail, resulting in a violent spectacle that Sloterdijk would no doubt

3. 'So wie in der Antike das Buch den kampf gegen die Theater verlor, so könnte heute die Schule den Kampf gegen die indirekten Bildungsgewalten, das Gewalt-kino und andere Enthemmungs-medien verlieren, wenn nicht eine neue gewaltdämpfende Kultivierungstruktuur entsteht.' Peter Sloterdijk, *Regeln für den Menschenpark*, Suhrkamp, Frankfurt am Main 1999, p. 46.

Hameau de la Reine, Versailles, 1783.

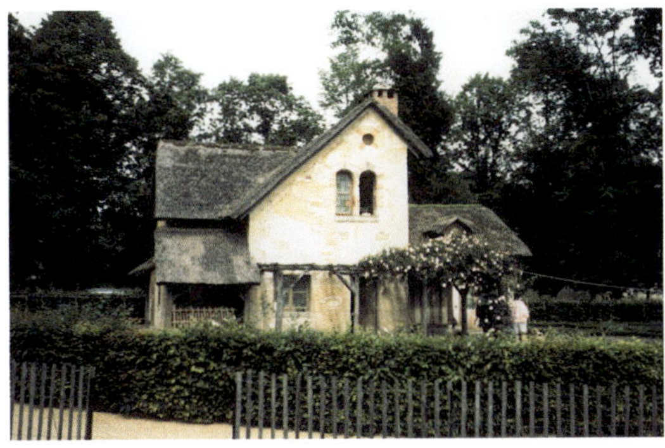

Jim Carrey in Peter Weir's <u>The Truman Show</u> (Paramount Pictures, 1998)
Photo Melinda Sue Gordon

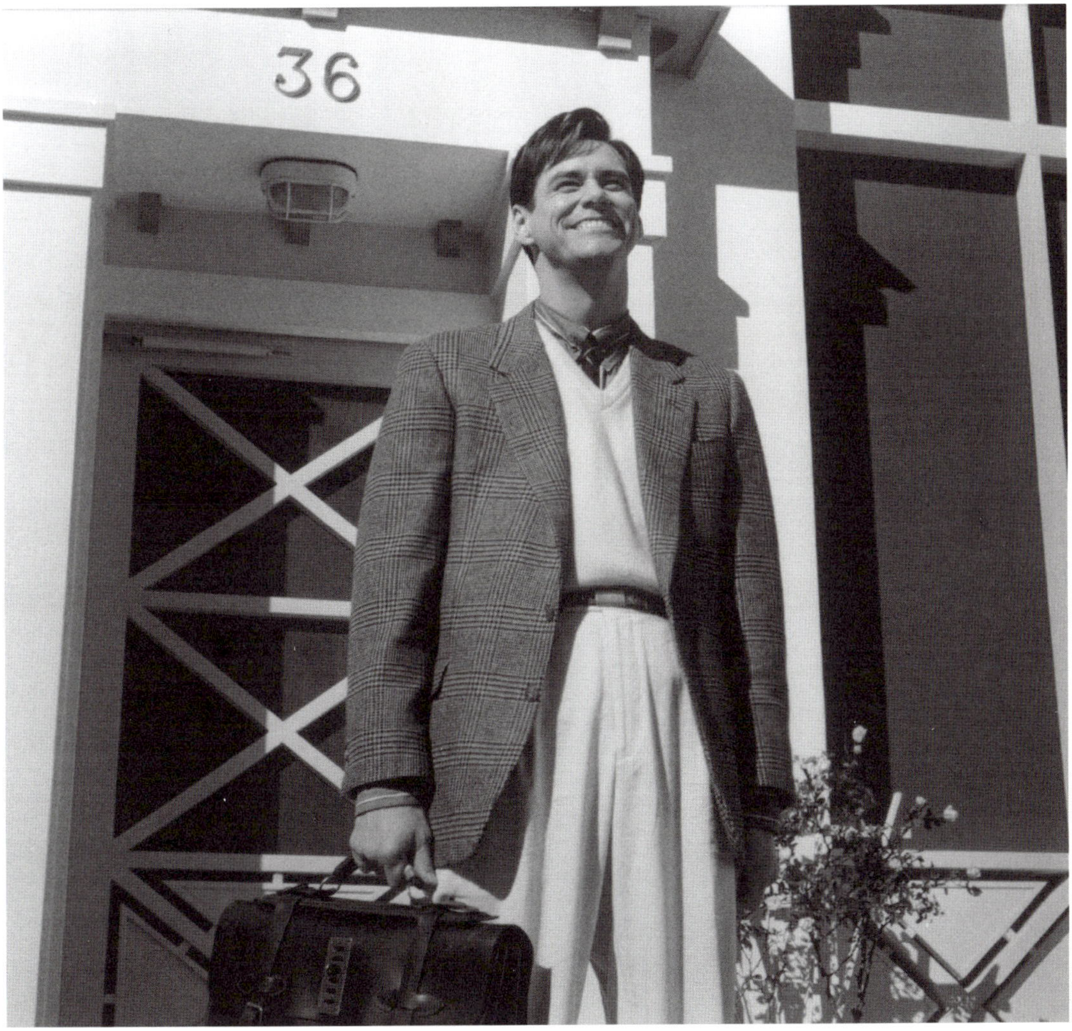

Still from <u>The Truman Show</u> (1998), filmed in Seaside, Florida. Seaside
is an example of a gated community for the wealthy.

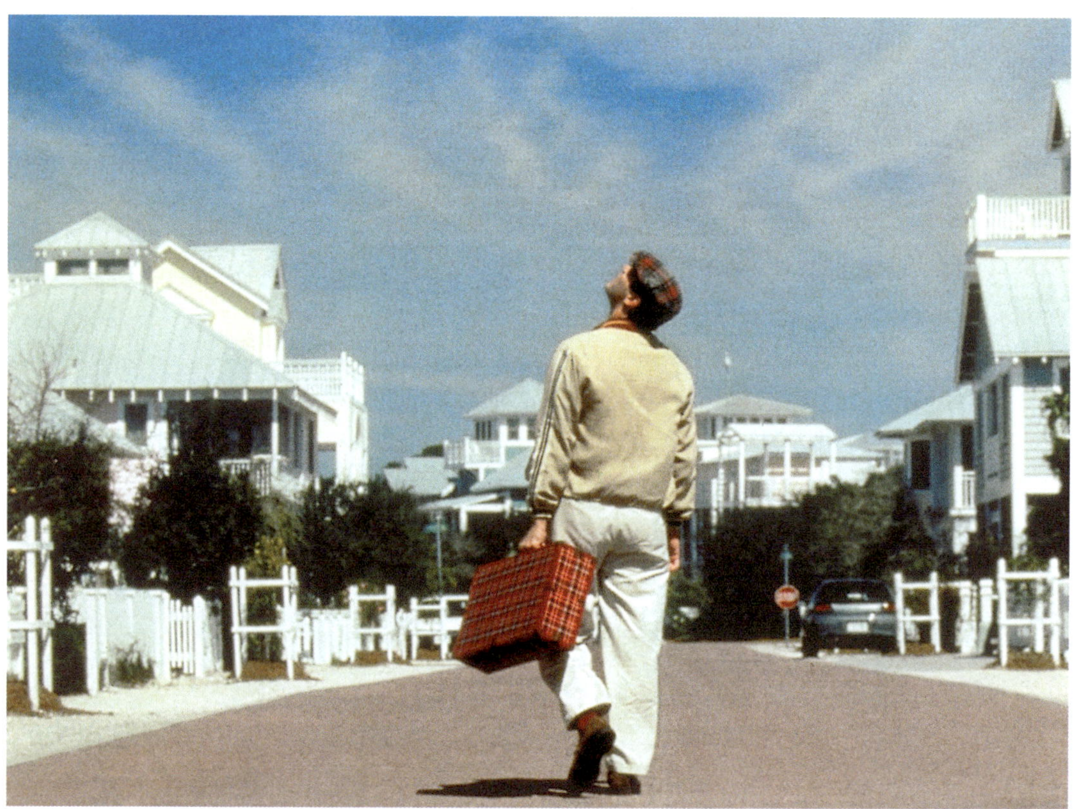

disapprove of. Whereas Walter Benjamin stated that the French Revolution saw itself as the Roman Republic returned, re-actualizing that era in a state of revolutionary *now-time* (*Jetztzeit*), today's culture seems to have a privileged link with the Roman Empire rather than with the republic.[4] Our now-time is an *imperial now-time*, not unlike that of the French Second Empire and of Victorian England: with a mixture of pride and fear of decadence and fall, these societies and their artists and architects mirrored themselves in (especially the late) Roman Empire. This passive and doom-laden now-time of empire cannot live up to Benjamin's criterion that the momentary link forged in *Jetztzeit* between present and past is transformative, active and revolutionary. But for some, this now-time of empire can also give rise to a new revolutionary now-time, in which the early Christians, especially Paul, appear as contemporaries.[5]

Although his view on contemporary society is dominated by comparisons with Rome, Sloterdijk's conception of society as a 'human park' has a pedigree leading back to Plato. But in his discussion of this 'pastoral' take on society, references to phenomena much closer to home seep in as well: 'Since the *Politikos* and since the *Politeia* there have been writings which speak about human society as if was a zoo that is also a theme park; from that moment on the keeping of people in parks or cities seems like a zoo-political task.'[6] Traditionally, parks are pieces of tamed, 'refined' nature, spots where nature has been made suitable for human consumption. Plants have been carefully grouped and groomed; if there are animals, these are either domesticated or – as in the *Tierpark* or zoo – put in cages. In theme parks, nature and its dangers are tamed by simulating them in all sorts of thrilling 'rides'; a visit to a theme park is presented as an adventure, but as safe as a visit to the zoo to see lions and tigers. In the 'human park' theory of society, society is a kind of zoo for people, where their dangerous instincts have to be curbed. Sloterdijk sees people as 'animals under the influence' of culture; the guardians of the park have to be careful to make sure that these influences are beneficiary.[7]

It was the question how stability inside these parks can be maintained now the influence of the Dionysian mass media is growing that led Sloterdijk to his remarks on genetic engineering. The polemics over this aspect of his speech have tended to obscure the fact that Sloterdijk's text, for all its phantasmagorical aspects – or indeed because of them – has the virtue of making a pervasive tendency in today's culture explicit. Sloterdijk may refer to Plato, and his technocratic paternalism may also remind one of the modern state in its various guises (communist, fascist, democratic welfare state), but his text is above all marked by contemporary preoccupations. Sloterdijk is closer to Disney

4. Walter Benjamin, *Über den Begriff der Geschichte* (1940), in: Rolf Tiedemann, Hermann Schweppenhäuser (eds.), *Abhandlungen: Gesammelte Schriften*, vol. I.2, Suhrkamp, Frankfurt am Main 1991, p. 701.

5. See Alain Badiou, *Saint Paul. La fondation de l'universalisme*, Paris: Presses Universitaires de France, 1997; Slavoj Žižek, *The Fragile Absolute, or, Why Is the Christian Legacy Worth Fighting For?*, Verso, London/New York 2000.

6. 'Seit dem *Politikos* und seit der *Politeia* sind Reden in der Welt, die von der Menschengemeinschaft sprechen wie von einem zoologischen Park, der zugleich ein Themen-Park ist; die Menschenhaltung in Parks oder Städten erscheint von jetzt an als eine zoo-politische Aufgabe.' Sloterdijk, op. cit. (note 3), p. 48.

7. 'Zum Credo des Humanismus gehört die Überzeugung, dass Menschen "Tiere unter Einfluss" sind das dass es deswegen unerlässlich sei, ihnen die richtige Art von Beeinflussungen zukommen zu lassen.' Ibid., p. 17.

than to Plato, though Sloterdijk's vision and Disney's urbanism of exclusion can both be seen as the return of a past that was never really superseded. The new comes in the shape of a return of the ancient. With Celebration, the Walt Disney Corporation has created a residential theme park where the disintegrating tendencies of a society that is seen to succumb to Dionysian *Enthemmungsmedien* are locked out as much as possible. And Celebration is not unique: it is just one famous example of a new kind of urbanism in which towns are created as a refuge from a larger community, from society. If the big human parks that used to be called nations have become unmanageable, than smaller, safer human parks must be created for those who want to live a quiet life. However, reality has a way of kicking in, and Celebration has had its share of crime.

Jurassic Park

In the nineteenth century, a new conception of the park was born in the United States: the National Park, where a large area of nature is placed under protection. In this kind of park, it is no longer man who tames nature and hence protects himself from the wilderness; it is rather nature which is protected from human interference. The park is, however, in principle open to 'the people', as long as they follow certain rules. This kind of park has become ever more dominant; nature has to be left untainted and pure, and if there is none left it has to be created (like the areas of pseudo-authentic 'new nature' being created in Holland). In his writings from the late 1960s and early 1970s, Robert Smithson attacked the nature park ideology, then getting a new impetus from the counterculture. In his view, conservationists traded one myth (the myth of progress) for another (the myth of 'untouched wilderness'). Smithson advocated a dialectical approach to parks, in which the human and the natural, the modern and the ancient co-exist and interact. Frederick Law Olmsted, the creator of Central Park in New York, was the master of this 'dialectical landscape'. Central Park is an artificial creation, a wasteland turned into a superior 'new nature' which kept evolving through the decades. Smithson described how in the early seventies the part of the park which is called The Ramble – with winding paths intended for thoughtful walks – teemed with 'hoods, hobos, hustlers, homosexuals,' whom he apparently regarded as the equivalents of wild animals: 'Olmsted has brought a primordial condition into the heart of Manhattan.'[8] Whereas communities like Celebration are be based on the premise that society as a whole (the big human park) has evolved into a scary place full of 'hoods, hobos, hustlers, homosexuals', Smithson delighted in a dialectical park that was far from 'well kept'.

Smithson's critique of the ideology of progress in postwar American culture went hand in hand with a fascination for the 'primordial', the prehistorical. The kitschy dinosaur paintings by Charles R. Knight were as compelling to him as anything in 'official' modern art ('Note impressionistic treatment of water').[9]

8. Robert Smithson, 'Frederick Law Olmsted and the Dialectical Landscape', in: Robert Smithson, *The Collected Writings* (ed. Jack Flam), University of California Press, Berkeley/Los Angeles/London 1996, p. 169.

9. Robert Smithson, 'A Museum of Language in the Vicinity of Art' (1968), in: ibid., p. 85.

Picture postcard with a painting by Charles R. Knight from the collection of the American Museum of Natural History, New York, reproduced by Robert Smithson as an illustration in his <u>A Museum of Language in the Vicinity of Art</u>, 1968.

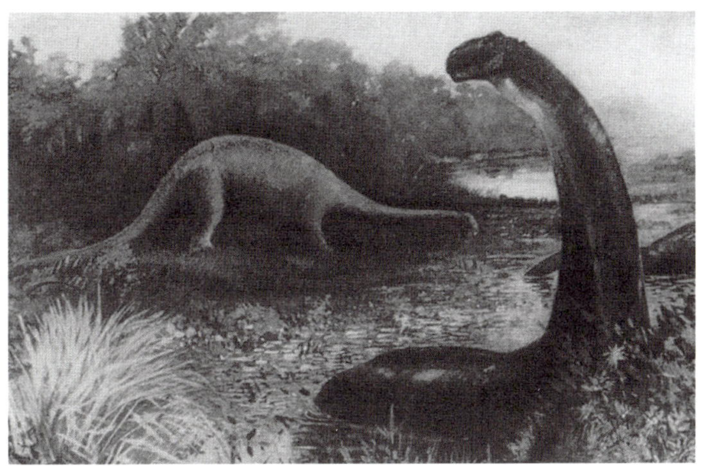

Stills from Steven Spielberg's <u>Jurassic Park</u>, 1993

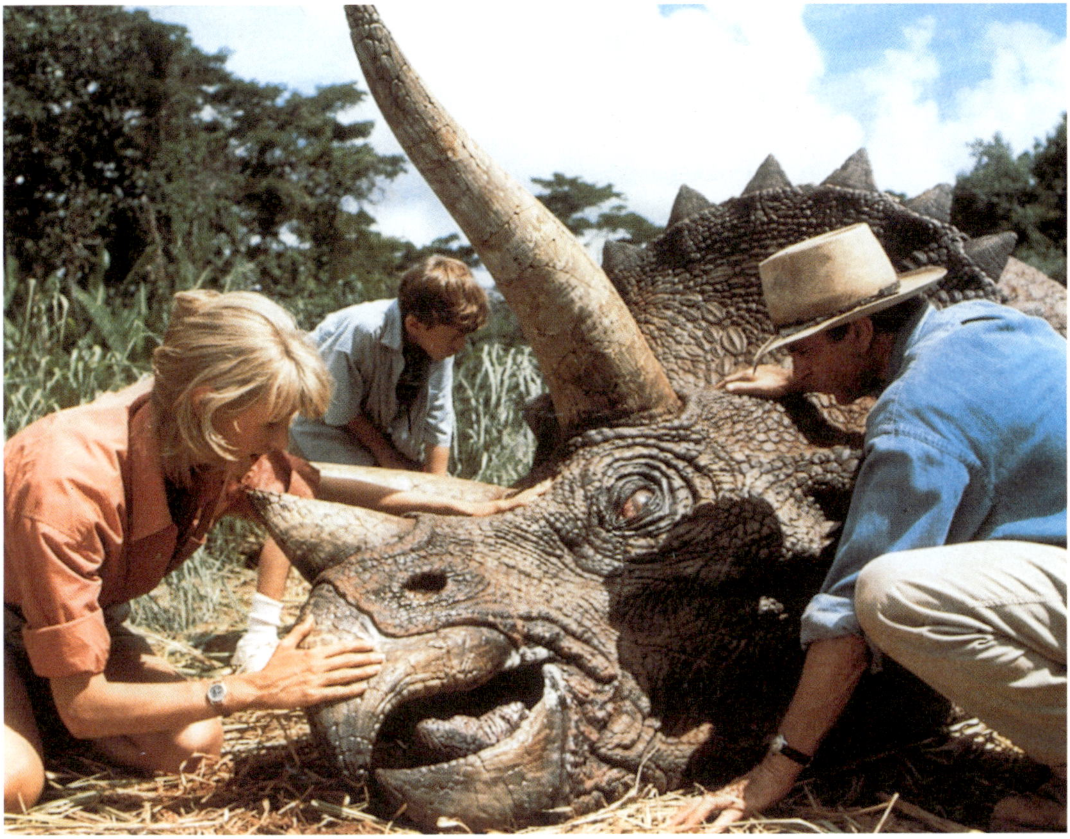

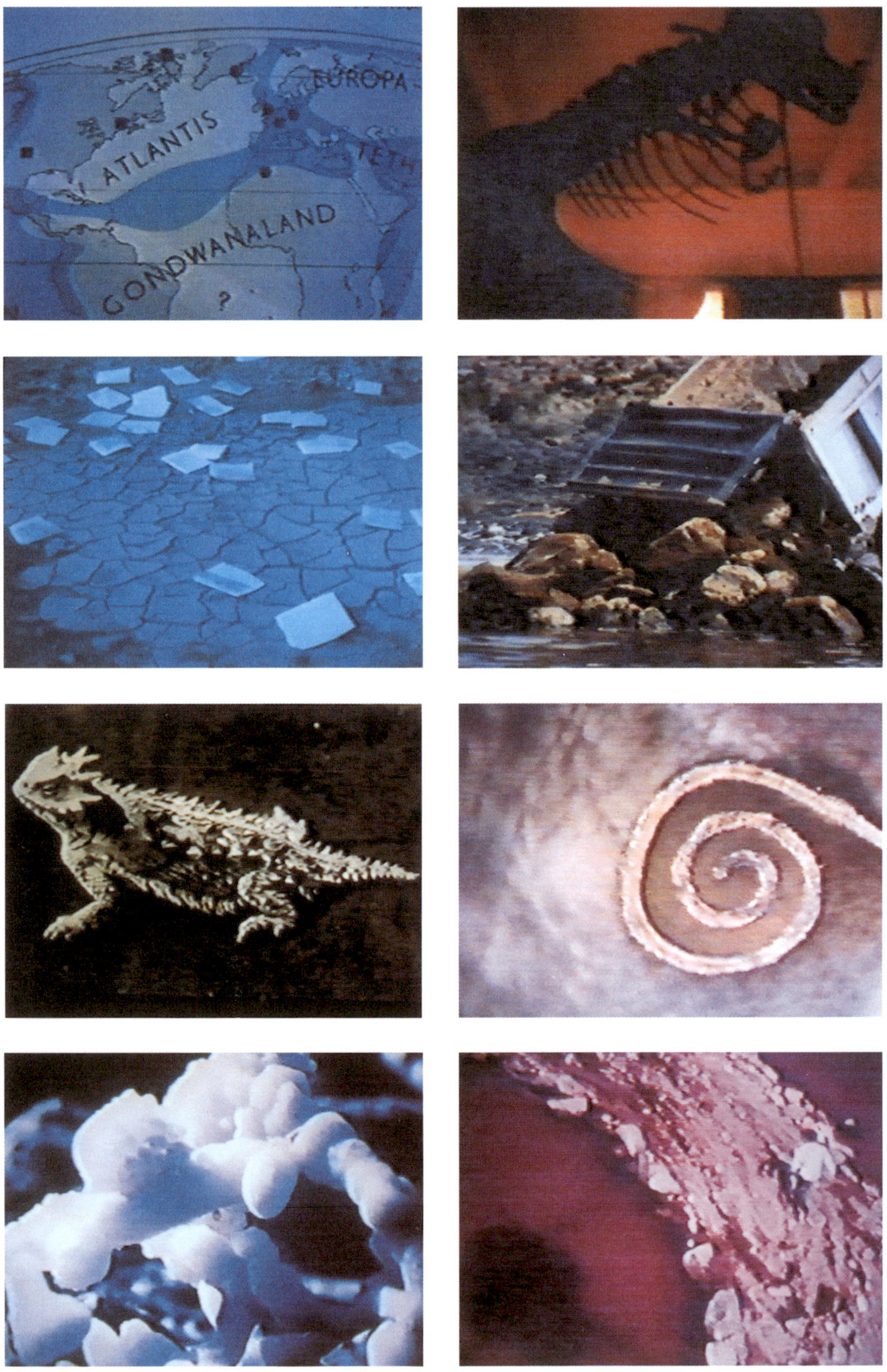

EUROPA
ATLANTIS
GONDWANALAND
?

Smithson did not so much oppose the ancient to the contemporary as try to show how and when the present becomes posthistorical, postapocalypic. He wanted to identify points where the limits of the conventional view of historical progress are exceeded, so that a posthistorical state is created that becomes one with its opposite, prehistory, which is also outside the bounds of conventional history. The industrial 'monuments' of Passaic, New Jersey, provided examples for this approach: 'River Drive was in part bulldozed and in part intact. It was hard to tell the new highway from the old road; they were both confounded into a unitary chaos. Since it was Saturday, many machines were not working, and this caused them to resemble prehistoric creatures trapped in the mud, or, better, extinct machines – mechanical dinosaurs stripped of their skin.'[10] In Smithson's view, opposites always converge and no enclosure can ensure purity – whether it is 'pure nature' or an idealized reconstruction of small-town America.

The last decade has seen the rise of a widespread fascination for amalgams of high tech and nature, of cutting edge technology and the primeval. However, this development has been marked more by the dream of a perfect convergence than by Smithson's insights into complex and messy co-existence. The Biosphere 2 complex, a system of linked greenhouses with a variety of climates, became a huge media hype when a group of scientists tries to live there autonomously in the early 1990s, without contact with the outside world. When it became apparent that there were difficulties and that the strict criteria (for instance with regard to ventilation) could not be met, the press turned against the project and its backer. Matters only calmed down when Columbia University took over the plant and promised to run it by strict scientific standards (recently, the university announced the end of the project). Whatever may be the scientific merits of Biosphere 2, it captured the media's attention because it was (also) something more than science: it was a phantasmagorical New Eden, the promise of a healthy, balanced ecosystem. If it were possible to create a stabile ecosystem in greenhouses, in an enclosed, park-like space, then perhaps it does not matter so much if the real biosphere – the global nature park, which mankind has managed rather badly – goes to the dogs. New paradises could be created on other planets once this one is defunct. The ideal human park in the age of ecological awareness would have to be a nature park as well: Paradise Regained.

The ultimate – fictional – nature park of the last decade is Steven Spielberg's *Jurassic Park* (1993) and its sequels. Smithson would probably have been mesmerized by this film, written by Michael Crichton: after all, the theme park entrepreneur in *Jurassic Park* uses advanced technology to re-create dinosaurs from their genetic material. Instead of creating peaceful inhabitants for the human park, as Sloterdijk hoped it would, the genetic revolution results in a new prehistoric age. This theme park is on an island, because the dinosaurs must under no circumstance leave their park

10. Robert Smithson, 'A Tour of The Monuments of Passaic, New Jersey' (1967), in: ibid., p. 71.

(the inhabitants of, say, Celebration would not be amused if a T-Rex stalked through their town). Of course the island soon becomes a deadly trap for the people on it, as the dinosaurs start breeding and take over 'their' theme park. The park management has screwed up, and Spielberg can stage a virtual bloodbath which would probably have thrilled the Roman audience in *Gladiator*. Since dinosaurs first became the subject of science and of the popular imagination in the mid-nineteenth century, they have often been used to comment on human society; hence it is hard not to see *Jurassic Park* as a human park in disguise.[11] After all, the dinosaurs' voraciousness and greed is matched by the ruthless park director and his financial backers. They are true creatures of capitalism. And how could new nature created by humans be anything else but a human park?

A Franchised Free State

For a few months in 2001, the 'free state' of AVL-Ville existed in Rotterdam. AVL-Ville was founded by Atelier Van Lieshout, the art/design/architecture studio headed by Joep van Lieshout. The main part AVL-Ville was the studio compound in the Rotterdam harbour area, which was sealed off by a wall consisting mainly of containers. On the lot itself there were various structures scattered around in a rather haphazard fashion – including a field hospital and a car turned into a chicken coop. There was also a farm nearby, called AVL-Ville 2. After less than a year, AVL-Ville was closed because the town of Rotterdam insisted that the buildings and restaurant in AVL-Ville met its regulations (thus making explicit the fictional status of AVL-Ville as a state). Drawing from the bag of 'radical' theoretical concepts, one might opt to characterise AVL-Ville as a *heterotopia*, one of the divergent, marginal spaces that Foucault contrasted with the abstract, homogenizing space of capitalism – or as a TAZ, the Temporary Autonomous Zone posited by Hakim Bey.[12] But for all the differences between these notions, both heterotopias and TAZs are *in* this abstract space, a part of it; they introduce difference, but they are not closed off. The fact that Van Lieshout envisaged a network of AVL-Ville 'franchises' throughout the world could be linked to Foucault's conception of a network of heterotopias, but by staging a secession from society in the form of a 'free' state, Van Lieshout effectively copied the logic of gated communities and other human parks.

AVL works like the *Atelier des armes et des bombes* (a shed for making bombs) have led critics to comparisons with the reactionary American Militia movement as well as with the Unabomber: deluded attempts to stop the permanent revolution of global capitalism and to recreate some 'normal', stabile society. AVL-ville has also been compared to David Koresh's compound in Waco, Texas – another secession from society, and a particularly ill-fated one. At the opening ceremony AVL-Ville turned out to be much more festive and friendly. But as a

11. On the dinosaur in modern and contemporary culture, see W.J.T. Mitchell, *The Last Dinosaur Book*, The University of Chicago Press, Chicago/London 1998.

12. Michel Foucault, 'Of Other Spaces' (1967), *Diacritics* 16, 1 (1986), p. 22-27; Hakim Bey, *T.A.Z. The Temporary Autonomous Zone, Ontological Anarchy, Poetic Terrorism*, Autonomedia, New York 1991, p. 95-134.

small settlement that takes the form of a demarcated compound, AVL-Ville is, however closer to Waco than to, for instance, Constant's *New Babylon* project from the 1950s and 1960s, which took the form of plans for immense structures that would have done away with the need to stay in a fixed place. Constant's vision could not be further away from Sloterdijk's view of society as a 'human park' which has to be kept in order, although Constant's Roussauist view of human nature may be as problematical as Sloterdijk's conservative one: Constant foresaw a nomadic *homo ludens* engaged in a perpetual *dérive*. Between New Babylon and AVL-Ville, something fundamental has changed: models for social reform (or revolution) are no longer aimed at society at large, but at small secessions from this society.

In the final analysis it is not Waco that comes to mind in the case of AVL-Ville, but Celebration, as incompatible as Van Lieshout's libertarianism may be with Disney's paternalist social vision – and as much as it may be inspired by commune experiments of the late Sixties and Seventies, which also followed the logic of secession. Both Celebration and AVL-Ville are small human parks that have split off from a society that is seen – although for different reasons – as a large human park that is run in an unsatisfactory manner. Both use the status of private property in the modern state to split a piece of land off from the state, to turn it into a micro-state. The concept of 'franchises' is also obviously derived from corporations such as Disney, who can effectively blackmail national governments, because they can always hop to the next countries. Multinationals are after all the true nomads; in the past decade it has become clear that perhaps only capital lives up to Deleuze and Guattari's romantic theory of nomadism; only capital is always on the move, without any definitive 'reterritorialization' taking place. In Asia, this has led to the establishment of 'free-trade zones' where normal law is suspended: in these zones, corporations (or rather their contractors) can pretty much do what they want (which includes barely paying their workers).[13] A discussion of AVL-Ville in this context may seem strange, as AVL-Ville was not about exploiting workers or evading taxes. It tried to use the human park approach to society against its aims, but it did not actually break with this approach. It was a human park dressed in the garb of a 'pirate utopia'.

13. Naomi Klein, *No Logo*, Flamingo, London 2000, p. 195-229.

Even more than books, films or inhabited theme parks (whether by Disney or by Van Lieshout), it is the medium of television that has exploited the fact that we have come to think of society as a human zoo. One successful 'reality TV' format was a show where a group of carefully selected people live with each other on an uninhabited island, a Jurassic Park for humans. In the even more popular *Big Brother*, the human park was been reduced to tiny dimensions: one house with cameras everywhere. It is the ultimate secession, the private home, turned into a peepshow. Meanwhile, reality soaps about Ozzy Osbourne and others reduce boredom by focusing on bizarre and famous individuals, rather

General plan drawing of <u>AVL-Ville</u>, Rotterdam, Atelier Van Lieshout, 2001

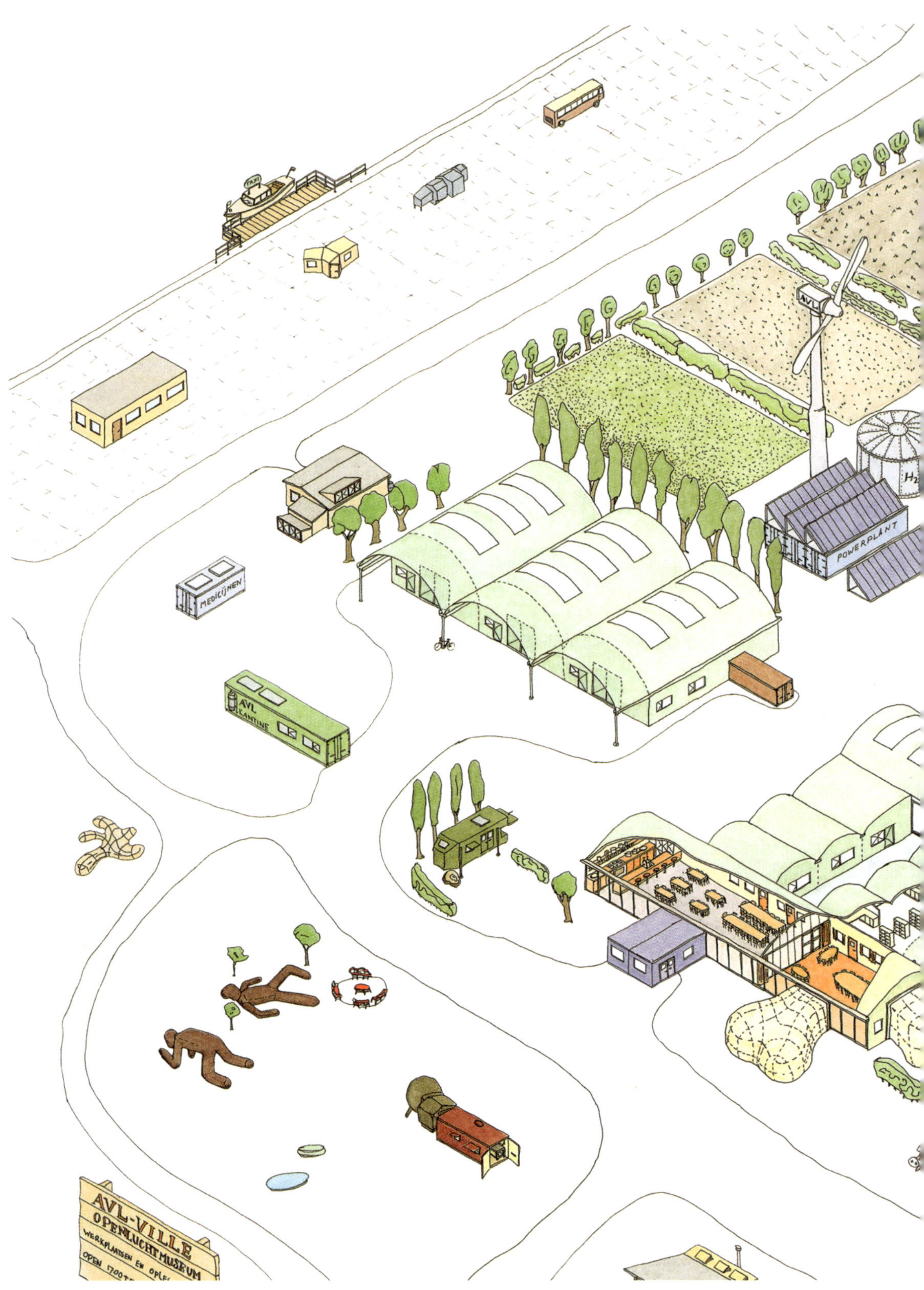

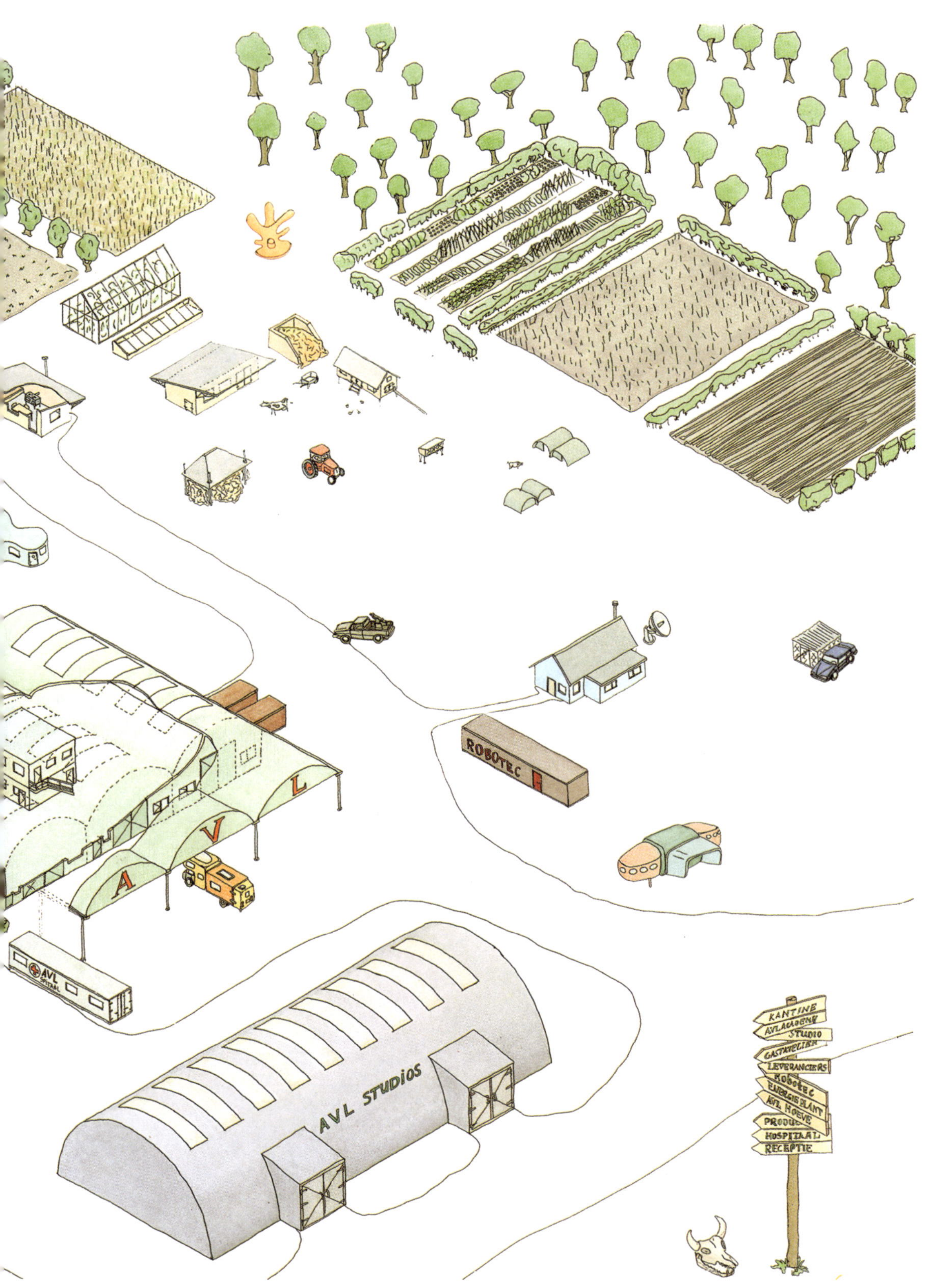
AVL
ROBOTEC
AVL STUDIOS
AVL CENTRAL
KANTINE
AVL ACADEMY
STUDIO
GASTATELIER
LEVERANCIERS
ROBOTEC
EMBALLAGE PLANT
AVL HOEVE
PRODUC
HOSPITAAL
RECEPTIE

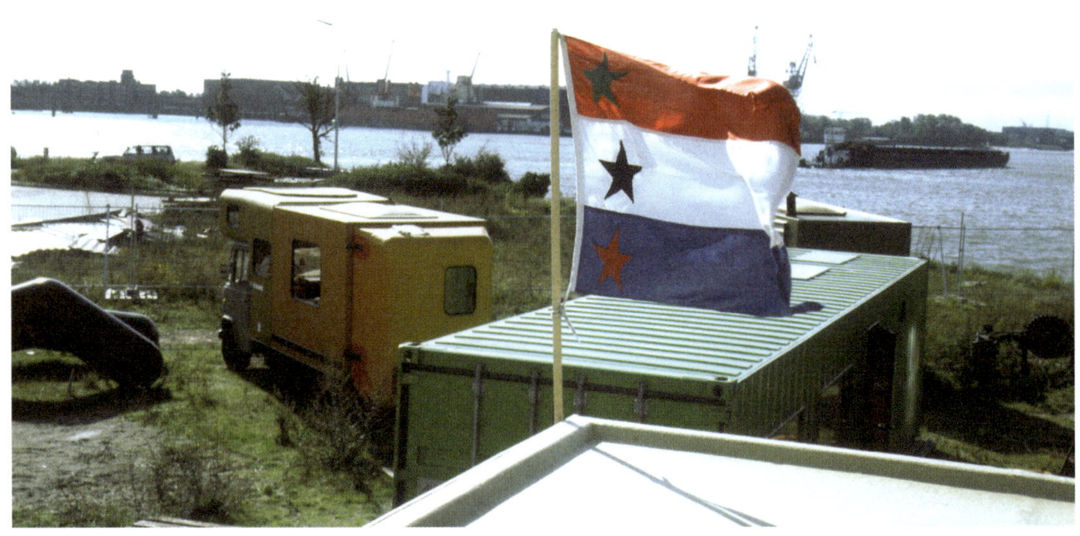

AVL-Ville flag, Atelier Van Lieshout, 2001. Photo D.J. Wooldrik

AVL-Ville, Atelier van Lieshout, 2001. Photo D.J. Wooldrik

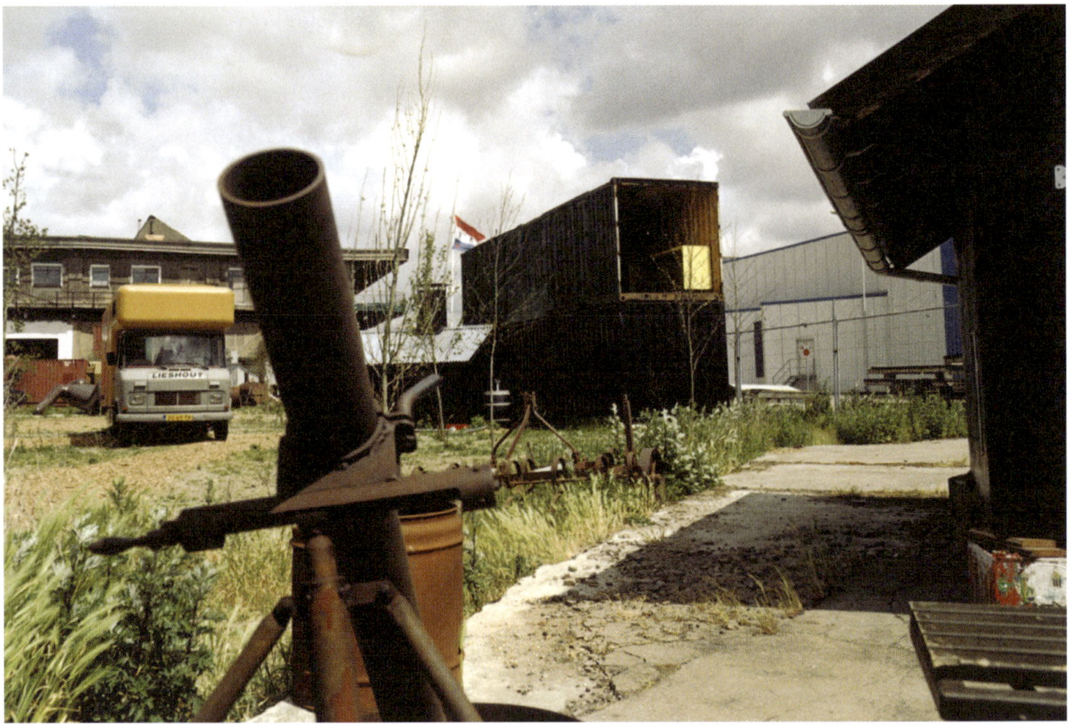

than on assorted nonentities. Having lost the faith in the manageability of society we watch how, in this microcosm, people just barely manage to get along; we watch how the secluded little human park turns out to be just as complex and unmanageable as the big human park that once used to be called society. As in *Jurassic Park*, the enclosed space turns out to be a trap rather than a way out.

This essay previously appeared in the *New Left Review*, no. 10, July/August 2001, p. 111-118 and has been specially revised for *Open*.

Harm Tilman

Architecture in Control Societies

Security as a Selling Point

As city authorities are confining themselves to their basic tasks and citizens are compelled to take the care of their living environment into their own hands, 'gated communities' like those becoming increasingly common in the United States may not be far off for the Netherlands, according to Harm Tilman. The development of a society of control in which the issue of security is high on the political agenda has opened the way for this in the Netherlands.

Your problem and everyone's problem in this village is that you think you have a right to be safe. You all know each other, and you're always telling each other everything. You all went to the same school and you shop in the same shops, and you know each other's parents and grandparents and great-grandparents. You all arrange everything among yourselves. You think that because you go to school, and to your work, and pay your taxes and don't break the law too blatantly, nothing can happen to you. And when something does happen, you're outraged. And then a scapegoat has to be found. It's time you woke up, Tessa. Just because you shower every day doesn't mean you can't get dirty.

Kristien Hemmerechts,
Donderdagmiddag. Halfvier, Atlas,
Amsterdam/Antwerp 2002

Not long ago, a village near the city where I live was shaken by the brutal murder of a petrol station owner. The loot totalled 100 euros and a few packets of cigarettes. The young perpetrators turned out to live around the corner and were quickly apprehended. A week and a half later, the village turned out for a silent march, yet another protest against random violence in the public space. It was not the first and probably not the last demonstration against reprehensible behaviour in public. They express a 'high level of common anger against the presumed and actual causes of evil' and constitute an escape valve for a society that is no longer what it was.

In the recent book *Sferen* ('Spheres') the German philosopher Peter Sloterdijk analyses various forms of anger in solidarity.[1] Sloterdijk argues that these are partly represented in scandals and expressions of indignation. This can even include the collective fuss about a former

1. Peter Sloterdijk, *Sferen, II. Globes, macrosferologie*, Boom, Amsterdam 2003.

Amsterdam city alderman's visit to the prostitution zone on the Theemsweg. These are exercises that are meant to banish evil from our midst. Together they define a communal inner space that can be called secure. The two processes are closely connected. Sloterdijk sees these efforts as attempts to create a safe distance between the immune space of the group and its banished spoilers. Security is a necessary ingredient for a society that has become highly individualized.

Societies of Control

The current growing focus on security or insecurity coincides with the transition from a disciplinary society into a society of control, as analysed two decades ago by the French philosopher Michel Foucault. The former type of society reached its high point at the beginning of the twentieth century. A characteristic of this is that the individual moves between closed environments, each with its own patterns, which succeed each other in a set order, from the family to the school, the military barracks, the factory, the hospital, the prison and the retirement home. In Foucault's view these environments slowly became mired in deep crisis. Well-intentioned but ineffective reforms are an expression of this. The school system in the Netherlands, for example, has been radically transformed various times since the implementation of educational-reform legislation in 1968, with little result.

The considerations developed by the Italian philosopher Giorgio Agamben in the book *Homo Sacer* outline the consequences of the emergence of a society entirely based on control.[2] According to Agamben the distinction between biological life (*zoe*) and the

2. Giorgio Agamben, *Homo Sacer. De soevereine macht en het naakte leven*, translation by Ineke van der Burg, Boom/Parrèsia, Amsterdam 2002.

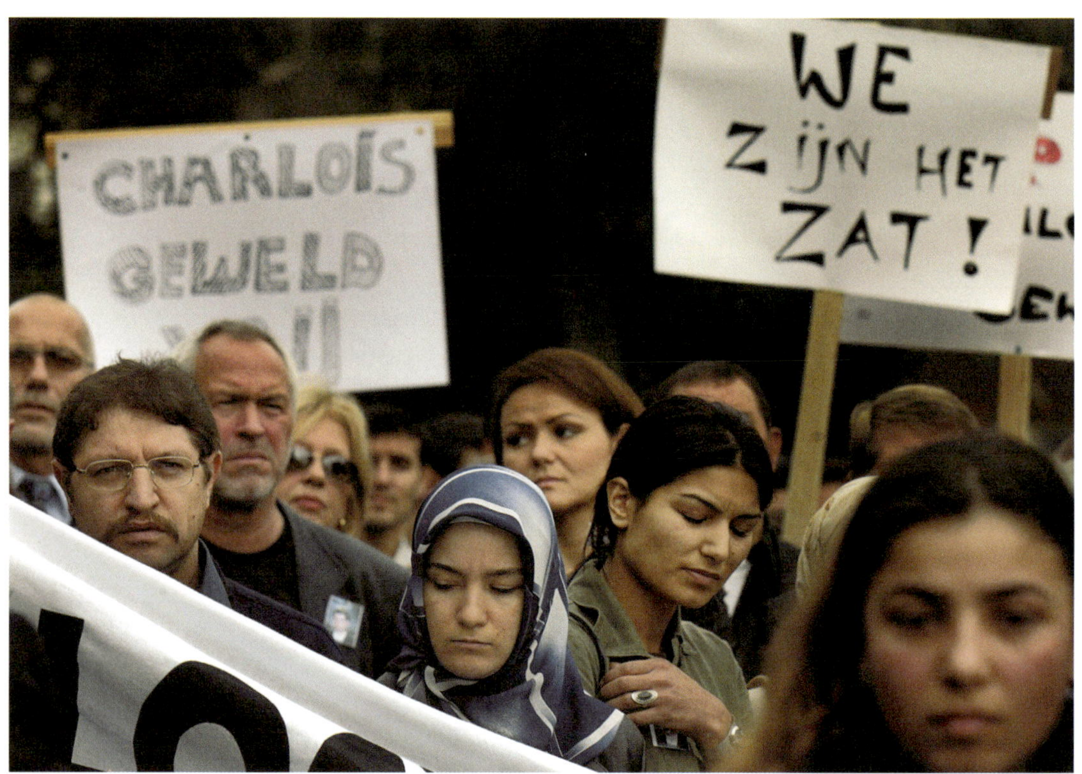
CHARLOIS
GEWELD
WE
Z IJN HET
ZAT !

qualified life of the citizen (*bios*) have disappeared, and all that is left is bare existence. Therefore it is no longer the city, but the camp in which life can be controlled down to the smallest detail, that forms the paradigm of contemporary politics. The camp has embedded itself firmly in the city, according to Agamben. At airports and stations, in shopping centres and asylum centres, a state of emergency is increasingly in force. Such 'non-places' are the epitome of modern camps, Agamben says. 'In all these cases an ostensibly secure place actually marks off (…) a space in which the normal order has effectively been suspended and the extent to which outrages are committed depends not on law, but only on the decency and morality of the police temporarily exercising sovereignty.'

A new urban reality is emerging. According to Paul Virilio, cities are being turned inside out, with sections of the public space becoming private and the private space becoming more public.[3] The design of the urban space is having to deal with demands for social safety. Insecurity is no longer confined to known bad neighbourhoods; it can be experienced anywhere and at unexpected moments. Conversely, the home, under the influence of the media, the computer and global communication, is turning into an increasingly public space. The traditional opposition of valuable public space versus secure private space has lost some of its importance. The sociologist Ioan Davies makes this clear using the example of the prison.[4] In prison there is no distinction between inhabitable and hostile space, as introduced by the French philosopher Gaston Bachelard. This space is both familiar and insecure.

3. Paul Virilio, *L'espace critique: Essai*, Christian Bourgeois Éditeur, Paris 1984.

4. Ioan Davies, *Writers in Prison*, Basil Blackwell, Oxford 1990.

Therefore, Davies argues, the use to which a space is put should be made into the starting point. The public domain (the prison) dictates the private domain (the personal everyday meaning) only superficially. In the spatial organization of the public domain, however, the centripetal and the centrifugal coexist, making its entrances and exits coincidental. This means that all spaces are insecure and therefore in one way or another hostile. We can see this reflected in the behaviour of urban dwellers in the public space. People make a detour if they do not trust a situation, or come to arrangements with neighbours and friends, for instance. 'Space is imagined, put into place, and resisted. The meaning and use of space are everywhere subject to strategic negotiation.'

The Netherlands is Slowly Being Secured

The promotional campaign 'Nederland veilig' ('Netherlands secure'), a joint initiative of the ministries of Justice and of the Interior and Kingdom Relations aptly plays into this. In it, the government is making it known that security is important for everyone. Exasperation about robberies, violence, vandalism and intimidation has reached unacceptable levels, as well as the resulting damage, according to the promotional message. By 2006, crime in and around contemporary non-places, such as stations, parking garages and shopping centres, must be reduced by a quarter. More police officers and more security personnel must ensure more security in the streets, as must surveillance cameras. Citizens are also being marshalled into the effort 'toward a safer society'. Official certifications, 'neighbourhood watch' projects and informant telephone numbers, including the option of

Henrik Plenge Jakobsen, <u>ANGST</u>, mural, 1999, 50 Lower Hall Lane, Walsall (UK). This artwork, according to the artist, addresses 'the condition of

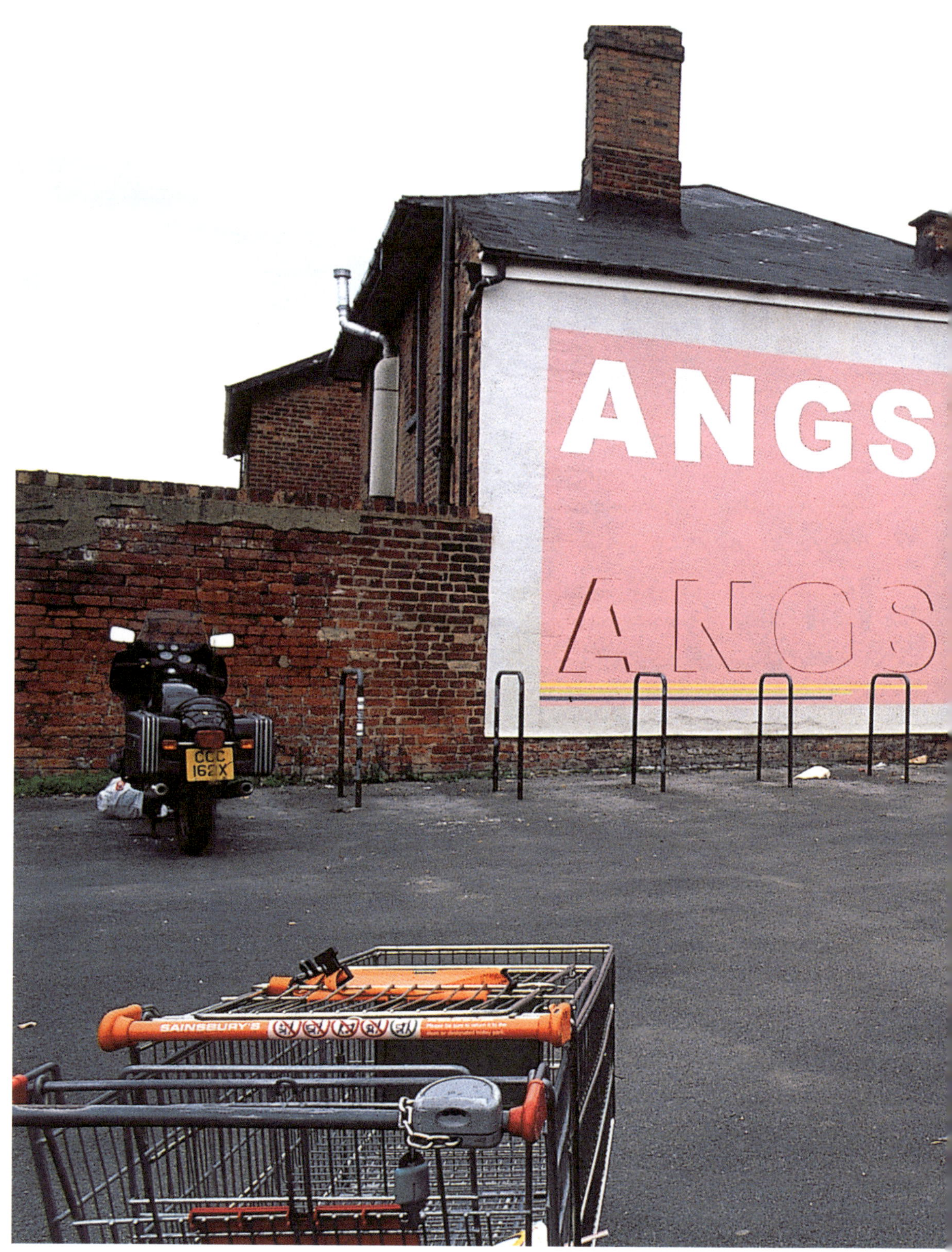

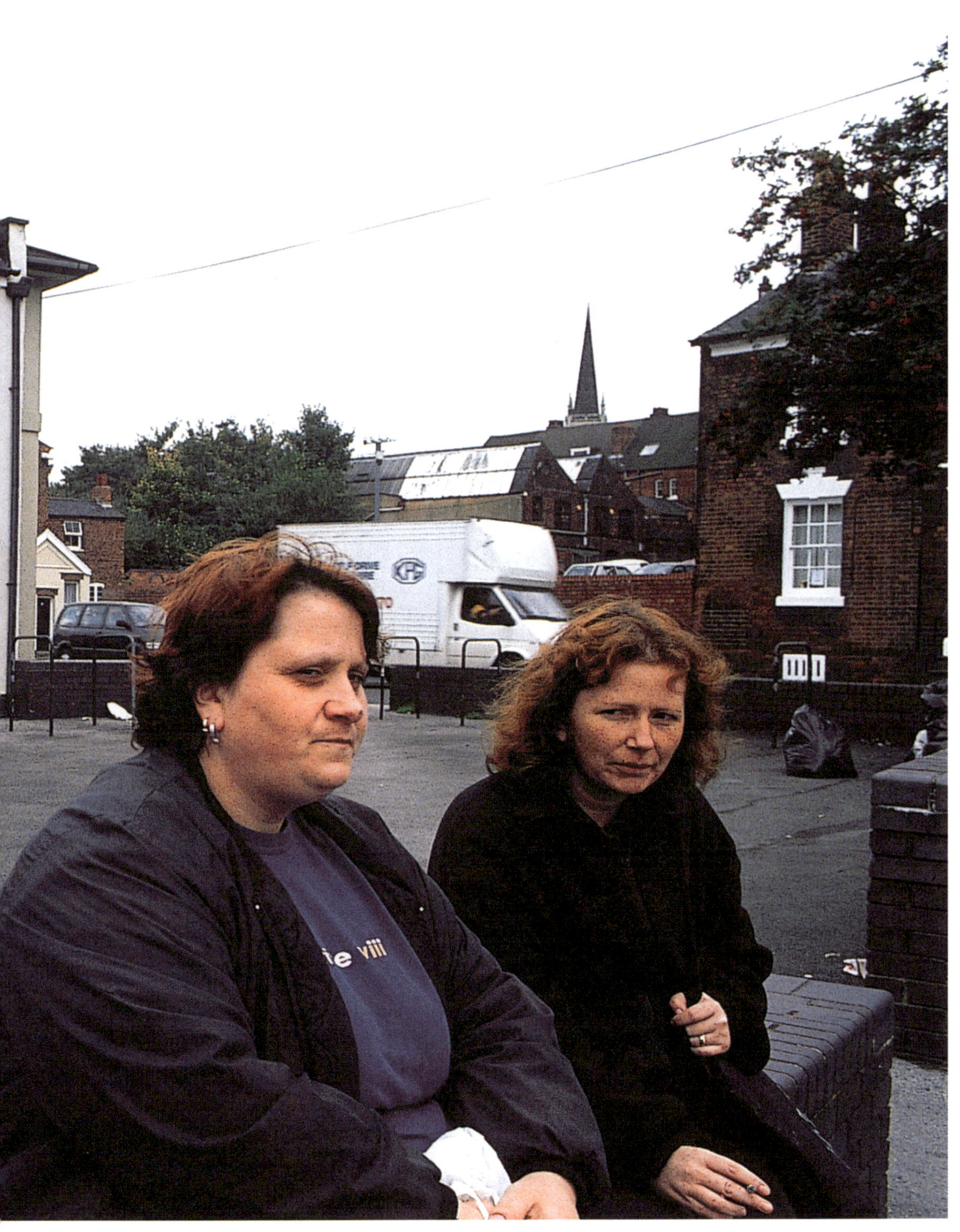

our societies, which undergo so many political, historical and
especially economic changes'. Photo Peter Baker. © Smith + Fowle

Public-service advertisement: 'We're going to be checking more. You stay alert as well.' Promotional campaign by the Ministry of Justice and the Ministry of the Interior and Kingdom Relations, published among others in <u>NRC Handelsblad</u>, 10 January 2004.

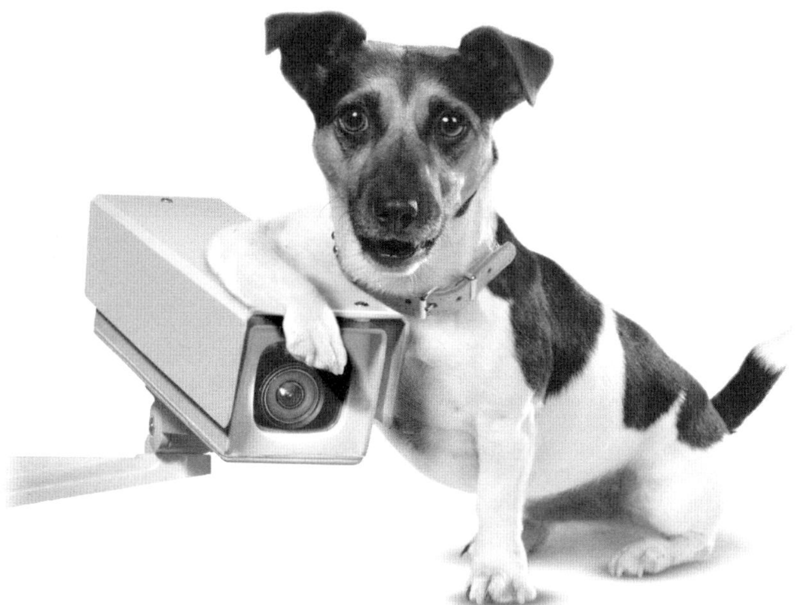

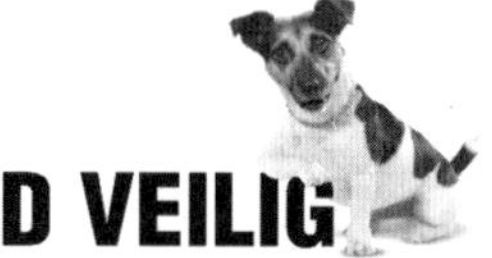

reporting crimes anonymously, offer diverse possibilities.

Security is saturating the micro as well as the macro sphere. The official police certification 'Politiekeurmerk Veilig Wonen' on house security is intended for owners and tenants of existing dwellings as well as new-build houses and flats. By bringing the dwelling into line with the standards of this certification, residents can be one step ahead of burglars. To achieve this they must adapt their windows and doors and change the locks on the front door and windows, to make them more difficult to force. They are also urged to change their behaviour by locking their doors at night, keeping their keys safe, shutting windows at night and making arrangements with neighbours. All of these measures are meant to result in a higher level of security in the home. This idea was derived from 'Secured by Design' in England. New-build dwellings that meet the security standards are granted a certification. In England this proved an effective concept, by reducing the chances for home invasion and turning out to be a selling point for potential house buyers.

But the security policy is now extending to the urban level. In Rotterdam, the city executive has developed an action programme intended to put an end to the deterioration of so-called disadvantaged neighbourhoods. According to the city authorities, these include those areas where too many poor, low-skilled people are settling and which too many well-off, highly skilled people are leaving. This is said to be placing a heavy burden on facilities as well as resulting in a concentration of poverty, nuisance and illegal activity. Key elements of the action programme are stringent residency requirements (such as the requirement that people moving in earn at least 120 percent of the minimum wage), strong-arm measures against illegal tenants and dodgy landlords, allocation of housing in problem areas through positive balloting and the establishment of economic development zones in which private parties receive tax benefits in return for investments.

The growing emphasis on security is also reflected in the use of security impact reports, comparable to environmental impact reports. These are tests on social safety for construction plans and urban projects. According to Tobias Woldendorp, social safety design consultant with Van Dijk, Van Soomeren and Partners, the design of a sustainable city falls within the jurisdiction of urban planners, architects and landscape architects. If the latter neglect security and liveability, a defensive-looking environment emerges, in which the degradation of the public domain can only be turned back through *ad hoc* interventions. Woldendorp therefore calls for every step in the planning process – from the Document on Basic Principles to the Definitive Design – to include a brief security test. He also wants to link a bottom-up approach to security improvement. The revitalization of city centres and neighbourhoods after all requires the participation of residents.

Toward an Ecology of Fear

The character of the city is changing. During the riots in the black ghettos in American cities, the mayor of Philadelphia observed that 'from now on, state borders go through cities'. The obsession with social safety and with the guarding of these societal boundaries is part of the *'zeitgeist'* of urban restructuring. One no longer enters a city via a station or a boulevard. Residents and visitors are now subject to systems of permanent surveillance. This phenomenon is particular prevalent in American cities, where one third of all suburbs are enclosed by security walls. St. Andres, for instance, a 'gated community' in Boca Raton, Florida, spends more than one million dollars a year on surveillance. Anti-terrorist barriers in the road surface are beginning to be part of the standard equipment of American residential communities. The obsession with security is greatest in Los Angeles, *the* city of freedom. Insecurity is not only related to vandals and street gangs, but also with the significant segregation that now characterizes the city.

Mike Davis, author of the book *City of Quartz: Excavating the Future in Los Angeles* (1990), has aptly characterized this phenomenon in 'the ecology of fear'.[5] Davis based this on the diagram used by the sociologist Ernest Burgess to represent the urban dynamics of Chicago in the 1920s. Around the Loop, Burgess drew concentric zones where processes of invasion and displacement were operating. Accessibility and property value are determinants in this scenario. Davis adds the factor of fear to this diagram. The Loop has evolved into a 'core' within which undesirables are placed in 'homeless containment zones'. The inner city, in the Chicago of the 1920s a 'melting pot', is now a disadvantaged area in which the police systematically scour alternating 'drug-free zones' for set periods of time. This core is ringed by the 'blue-collar suburbs', where citizens provide for their own security by means of 'neighbourhood watch' programmes. Further out are the 'gated affluent suburbs'. In the periphery of this city, there are various opportunities for

5. Mike Davis, *Ecology of Fear: Los Angeles and the Imagination of Disaster*, Metropolitan Books, Henry Holt and Company, New York 1998.

containing minorities within various ghettos.

As far back as the 1980s, Hollywood films, such as *Running Man, Blade Runner, Die Hard* and *Colours,* showed to what extent the theme of security had displaced that of social integration. Security is what the economist Fred Hirsch calls a 'positional good',[6] a good defined by the extent to which people have access to private 'protective services' and secured residential enclaves. Moreover, social safety is a self-fulfilling prophecy. As the sociologist William H. Whyte once said, 'Fear proves itself'.[7] We can see this in the Netherlands as well. Although the statistics have not changed dramatically, the suddenly increased perception of threat is dictating the measures now being taken in the area of social safety. The military phraseology used makes references to potential violence and alludes to imaginary dangers.

6. Fred Hirsch, *Social Limits to Growth*, Routledge & Kegan Paul, London/Henley 1977.

7. William H. Whyte, *The City, Rediscovering the Center*, Doubleday, New York 1988.

The Design of New Collectivism

This places repairs to the most intimate of spaces high on the agenda. This is coupled, as made clear by Sloterdijk, with an expansion of the private sphere. This is also happening in the Netherlands. Does this mean that the Netherlands, like the United States, will see 'defended neighbourhoods' and 'gated affluent communities'? The question is not whether, but rather how this phenomenon will manifest itself in the Netherlands. The Dutch housing market has changed from a supply into a demand market, and security is an important 'positional good' in this market. This will also find expression in design.

The role of security is different on the outskirts of cities than within existing cities.

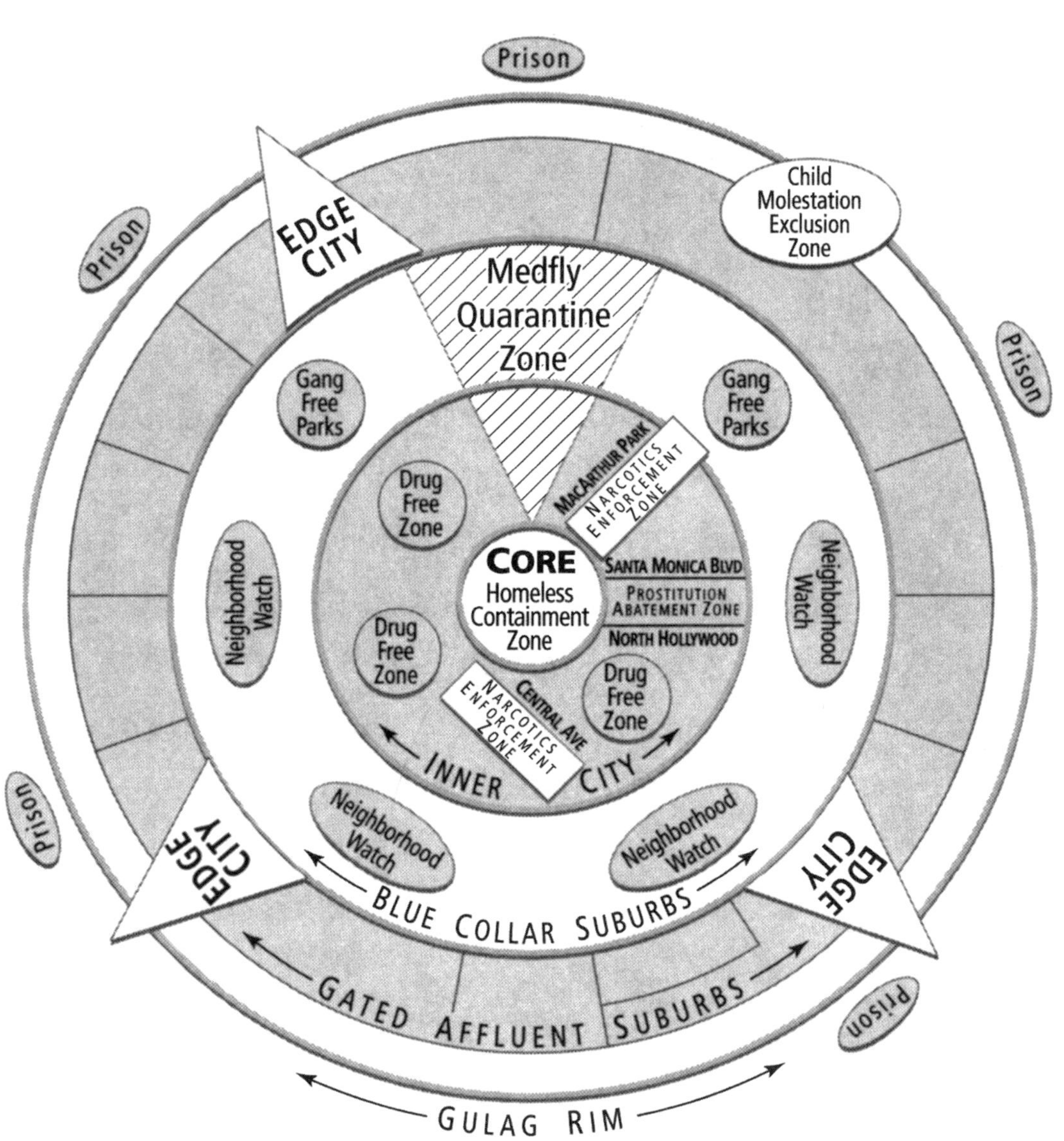
Prison
Prison
Prison
Prison
Prison
Prison
EDGE CITY
EDGE CITY
EDGE CITY
Child Molestation Exclusion Zone
Medfly Quarantine Zone
Gang Free Parks
Gang Free Parks
Neighborhood Watch
Neighborhood Watch
Neighborhood Watch
Neighborhood Watch
Drug Free Zone
Drug Free Zone
Drug Free Zone
MacArthur Park
NARCOTICS ENFORCEMENT ZONE
CENTRAL AVE NARCOTICS ENFORCEMENT ZONE
CORE
Homeless Containment Zone
SANTA MONICA BLVD
PROSTITUTION ABATEMENT ZONE
NORTH HOLLYWOOD
INNER CITY
BLUE COLLAR SUBURBS
GATED AFFLUENT SUBURBS
GULAG RIM

Example of a 'gated community' in the United States
Photo from <u>Mutations</u>, Bordeaux

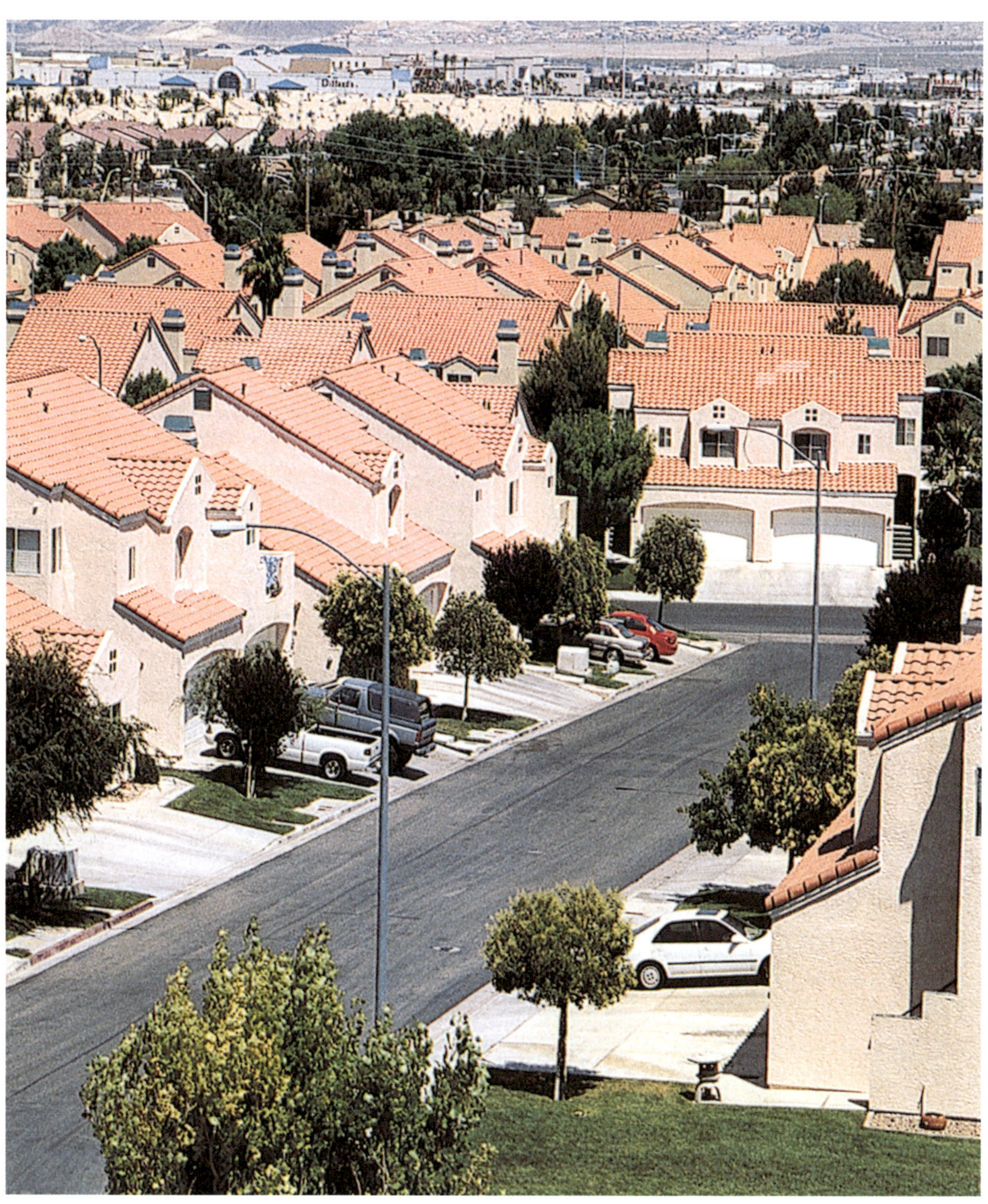

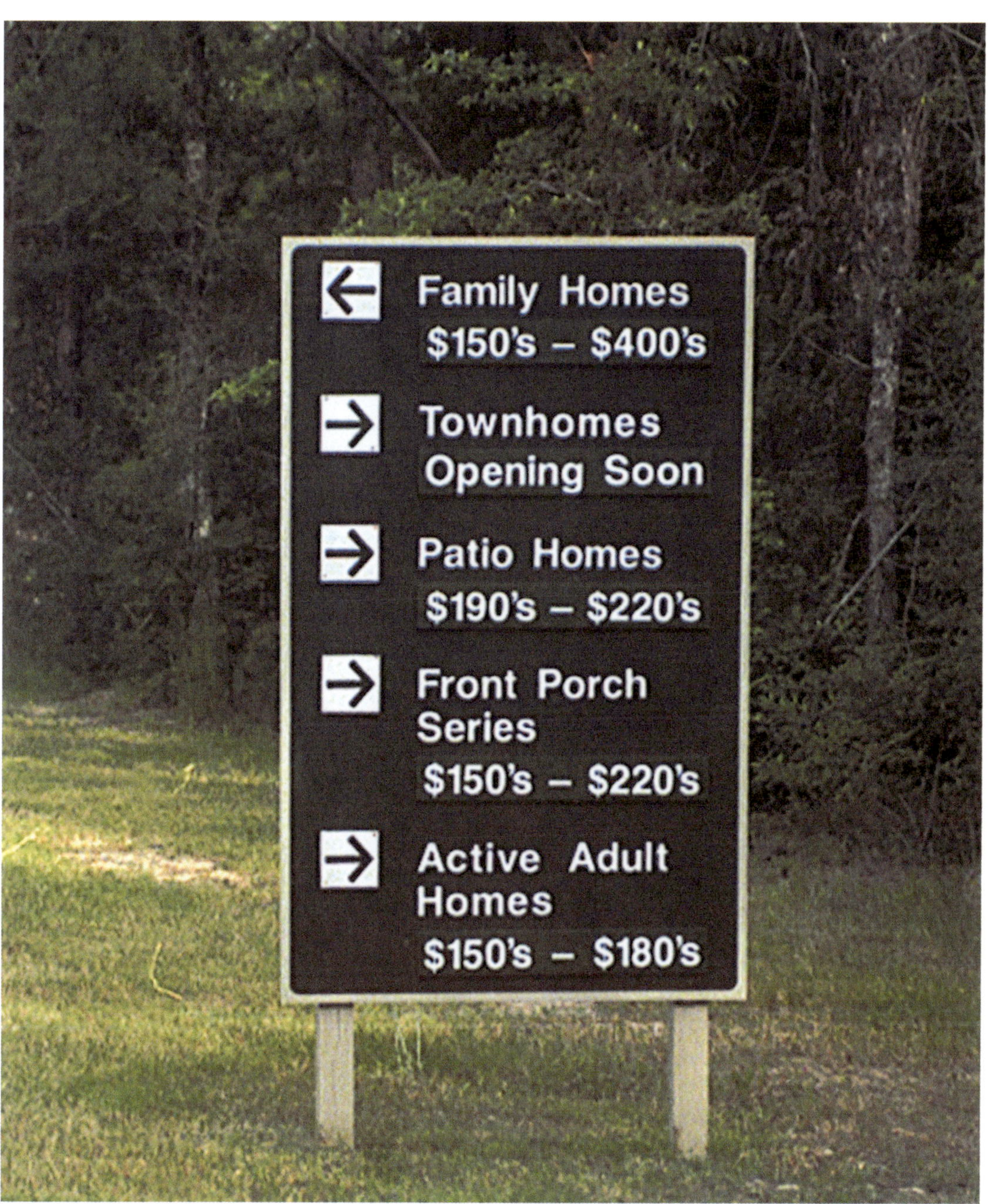
Family Homes
$150's – $400's
Townhomes
Opening Soon
Patio Homes
$190's – $220's
Front Porch
Series
$150's – $220's
Active Adult
Homes
$150's – $180's

Individual subdivisions in Vinex developments distinguish themselves through great physical and cultural homogeneity. This is reinforced by the name or metaphor which lends the subdivision its own identity. This allows these subdivisions to exude a strong sense of unity, which gives 'undesirable visitors' the impression that they do not belong here. The villa subdivision Park Boswijk in the Vinex development of Ypenburg, for example, stands entirely alone. It has its own identity, primarily one of luxury. The high prices that must be paid for the parcels and dwellings do the rest. Haverleij, near Den Bosch, goes a step further. It consists of islands of luxury dwellings in an attractively designed landscape. Here, cultural homogeneity has also been physically expressed, in that the 'manors' are walled in.

In inner cities, large, 'thick' buildings are being created, which can be closed off entirely and offer residents a sense of safety and security. The core here is a collective (or semi-public) space that functions as an inner world within the complex and forms the link between dwelling and city. This collective space provides a controlled oasis or resting place within the dynamics of the big city. It is usually designed as an inner garden, but it can also be a swimming pool or a tennis court. Spectacular examples of this form of housing include the building by Neutelings Riedijk Architecten on the Mullerpier in Rotterdam, KCAP's 'Commissaris' in Venlo and the Baekelandplein project by Paul Diederen of Diederen, Dirrix van Wylick Architecten in Eindhoven. These complexes offer the target group of senior citizens the quality of a 'protected community' within an urban environment.

There are as yet no 'gated affluent communities' in the Netherlands. In such a community the neighbourhood or the building is enclosed by walls and the area within the walls is fully private (and thus not semi-public). The residents themselves are responsible for the arrangement and maintenance of their domain. Life is subject to strict rules of behaviour, which must be accepted upon purchase. Municipal democracy has been eliminated in these enclaves. It has not come this far in the Netherlands yet. Even when neighbourhoods are walled in, they are not closed off. Yet we are moving in that direction, as municipal authorities are limiting themselves to their 'core activities' and citizens have to care for their own living environment. Thus we will not have to wait long for this phenomenon.

Diederen Dirrix van Wylick Architecten, Baekelandplein, Eindhoven (project architect Paul Diederen). The location forms a link between the centre and the former working-class neighbourhood of Woensel-West, which is now seen as a disadvantaged area with high levels of crime, immigrant numbers and prostitution. In the project, the accumulation of the diverse programme components, conflicting in themselves, is used to create a special cohesion between the building and spaces. The plan is organized around a collective space positioned four metres above the surface level and providing access to all the components.

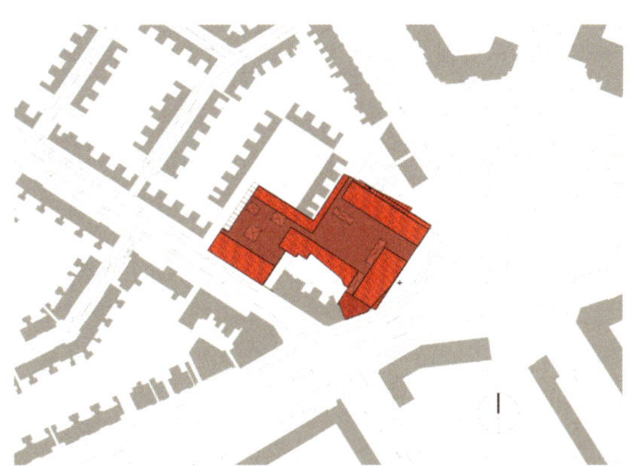

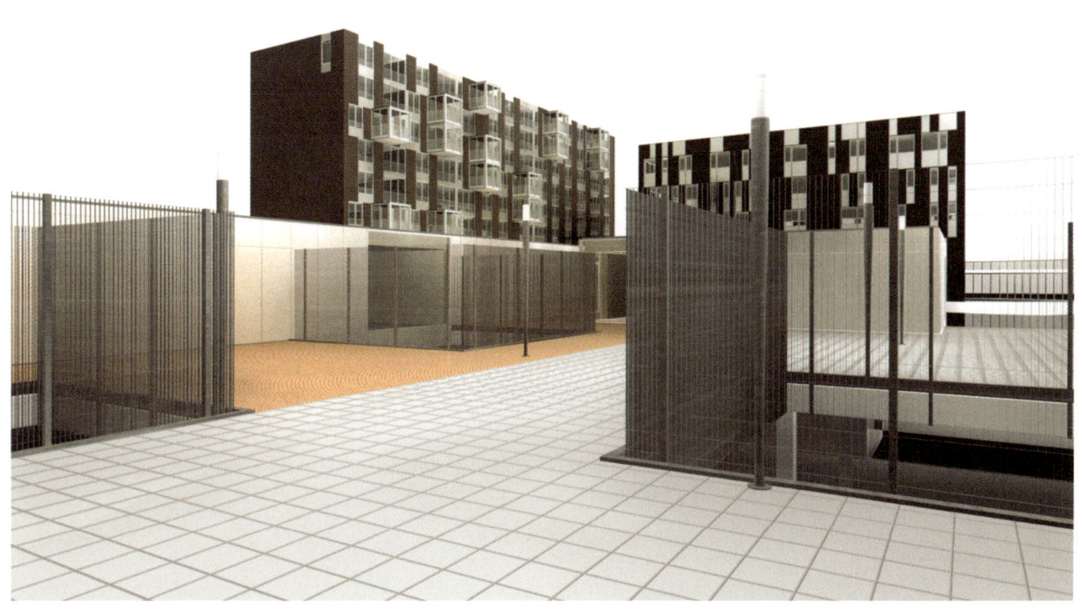

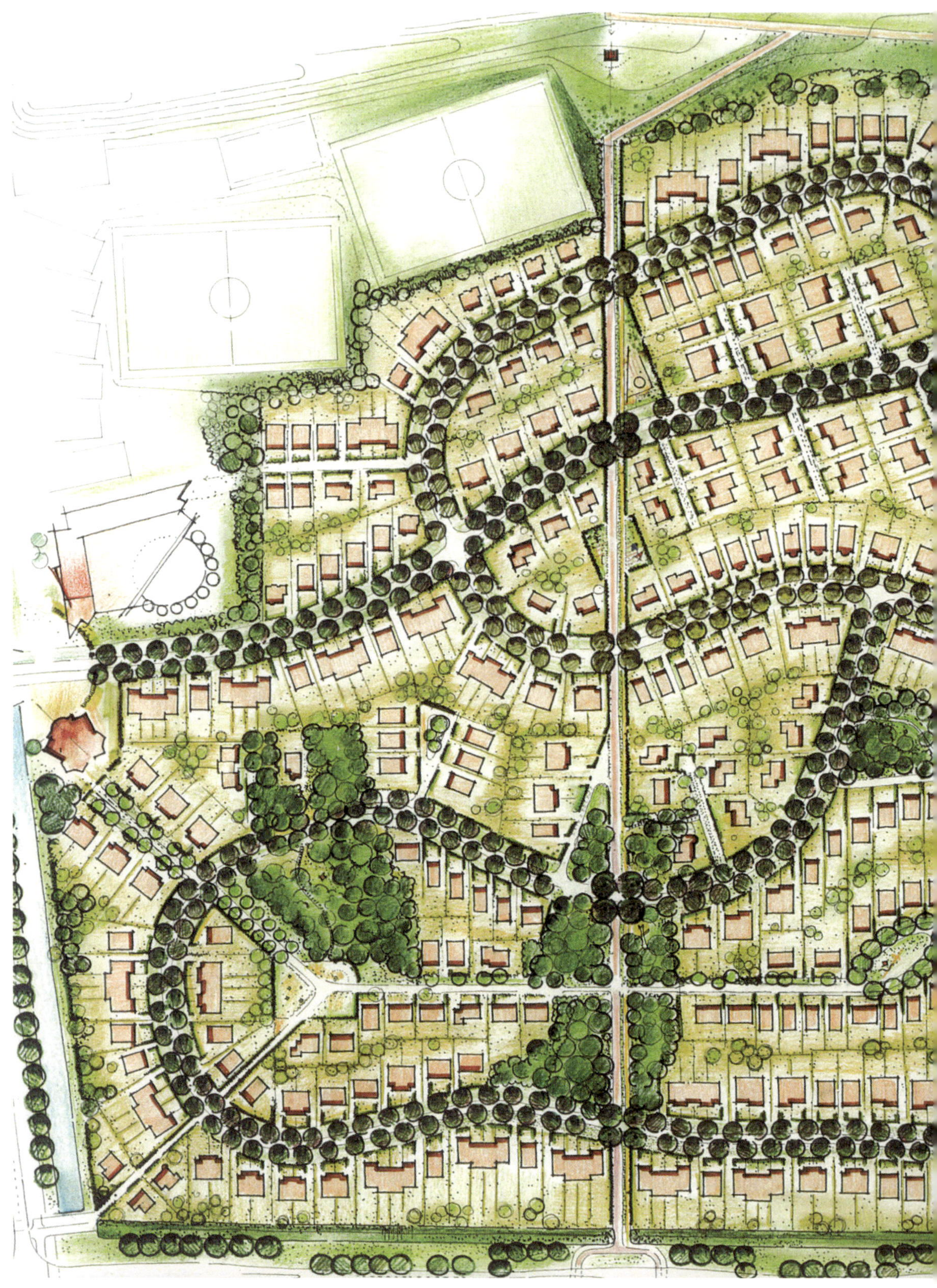

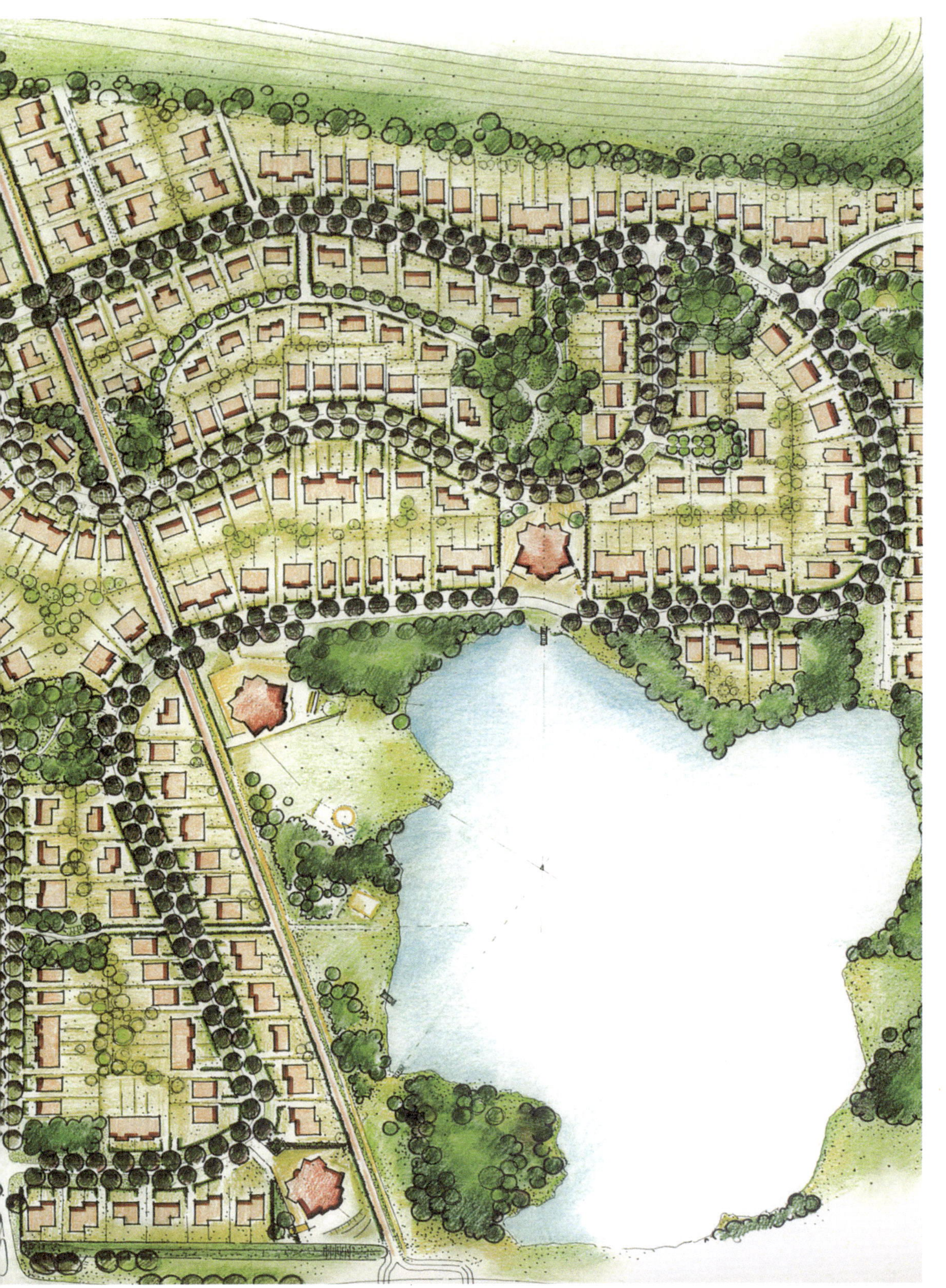

Mark Wigley

Insecurity by Design

WTC New York

The idea that architecture keeps danger out seems a fable since the attacks on the World Trade Center buildings in New York. Therefore, architects should stop pretending architecture offers security and protection. So long as they refuse to see that architecture is not neutral, they will keep on building new targets.

A very tall building absorbs a plane and collapses after 105 defiant minutes, having watched its twin suffer the same fate. Everyone sees it. Again and again. It captures every eye and ear in stunned amazement.

When the towers fell, the world shook. Nobody could accept what they saw. Such a vertical drop seemed impossible. And no amount of analysis of the mechanics of the collapse, the simple way the attack was carried out, or the strategic mission of the attackers can ease the incredulity. The event remains unbelievable, surprising even to those who initiated it.

People turn to architects for answers. Surely those responsible for shaping structures could help explain the meaning of this traumatic event. Emerging from relative obscurity, architects were featured in magazines and extensively quoted in newspapers. They appeared on television talk shows and were interviewed on news broadcasts. It was hard for any designer or critic to remain thoughtfully silent. Yet so little is said in the end. Everyone pretends to find in the event the clearest evidence for what they have been saying all along. Mainly it is a kind of disciplinary therapy, a reassertion of the traditional figure of the architect as the generator of culturally reassuring objects, an ongoing denial of the fact that architects are just as confused as the traumatized people they serve.

Why did our seemingly hyper-aware and congenitally paranoid world become so shocked? Not because of the number of people killed. Such numbers are tragically all too common on a planet routinely tormented by starvation, war, disease, and genocide. Nor is it simply the terrorist assault on a large metropolitan building. Buildings are constantly being targeted. Yet while the front pages of newspapers regularly feature the lethal rubble of flattened modern buildings, none of these collapses has stimulated any kind of debate about architecture. Only with the destruction of the World Trade Center have the designers and critics swarmed down like vultures to pick over the site of collapse, unable to offer much because the ancient intimacy between architecture and violence has for so long been off-limits in their discussion.

A Reassuring Witness

To grasp the event, we need to appreciate the intense fantasies people have about buildings in general and the twins in particular. To begin to understand the depth and complexity of the reaction, we need to go back to the simplest level. In the simplest terms, buildings are seen as a form of protection, an insulation from danger. To be hurt by a building is unacceptable. Even the most minor fragmentation of a structure is front-page news. And fatal collapses are international news – death by architecture is intolerable. Furthermore, buildings are traditionally meant to last much longer than people. It is the sense that buildings outlive us that allows us to have a life.

Buildings shelter life by sustaining a collective sense of time, a form of cultural synchronization. Buildings act as a reassuringly stable witness of whatever we do by surviving longer than us and evolving more slowly.

This sense that our buildings are our witnesses depends on a kind of kinship between body and building. Not only should buildings protect and last longer than bodies, they must be themselves a kind of body: a surrogate body, a superbody with a face, a façade, that watches us. We use buildings to construct an image of what we would like the body to be. Buildings are thereby credited with considerable representational force. This force can be seen in the everyday notion that the place where you live continues to represent you when you are hidden within it, away, asleep or dead. Like your clothes, your building projects some kind of stable image regardless of what you are doing or feeling.

Terrorists know this, have always known this. They play with these basic fantasies about architecture, wounding buildings as often as people. Damaged buildings represent damaged bodies. And it is the representation that counts. Terrorism is not about killing people, but about dispersing the threat of death by producing frightening images. Particular sites are targeted to produce a general unease. If you can identify with the target, then your own buildings become unsafe, and everybody becomes vulnerable. This tactical use of images of assaulted buildings plays with precisely the representational capacity of buildings that architects have devoted themselves to for millennia. In this, the terrorist shares the expertise of the architect. The terrorist mobilizes the whole psychopathology of fears buried beneath the architect's obsession with efficiency, comfort, and pleasure.

The Humanity of Buildings

The attack on the towers was an extreme yet textbook example. What was unique was the size of the audience and therefore the size of the threat. Symptomatically, the video statement by the structural engineer Osama Bin Laden refers to striking the 'softest spots' of America, its 'greatest buildings', and not the people within them. The real threat is to the architecture, or rather to an architecture that represents a much wider population than its physical occupants. In a classic sense, the targeted buildings represent the bodies of a global constituency, assuming the humanity of all those who watched. Again and again, the towers are described with the same terms used for suffering people. In the grieving for those who died, there is also grieving for the buildings themselves. In all the improvised memorials and media coverage, images of the towers' faces share the same space as images of the victims' faces. The buildings became victims, and in so doing victimize those who watch them suffer.

If everyday cultural life makes an unconscious association between body and building, it is enormously frightening when the confusion becomes literal. The devastating spectacle of September 11 was a simultaneous destruction of body and building and the distinction between them. 'He became part of the building when it went down', as one distraught parent lamented. The buildings became lethal elevators, dropping in on themselves at the same speed as any object free falling in the air. No resistance: 415

meters of structure compressed into 20 meters of rubble in 10 seconds, generating a level of energy comparable to nuclear blasts or volcanic activity. Buildings and bodies were instantly compacted into an extraordinarily dense pile or dispersed to the wind. In lieu of remains, family members received small boxes of the dust. The bodies themselves were mainly lost, and even the number of victims stayed a mystery. The few bodies that were found were kept invisible. Despite all the intense and endless media coverage, no bodies were shown. No broken, bloody, burned, or fragmented people. Just the desperate flight of those who could choose to jump, and the shocked, dust-laden bodies of the survivors.

Millions streamed downtown to look, partly driven by the voyeuristic compulsion to see the site of such a huge crash and partly like loving family members of the buildings themselves who needed to see the actual body of the buildings to accept their loss.

Perplexing Popularity

The towers had of course been designed to produce such a global audience. The whole point was for them to rise up above the city at the end of the island facing Europe to capture world attention. Which they did. They were the centrepieces of billions of images. More postcards were sent of the towers than of any other building in the world. And what was constantly looked up at by so many was also looking back. Whether we were on the streets of Manhattan or watching TV in living rooms on the other side of the world, the Twin Towers had an eye on us. But there is now a palpable sense on the island of having lost a crucial witness that could see you wherever you were: an architecture of image that was understood, and enjoyed.

This popularity was never understood by architects, who are now being asked to talk about buildings they never embraced. Indeed, the Twin Towers were mercilessly slammed by architectural critics, particularly those who led the support for so-called 'postmodern' architecture. For them, the towers personified the inhumanity of modern architecture. Ironically, the critics spoke in the name of popular sensibility. But in the end ordinary people simply had stronger feelings about the buildings than architects, to whom they rarely listen anyway. The Twin Towers played a much bigger role in everyday experience than in architects' discussions. At some level, an extraordinary identification with the buildings took place that exceeded the expectations of both the boosters of the project and the architectural critics. Precisely because their brutal scale did not fit into their surroundings, they perfectly belonged in a city of refugees and misfits of every kind, the city that is at once the most and the least American.

The key symbolic role of the World Trade Center, the rationale for both its design and its destruction, was to represent the global marketplace. In a strange way, super-solid, super-visible, super-located buildings stood as a figure for the dematerialized, invisible, placeless market. In this, architecture was surely a vestigial symbolic system, as demonstrated by the fact that the markets reopened within days after the attack. Supposedly fragile digital patterns have long assumed the solidity once associated with buildings. Electronics have taken over from architecture as our primary witnesses and storehouses of collective memory, allowing buildings to assume new roles. Not by chance were those who first described the architectural role of electronics in the 1950s and 1960s also those who insisted that buildings should become as expendable as dishwashers and toasters. Yet the traumatic reaction to the loss of the towers themselves, beyond the terrible loss of life, shows that even the vestigial system of architecture had more force than anyone expected. Still, it is as yet unclear what it means to threaten a building in an electronic age.

Representation

We need to look more closely at exactly how this seemingly outdated representational system worked. The World Trade Center was a hyper-development of the generic postwar corporate office tower. The corporate building provides a fixed visible face for an unfixed, invisible and carnivorous organization. Typically, there is no sign of the company on the building. The lack of a literal sign becomes the sign that the corporation is nothing more than an open network. As is written into the very word, the 'corporation' is an abstract body, a corpus composed of many bodies networked together into a single organism. It is an invisible collective network that may be made visible on a particular site by a building.

The shiny glass 'curtain wall' is not a showcase revealing the workers inside. During the day, reflections usually render the interior mysterious. At night, when the interior becomes visible, it is the horizontal grid of fluorescent lights visible through the vertical grid of the façade that is put on display, not the workers. The fluorescents, which are never turned off, are more important than the workers. Not by chance is the corporate office building one of the first building types to be routinely photographed at night by architectural publications. Of course, there are internal spaces occupied by workers, and a whole range of tactical design strategies for accommodating them, but this remains subordinate to the polemic of the outer screen. At the ground level, the façade is thinned down to the absolute minimum and the resulting walls of glass invite the eye and body in. But all that is revealed is a huge lobby space that usually continues the pattern and materials of the exterior plaza. What promises to be the interior turns out to be an exterior bathed in eternal artificial sunlight and inhabited only by the elevator core. The elevators are the only substantial objects. If you look up, you don't see the solid underbelly of the building's main volume but an artificial sky, a continuous, brightly glowing, horizontal surface that veils even the shape of the fluorescent tubes that activate it. The hidden office floors above often have the same kind of singular glowing ceiling. And even when the fluorescents

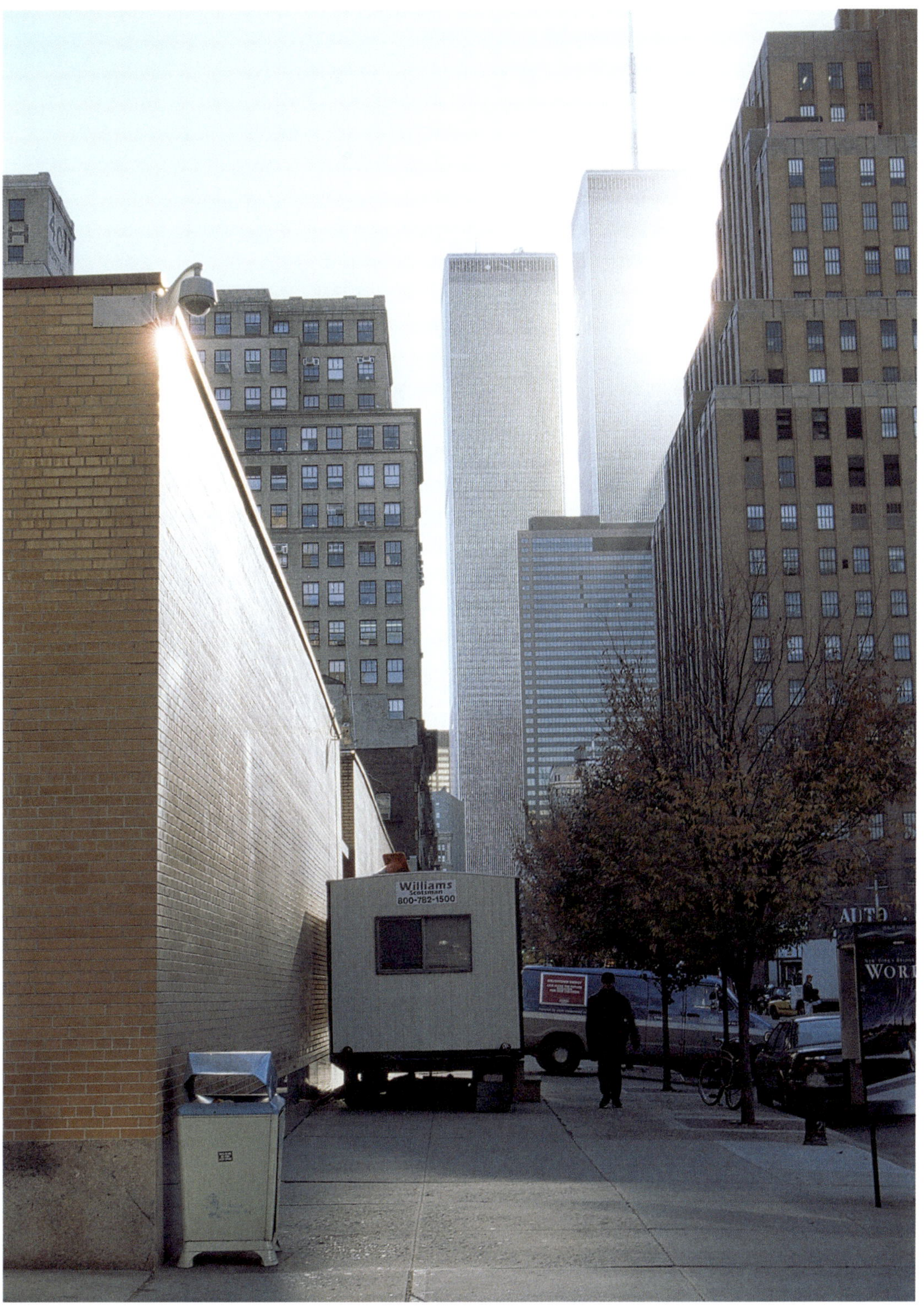

are discrete fixtures arrayed across an opaque surface, workers do not inhabit rooms but are distributed across a 'landscape'. In the most fundamentalist sense, the corporate building has no interior.

The Neutral Screen

The Twin Towers took this to the limit, perfecting the logic of the 'neutral' screen, stretching it to the clouds and exemplifying the culture of the invisible body. The towers were at once sealed yet porous, intimidatingly heavy yet floating. The twins were at their most beautiful at night as a complex pattern of lights hovering above the city, framed by the sky-lobbies and observation levels which turned into thick dark bands. The lights simulated occupation, but not by people. For the first decade, 23,000 fluorescents always remained at their posts, working around the clock. There were not even light switches in the towers until 1982, when the endless stacked layers of light started to fragment into an elusive and seductive figure.

The two mysterious, gargantuan shafts connected a vast, crowded, horizontal slab of shopping and eating in the ground to equally crowded platforms for viewing, eating, and drinking in the sky. Below the shopping level was a physical communication hub that radiated multiple underground rail systems. Above the viewing level was an electronic communication hub that radiated television, telephone, microwave, and radio. The result was a density of bodies in the spaces of consumption below and above, framed by communication networks binding the structure to the city and the rest of the planet. In the space of production in between, the two shafts, the body simply disappeared. Tourists rocketed through it in America's largest and fastest elevator, suddenly aware of the inside of their own flesh but oblivious to the spaces and people that surrounded them.

Even the workers did not simply enter or appreciate the space. Isolated in their express elevators, they went to separate sky-lobbies from which they took local elevators to their respective floors. Yet in the deluge of countless images of the building in loving reaction to their unbelievable disappearance, it was symptomatic that not one showed the interior of the workspaces.

The design of these hidden spaces was celebrated in the press as highly innovative when the buildings first went up. The invention of sky-lobbies had freed up an unprecedented amount of usable floor area. Concentrating all the structure into a tight ring of huge columns around the elevator core and another heavy ring around the outside of the building made the workspace column-free. Starting with their own choice of lighting pattern, each of the huge number of tenants could organize their slice freely and differently, setting up a whole array of different relationships to the famous façade, a heterogeneity that was masked by the unified exterior, and only subtly implied by the different intensities and rhythms of the light pattern at night.

The towers had no front, back, or sides. Each face was the same.

Furthermore, the buildings had no depth. There was no simple view of them in perspective. The smaller buildings ringing their base blocked the view upward, and the windswept plaza on top of the shopping mall was typically deserted. The buildings were meant to be seen from a distance, as pure façade. They were made to seem flat, as can be seen in the architect's original renderings. Each typical view, the cliché embedded in a worldwide consciousness, had two seamless screens side by side: each a shimmering blend of aluminium and glass, subtly modulated by the Gothic- and Arabic-inspired details of the stretched floor heights at the bottom and the top, and the even subtler change of dimension produced by two sky-lobbies. The curved grafting of the columns at the base could be read from a distance, but the details in the higher floors were so discrete that only their effect was visible, and then only just. Setting the glass back in the recesses between the huge columns meant that the colours and texture of the face changed continuously with each new angle of view or sun – a minimalist composition that achieved a maximum array of effects.

The Twin Towers were a pure, un-inhabited image floating above the city, an image forever above the horizon, in some kind of sublime excess, defying our capacity to understand it. The unfathomable trauma of their destruction simply deepened the mystery. And despite the earthshaking intensity of the collapse, the dust finally settled to reveal large sections of the façade improbably left standing, the whole spirit of the building encapsulated in a lonely porous screen whose subtly grafted curves may well have become the most famous architectural detail in history.

Haste

The eventual demolition of this poignantly defiant screen was itself foolish and painful. There was an obscene haste to remove all the traces and rebuild in a desperate attempt to fill the void in so many hearts and bank accounts. But the question of how to replace nine million square feet office of space is irrelevant. If anything, the issue is how to replace the more than two million square feet of façade – those vast, uncannily duplicated screens. When the facades came down, the faces of the invisible occupants who were lost came up, filling the vertical surfaces of the city in pasted photocopies and covering the surfaces of televisions, computers and newspapers all around the world. They formed a new kind of façade, a dispersed image of diversity in place of the singular monolithic screen. In contrast, survivors were covered with dust, all differences between them concealed by a uniform coating, screened by a thin layer of the building. The old façade still at work. It was precisely those who were missing, those the buildings did not protect, who had their horrifying disappearance marked by a sudden visibility. When architecture rises again, it will probably rebury what was exposed. Another defensive screen will be placed between us and our fears.

This new screen, even, if not especially, that part of it devoted to 'memorial', will insulate us from what happened. A city that was able to so completely forget that a third of it was destroyed by a deadly downtown fire in 1776 ('a scene of horror beyond description' said the newspaper of the day) and forget that a quarter of it (700 buildings) was destroyed by another downtown fire in 1835, will be able to forget this latest trauma remarkably quickly. The whole financial district that acted as the site of the latest catastrophe was itself entirely built within a year of the 1835 fire – the first architect having been hired only a day after the fires were put out. Surely a city shaped only by greed will once again find ways to profit quickly from its pain. Appeals to memory and solidarity will be but excuses for multiple forms of local and global restructuring. New shapes of building and social control are easily promoted in the guise of healing the physical and psychological wounds.

The Illusion of Security

Before any such talk about rebuilding, there should have been a patient attempt simply to understand exactly what happened. After all, what occurred is not simply the tragic loss that we can point to, no matter how dramatic and clear-cut it seems. Nothing was easier to point to than the Twin Towers and their collapse. Yet amidst the obvious horror, there is another level of trauma that is even more challenging because we are unwilling to acknowledge it, let alone comprehend it. For what might be really horrifying in the end is precisely what was already there. The collective sense that everything changed that morning

may have more to do with no longer being able to repress certain aspects of contemporary life. Things that we have been living with for some time were disturbingly revealed. The everyday idea that architecture keeps the danger out was exposed as a fantasy. Violence is never a distant thing. Security is never more than a fragile illusion. Buildings are much stranger than we are willing to admit. They are tied to the economy of violence rather than simply a protection from it.

When the design of the twins was first revealed in 1964, the architect said that they would be a physical manifestation of 'the relationship between world trade and world peace'. Did we really think that the emergent forces of globalization were so innocent, and that architecture could embody that innocence? Did we really think that buildings could be in any way neutral? Or did we just agree to pretend? The rationalizations of the rebuilding are just as naïve – and just as successful. Once again, business will appear to be separated from memory, a clear prophylactic line will be drawn between 'memorial' and routine industrialized spaces for offices, shops or residences. We will again pretend to understand the structures we occupy and observe. The only challenge will be to select the collective forms of denial. And in burying our fears so earnestly, we also bury our pleasures. Architecture will be neutralized and returned to the background.

Architects are in fact filled with doubt, and often share it when they passionately discuss their designs amongst themselves, but they are called

Elevation of crown detail between the 108th and the 110th floors (working drawings for the North Tower) © Yamasaki and Associates

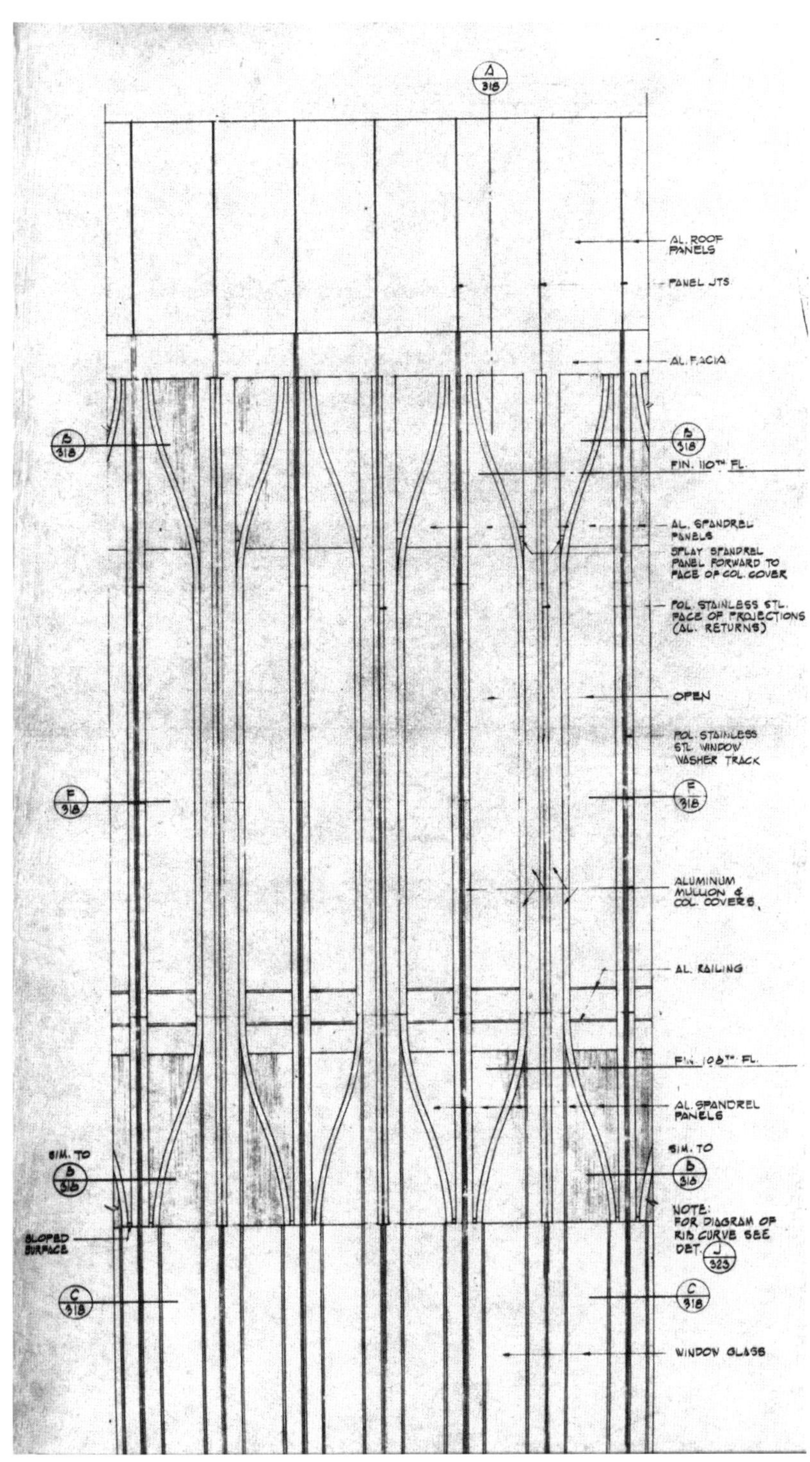

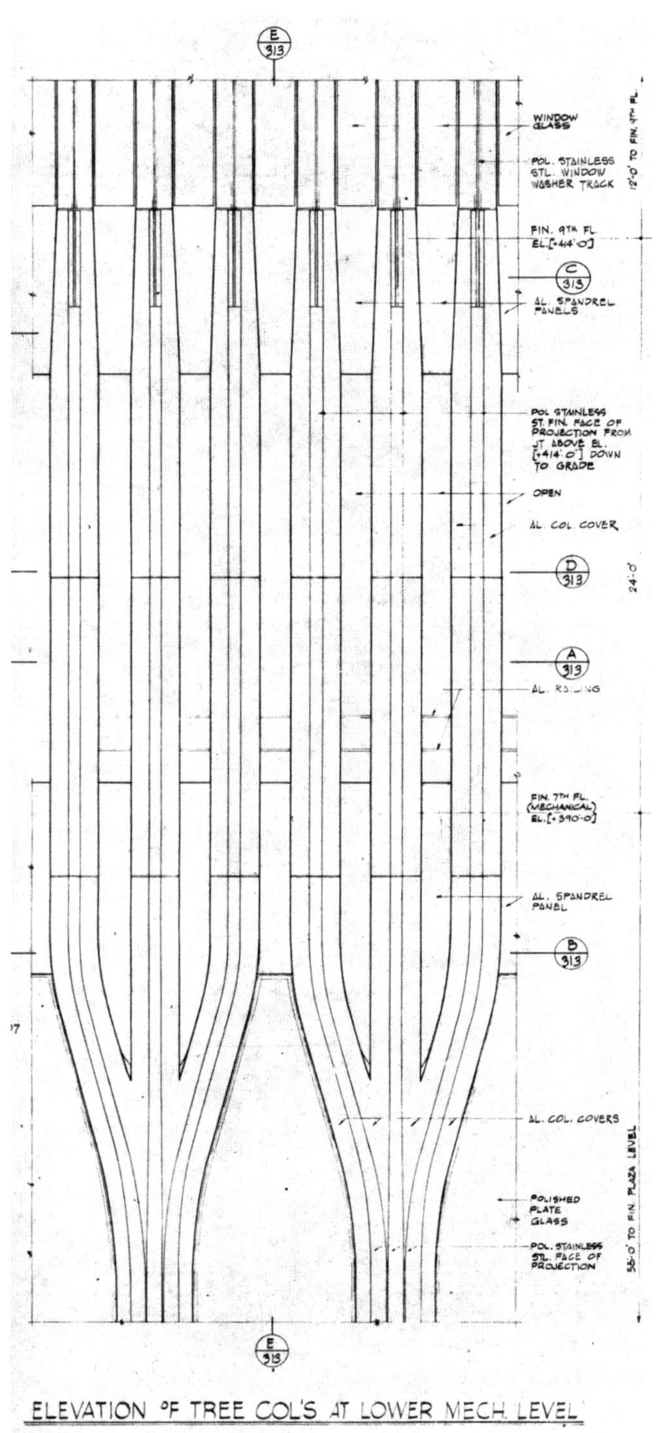

E
313
WINDOW GLASS
POL. STAINLESS STL. WINDOW WASHER TRACK
FIN. 9TH FL. EL.[+414'-0"]
C
313
AL. SPANDREL PANELS
POL. STAINLESS ST. FIN. FACE OF PROJECTION FROM JT. ABOVE EL. [+414'-0"] DOWN TO GRADE
OPEN
AL. COL. COVER
D
313
A
313
AL. RAILING
FIN. 7TH FL. (MECHANICAL) EL.[+390'-0"]
AL. SPANDREL PANEL
B
313
AL. COL. COVERS
POLISHED PLATE GLASS
POL. STAINLESS STL. FACE OF PROJECTION
E
313
12'-0" TO FIN. 9TH FL.
24'-0"
56'-0" TO FIN. PLAZA LEVEL
ELEVATION OF TREE COL'S AT LOWER MECH. LEVEL

The subtle widening of the columns between the 41th and the 43rd floors and between the 75th and the 77th floors (working drawings for the North Tower) © Yamasaki and Associates

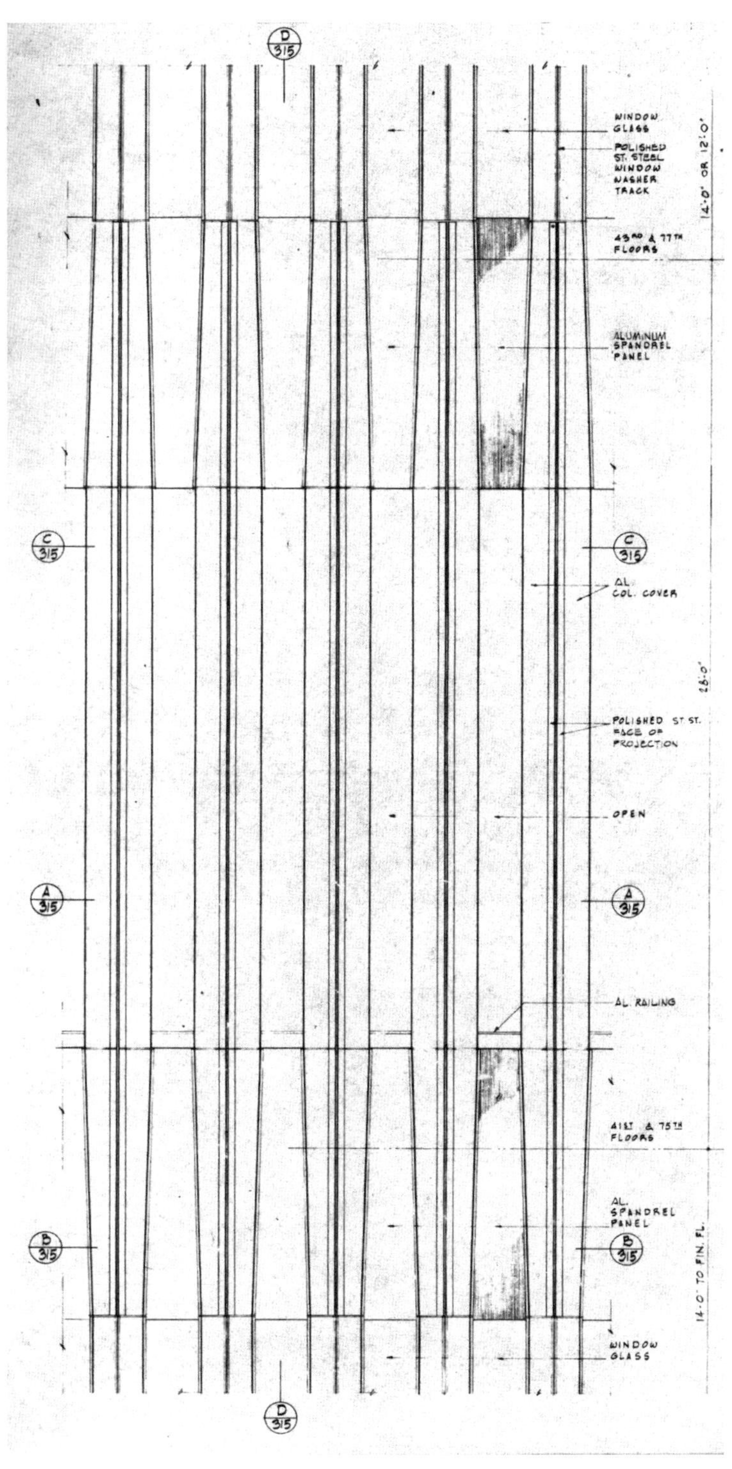

Section showing the uninterrupted slice of office space between the elevator core (right) and the façade (left) (from the architect's set of working drawings for the North Tower) © Yamasaki and Associates

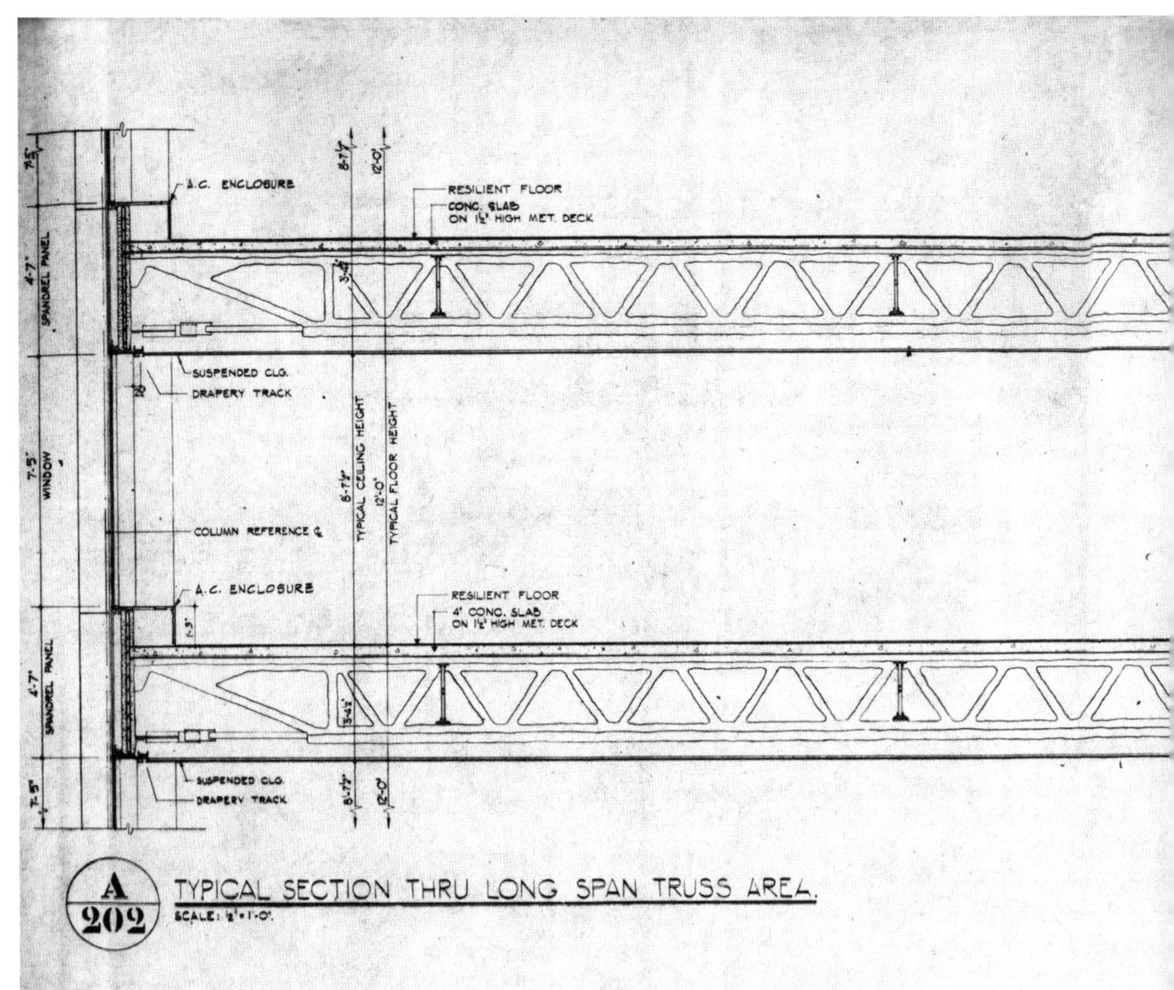

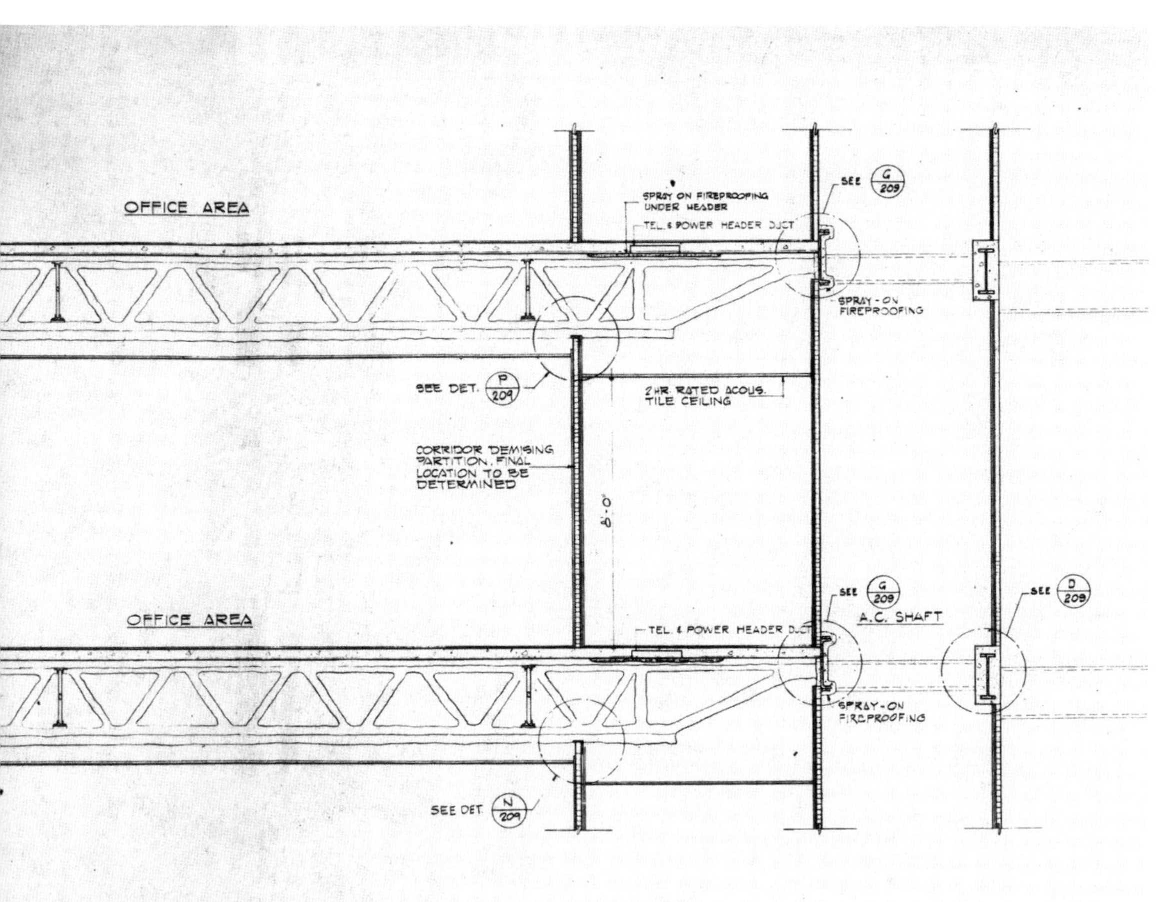

OFFICE AREA
SPRAY ON FIREPROOFING UNDER HEADER
TEL. & POWER HEADER DUCT
SEE G 209
SPRAY-ON FIREPROOFING
SEE DET. P 209
2 HR. RATED ACOUS. TILE CEILING
CORRIDOR DEMISING PARTITION, FINAL LOCATION TO BE DETERMINED
8'-0"
OFFICE AREA
SEE G 209
TEL. & POWER HEADER DUCT
A.C. SHAFT
SEE D 209
SPRAY-ON FIREPROOFING
SEE DET. N 209

on to exude confidence in public. If our
buildings are meant to give us confidence, their producers apparently have to
embody it. But if architects are not used
to bringing their doubts about the status
of buildings into public discourse, they
are unable to contribute to the much-
needed discussion of architecture's
intimate and complex relationship to
trauma. All they can do is once again
collaborate on the production of images
of security, comfort, and memory. The
embarrassing truth is that the traditional
architect is empowered rather than challenged by such events. Architects are in
the threat management business. For all
their occasional talk about experimenta-
tion, they are devoted to the mythology
of psychological closure. But the only
architecture that might resist the threat
of the terrorist is one that already
captures the fragility and strangeness of
our bodies and identities, an architecture
of vulnerability, sensitivity, and pervers-
ity. Ignoring this, architects will unwit-
tingly get on with the job of making the
next targets.

This text is a version, specially
adapted for *Open*, of a text previ-
ously published in: Michael
Sorkin, Sharon Zukin (eds.),
*After the World Trade Center:
Rethinking New York City,*
Routledge, New York 2002.

column

HANS BOUTELLIER

CREATION

We live in a time without illusions. Its utopian yearning is for security. Fear and unease are so prevalent that we can think of nothing else but fighting them. The police and the criminal justice system have become the agents of our yearnings, and we cannot get enough of this. We are trapped like a rabbit in the headlights: paralyzed with fear and unable to get away. I expect artists to manage to escape the powerlessness of the present time. Art does not have to please, but it could offer some support.

A few months ago I saw a performance of the oratorio <u>Die Schöpfung</u> by Haydn at the Finlandia Hall in Helsinki. The musical composition of the Creation story was simply overwhelming. But what especially struck me was the unembarrassed sense of jubilation about the beauty of nature and of humanity. It dawned on me that the power, the joy and the solace this composition expressed are out of date. I think few artists these days feel compelled to celebrate Creation in such an exuberant way.

But why? It seems art is being guided by the idea that there is little to celebrate. It prefers to focus on the Fall and on the unmasking of beauty as kitsch, of love as a trap and of human motives as terror. I realize general statements about art are dilettante-ish and criticism of modern art practice quickly smells of grousing. And yet I am often unable to shake off a feeling of disillusionment upon visiting a museum of modern art. A lot of concepts but little inspiration.

In essence there are three sources for providing impulses to a culture devoid of illusions. We cannot expect this of politics — the first candidate. Its pragmatic and mediagenic course can no longer be turned back. Something similar applies to the second candidate, religion. Religious faith is an individual matter and will not experience a revival as a cultural factor. From the Muslims we would prefer no organized religious movement.

When it comes to inspiration, I still base my hopes most on the art and culture sector. For a long time — too long — this has been dominated by the motif of unmasking. The inquiry into the deepest if not the lowest motives of human beings (Bataille!) seems to me to have been sufficiently carried out by now. Indeed, if we look at some commercial television programmes, the results of this examination have become common property. The inquiry into human perversion has made it commonplace and thereby become superfluous.

Pornography and violence have become normalized and thereby have acquired a new significance. They _abnormalize_ restraint, vulnerability and the inquiry into moralities. This is not a call for decency in art or for a reintroduction of hypocrisy. It is, however, a plea for a new cultural élan, which must come from the people who have traditionally dared to venture down unbeaten paths. I yearn for new (or in fact old) representations of – ahem – love or reformulations of the battle between good and evil.

The old culture has been sufficiently dismantled to look for new potential in its foundations. This requires time (and means), which might best be used in studying texts and images that have survived, or in fact in making new ones that have not yet been appropriated by the culture of security. In the current utopian yearning for security lurks the danger of a totalitarian dream of power, but also a spark of hope. I yearn for the hope of creation.

Jouke Kleerebezem

Beware of the Dog!

The Public Domain in the Information Society

Fear is a poor counsellor if we want to examine the potential of the information society. If we let ourselves be led by it we will remain stuck in a mass-media society, in which obsolete systems of power and knowledge still operate. According to Jouke Kleerebezem we must above all be vigilant ourselves and test the limits of the possibilities offered to us in a network society.

At the first 'Doors of Perception'[1] conference in Amsterdam in 1993, Bill Buxton, at the time a software engineer with the Xerox PARC research laboratory, introduced a powerful mantra when he explained what his interest in ubiquitous computing, better known as *ubicomp*, is based upon. Buxton's 'I want my desktop back' became a modest hit in Mediamatic's version, on the CD-ROM issued as a report of the conference.[2] The encroachment of the computer out of its beige plastic housing, to occupy other parts of our physical environment – 'in the woodwork', as Buxton put it – has always been the goal of *ubicomp*. The computerization of the everyday environment is drawing the networks out of the house and office and into the street. The Internet and the telecommunications networks connect people and places on a rapidly expanding scale, creating new public and private spaces. Activities that used to take place primarily in the domestic environment, such as telephoning with a 'fixed' telephone, have become public. Activities that used to require visiting public places, such as obtaining information from government authorities or in libraries, on the contrary have moved into the private environment. With the rapid increase in so-called 'hot spots',[3] the streetscape is increasingly being taken over by not only the mobile phone but other portable digital devices as well. The architectural, landscape, and information spaces are beginning to overlap. In optimal mobility, we are expected to communicate as much as possible. Commerce and industry are expending great effort in making all digital products and services available in any location. The advent of communication networks, in which public infrastructure has ended up above ground rather than below it, has ushered in a new era in the Early Information Age.

Computerization is moving forward unabated, without taking on the form of our familiar computer – box, screen, keyboard. Unlike what happened with the personal computer, the new computerization is geared to the computerization of the everyday physical environment and incorporates various objects and environments in digital networks. A habitat rich in data is put at our disposal, in which a dense network of connections encompasses and provides access to our everyday environment. The design of the public space, however, is still scarcely adapted to the manipulation of a flow of information. The woodwork offers sufficient space for processors, screens and simple control panels, yet it neither reflects nor facilitates in a more considered form the gradual emergence of what I call an *information habit*.[4] The public space does not yet really provide room for the public collection and production of information. To genuinely be able to speak of an 'information society' in terms of

1. The 'Doors of Perception' conference was initiated by the former Design Institute in Amsterdam and is now an independent foundation under the directorship of John Thackara. The conference, bringing together interested participants from the design, media and business worlds, has been held alternately in the Netherlands and India since 2000.

2. *Doors of Perception* CD-ROM, produced independently and bundled with *Mediamatic* vol. 8, no. 1, Amsterdam 1994. This highly praised conference report offers the user the possibility to put together his own Doors using lectures and contextually relevant content. No longer available.

3. 'Hot spots' are locations in the public space where, within the range of a wireless network, one can get access to the Internet. Some of these places are publicly available; others, for instance private or commercial networks, are mapped and publicized by network nomads. See for instance http://warchalking.org; http://wirelessbandit.nerdsunderglass.com.

4. 'Remember Home?' (1994) for Doors of Perception 2 'Home': 'Communication media pierce our dwellings to facilitate the settling of home in information technology. The poetics and politics of home in the age of information will equally guide the architecture of built and electronic space. The memory of architecture will model electronic space to the same extent as the hot links of new media will model different buildings. Thus a new set of practices, which will be known as our information habit, will come into being.' (http://nqpaofu.com/nqp/ciw_nqp6.html#rememberhome)

meaning as well as function, this will have to change. We will not only have to have the option of collecting information in any location, we also have to be able to produce it. To this end, the nature of the transaction must be clearly readable from the activities undertaken and therefore from the technology used.

Sometimes the means of communication vaguely recall the unwieldy boxes that once gathered dust on or under our desks. Thanks to miniaturization the new devices have become elegant and highly fashion-sensitive gadgets. We find adapted versions of screen, keyboard and track ball (a classical mouse turned upside down) in mobiles, personal digital assistants, GPS scanners, automatic tellers, dashboards, kitchen appliances, remote controls, video and photo cameras, portable and household audio and video appliances, game consoles and of course in the laptop as well. The connecting networks are for the most part wireless and can find us anywhere. With the devices mentioned, information (sometimes co-ordinated by satellite and thus location-specific) is received by us and potentially made available to the network. 'Computing' is no longer something we do exclusively in our places of work or in our hobby rooms, at times set for the purpose. These days we 'compute' day in and day out, during work and in our free time. Thanks to the connecting networks we leave behind trails of information through physical reality.

Different Speeds

Information moves at the speed of light. Products and services that enrich our daily lives will try to accelerate to this standard. We want our wishes attended to. 'Click and Go'. But physical reality is slow. Our own mobility and that of our goods is stuck at best at the speed of sound, and that, since the Concorde has been retired, is reserved for such professional speed demons as jet-fighter pilots and astronauts. The rest of us move slowly around the world, covering long distances over many hours and at the cost of a huge expense of energy. Our information is always one step ahead of us. Reservations precede us, our presence is widely announced in the network that organizes our movements and reported at the destination. Once we arrive we are logged into new networks, our mobile phones adapt to another environment, in which our credit cards are also accepted. While we get over jet lag with a fuzzy head and unsteady stomach, our chips are already fully at home in their new surroundings and working for us. The professional staff treats us with international courtesy, but the glances we exchange in the street are still somewhat uncomfortable. Meanwhile the local ubicomp has accepted our devices without distinction as to origin. Our data is absorbed into new databases. At each new contact with the network, they are recognized and fitted in without any problem.

In Bruce Sterling's *Islands in the Net*, and in Neal Stephenson's *The Diamond Age*, the main characters live in parallel realities in real time, 24 hours a day, seven days a week. They are never disconnected from the information network that tracks them, makes them visible and makes contact with others possible.[5] The science fiction of the last 10 years is fast becoming everyday reality. Our presence is being reported and processed beyond the flow of information we set into motion ourselves. Surveillance cameras watch us as we go in or out, and the cameras of fellow travellers repeatedly record us and send these images on to other public environments. We are no longer merely anonymously present in holiday photo albums with a limited distribution; we appear increasingly on holiday and other personal websites, in weblogs and photologs – thus in the public information space. Mobile phone cameras have already been banned in many swimming pools, and in some countries, including Saudi Arabia, a general ban is even in place. The democratic potential for producing information in picture, sound and text, and its distribution to (semi-) public popular media perhaps challenge the norms of our privacy more than the ubiquitous surveillance cameras in the urban environment.[6]

5. Bruce Sterling, *Islands in the Net*, Arbor House, New York 1988; Neal Stephenson, *The Diamond Age*, Bantam, New York 1995.

6. A new sort of street theatre is operating in New York, the Surveillance Camera Players: see http://www.notbored.org/the-scp.html.

The information society is a society in which the citizen consumes and produces information in equal measure. He or she is as much the object of uninterrupted observation by digital devices as the author and distributor of digital information. 'Look up and smile', read the headline, in *Wired* in November 1999, to an article about low-orbit surveillance satellites.[7] But a Siemens MC60 or Nokia 7600 gets a lot closer. Every day thousands of private lives are being recorded in tens of thousands of photos in photologs and made public on the web.[8]

7. For more information on the technology used, see for instance http://www.notbored.org/surveillance-technologies.html or http://www.spaceimaging.com

8. See for instance http://www.fotolog.net.

Communications networks are always open to traffic, without applying particular demands on the message, or checking its content. The Internet is no 'sir', as the newspaper once was. The network merely links the many ladies and gentlemen who are individually using information. The mobility of 'our' data – both in the sense of actively generated by us and passively applicable to us – knows no limits in speed and aspect. Our personal information is instantly available all over the world and we can be traced anywhere. Already, some products and services are also moving at the speed of information – products and services that can be computerized, such as text, images and sound, but also products and services that materialize virtually *ad hoc*, for instance 'rapid prototyping' or three-dimensional print processes.[9] Any material that can be read or written through the intervention of digitization can thus move just as fast as the information with which it is written (coded). In this way a physical, everyday reality accompanies us to some extent, and environments adjust to our presence.

9. For 'rapid prototyping' see for instance http://www.cc.utah.edu/~asn8200/rapid.html.

Ubiquitous computing plays a role in this. Environments become interactive. Although our velocity does not increase, the adjustments of our environment to our presence make it relative. After all, we prefer to be where our information is, and at the moment it gets there, as well. This is the fulfilment of an 'information habit'.

The illustrations are by the Indian artist Abhishek Hazra. Abhishek attempts for a praxis that locates its conceptual trajectory within the interstices of theoretical discourse and visual arts. His affiliation to the discipline of his training – graphic design – finds expression in

Abhishek Hazra, <u>Infobot</u>. 'We are at home with our information.'(JK)

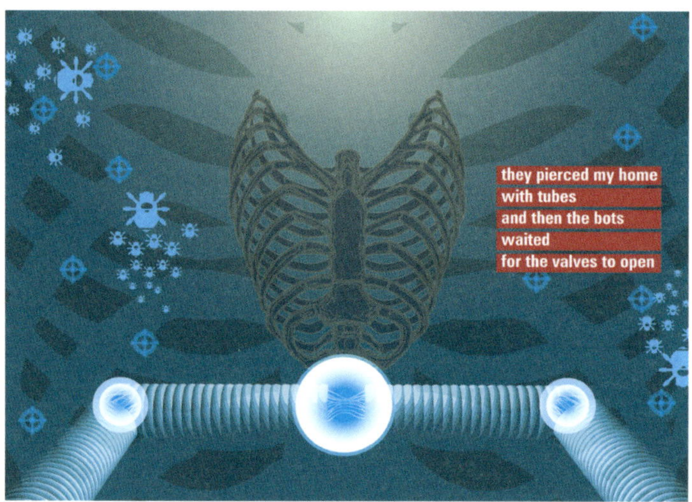

Abhishek Hazra, <u>Gesturemask</u>. 'Identity and anonymity are measured in visibility.' (JK)

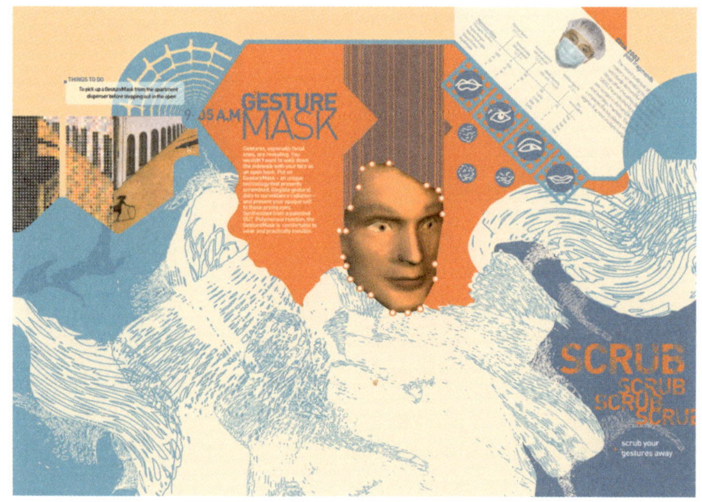

the formal language that informs his work. Abhishek works with the Center for Knowledge Societies, a Usability and Ethnographic Research organisation based in Bangalore, India. (see http:/www.ict4d.info).

Abhishek Hazra, <u>Mining</u>, 'Our data are our greatest possession.' (JK)

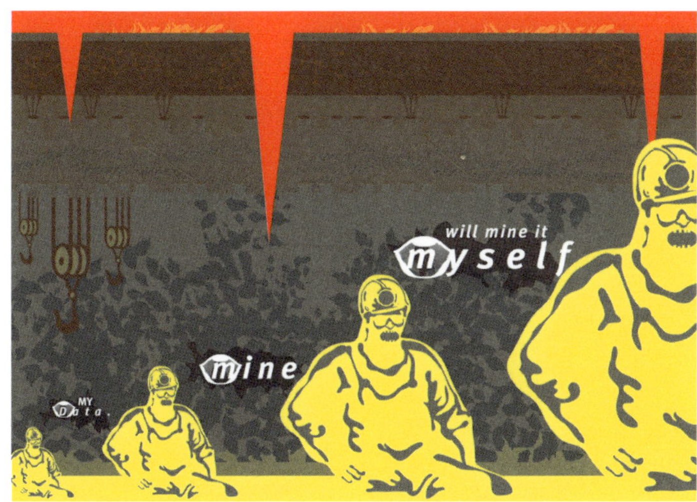

Abhishek Hazra, <u>Memoryblog</u>, 'The access to our own and others' memory is formed by interaction.' (JK)

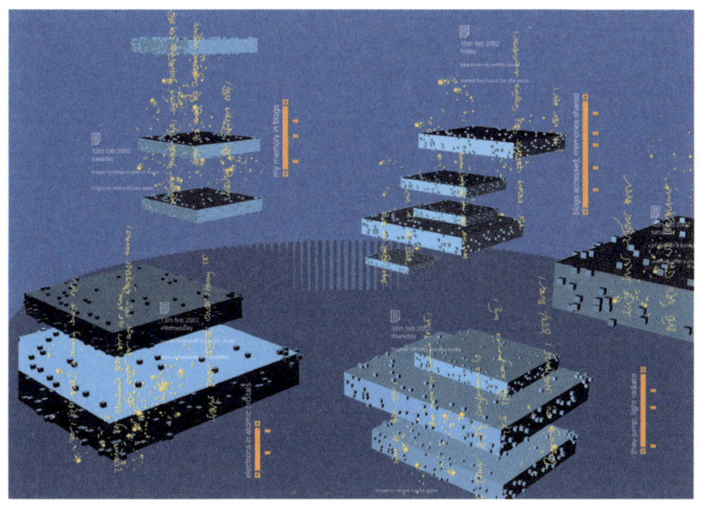

To be seen or to remain unnoticed – that seems to be the question. Yet it will not be easy to remain unnoticed in a network society. The relationship between identity and anonymity is once again relevant, and the advent of so much new technology is making it the focus of debate. Unease and irrational fears arise because information and everyday experience are not synchronous. The confusion between 'real' and 'virtual' is leading many critics of new media and the Internet to spurious conclusions. For example, a virtual world is supposed to be lonely and antisocial, the Internet is supposed to be dominated by commerce or to primarily provide outlets for criminal activities. But at the same time the positive achievements of the Internet are generally grossly exaggerated. Making this confusion the subject of debate, however, is the last thing we should do. After all, the condition of the information habit is 'real'. The conjunction of the architectural, landscape and information spaces is real. The confusion between private and public is not only real but also fruitful and can have emancipating developments. Our traceability is real as well, and the need to produce and consume information in equal measure is definitely real. If social and instrumental conditions do not develop to address this, we will never live in an information society, but in a traditional twentieth-century mass-media society, in which we once again get mired in traditional fears about already obsolete power mechanisms. Fears that are naive in a general, radical computerization, because they entail far too mechanical an idea of the organization of power. While the threats remain the same – discrimination, domination, exploitation, assault, extortion – in short, abuse of power – the form in which great and small evils touch us is continually changing. Traditional authoritarian power was often embodied by institutions and could be identified – and fought – through its central location and the apparatus of its domination. We should not forget that the forerunner of the Internet, the ARPAnet, was designed to make the military machinery and the military intelligence of the United States less vulnerable.[10] However, in distributing the intelligence and the machinery of power we also distribute the danger, just as, according to Paul Virilio, we designed the crash when we designed the aeroplane.[11] A network society offers neither the stability of the institutionalized good, nor a clearly localized evil. Knowledge and power are no longer concentrated in institutions and then distributed. They merely form occasionally recognizable patterns in the network. The individual development of an information habit will have to adjust to this kind of organizational and logistical innovations.

10. For the history of the ARPAnet, see for instance http://www.zakon.org/robert/internet/timeline/ or http://www.netvalley.com/intval1.html.

11. Paul Virilio, 'Le musée de l'accident', in *Un paysage des événements*, Galilée, Paris 1996

Investigating Possibilities

General information skills can certainly be learned. If they are not yet taught in traditional educational institutions, which mainly teach goal-oriented, training-related applications, they must be picked up in practice. This practice offers, as we have seen, a highly varied landscape of new conditions, in which the public and the private spaces are tested against one another, in a physical as well as an informational sense. Our use of and behaviour in these spaces is not without risk – but there is no alternative. Computerization is expanding at all levels of society. This does not mean that no alternative applications of our new environments should be attempted. They should be used and abused to investigate new possibilities and testing their limits. As producers more than as consumers of information, we shall have to realize that we are our own guard dogs here, that we must be alert users. The 'we' and the 'here', however, are relative concepts within a network, constantly in motion and constantly changing in composition and location. The integrity of our alertness is thus less dependent on a set group or a set place; in other words, it is not dependent on 'institutionalization': alertness means the openness with which we engage individually with constantly changing groups in constantly changing locations. Even our alertness is thus becoming mobile. After all, in the information society my data are my greatest possession. They are the building blocks of a society that still has to be invented. It is precisely this awareness that must be safeguarded from systems that fail to appreciate an informed and informing consumer as a full-fledged producer.

N.B.
Recent thematic projects on the integration of the information space and public infrastructure include *Fused Space* (Stroom, SKOR and Premsela, http://www.fusedspace.org) and *Ubiscribe* at the Jan van Eyck Academie, Maastricht (http://www.ubiscribe.net). *Fused Space* is a competition, open to artists, designers and architects for 'inspirational applications of new technology in the public space'. *UbiScribe* is a research project in which the limits of 'publishing' personal information in a network environment are examined.

Willem van Weelden

Insecurity as Absolute Zero

<re-start> by Jan van Grunsven and Ineke Bellemakers, Kanaleneiland, Utrecht

The <re-start> project by Jan van Grunsven and Ineke Bellemakers is being conducted in the Utrecht problem area of Kanaleneiland, a place where insecurity is readily linked to immigrants. <re-start> attempts to make young people aware of the role of the media and, in Willem van Weelden's words, 'enables them to effect an expressive correction to the images pandered by the media, which represent this "insecurity" '.

It is remarkable that almost no opinion piece published about the so-called immigrant issue broaches the question of how a sense of insecurity, threat, intimidation or outright fear are experienced among immigrant sections of the population – all the while the social debate, in a pseudo-logical conglomeration of concepts, regularly lumps 'insecurity' together with the 'immigrant problem'. For, these days, as an average Moroccan, you need not, in essence, have committed any crime to elicit significant 'insecurity'. The ecumenical miracle of the insecurity hysteria is that there is no difference between the native-born and immigrants in how they must adapt to the monumentality of this one-sided combination of quantities. Meanwhile, the thought that this same Moroccan, perhaps with better reason, may be terrified by intimidation, by discreet and bureaucratic racism and by economic and political inequality, is difficult to reconcile with the usual discussion of the issues. It seems the phenomenon of 'insecurity', difficult to grasp yet ubiquitous, is thought about in extremely secure terms.

The fact that this new course, in which security has become the spearhead of policy, is primarily seen within the same social debate as a statistical given, indicates that there is an urgent need for 'objective' and 'hard' information. Surveys and samplings regularly come out, using fresh data to unearth the confirmation of something that has already been demonstrated: the significant cause for 'a sense of insecurity' is the presence of immigrants. The principle of the self-fulfilling prophecy is nowhere so efficient as in statistics and expert rhetoric.

The hardening of society, violence in the street for no apparent reason, brutal acts of destruction and intimidation, rising racial hatreds easily buttress a repressive trend in policy, which definitely can count on broad public support after the murder of Fortuyn. In this repressive scenario there is little room for nuance and inquiry into motives, for ultimately these can only show up a guilty conscience. After all, despite all the decisive language and propaganda in favour of an active, problem-solving policy, people quietly assume that the problems can at most be regulated, but certainly not resolved. Let alone that from a broader perspective any thought should be given to what is causing this hardening and this sense of insecurity. Just as in the management of the traffic congestion problem, the management of the 'sense of insecurity' is intended to reduce this socially undesirable phenomenon to a tolerable quota of incidents, or, in a Newtonian exercise (cause-and-effect thinking) to make the case that the policy has caused the freezing of a previously measured percentage. It might be acknowledged behind closed doors that a deeper set of problems underlies these inventoried incidents and percentages. In an atmosphere of zero tolerance, however, delving into the unfathomable depths that lie hidden behind these numerical translations of expertly dissected *Volksempfinden* would be media and political suicide. Policy, after all, is not based on inquisitiveness but on numbers.

The politics of combating 'insecurity' have become a mathematical equation approaching zero.

Insecure Governance in Repressive Times

At an unsafe distance from the general debate, entirely different problems apply to municipalities that must formulate local policy for (immigrant) problem areas. Percentages and rhetoric apply here as well, but compared to the national government, there is greater urgency to gauge the effectiveness of policy. The popularity of the issue is not congruent with the resources that are devoted to the policy – certainly not when a radical, multi-million-euro restructuring of such an area seems the only solution to the problems. Often, the problems in these areas are the result of years of delay in tackling degeneration, the collapse of the socio-economic infrastructure, the exodus of better-educated residents, problems in education – problems that, certainly in combination, engender gigantic costs. Yet delay does offer some solace. Indeed, from a 'silent reserve' standpoint, these degenerated city areas offer potential for further urban development within the existing city limits. In an adapted variant of the slum-creation theory, one might speak of a strategy of pauperization in order, subsequently, to legitimately demolish and (prestigiously) rebuild – with the hope that this will also instantly 'solve' the socio-cultural problems. Financing for such prestigious projects can be found, not by applying to the national government, but to the private sector. This has turned public housing into a market-driven component of city policy and thus removed it from the sphere of social policy.

Utrecht has just such a prototypical problem area: Kanaleneiland. Once a model of modernist urban planning and architecture, it has long since become an impoverished enclave, wedged in between the prestigious Leidsche Rijn Vinex development and the old city centre. When the area, with its high concentration of immigrants, gets any media coverage, it is invariably negative in the extreme. One of the problems the city has with this is that it is difficult to contradict this negative coverage. The city has been promising for years to improve the living climate in this area, and has demonstrated its readiness to provide needed maintenance to its buildings and surroundings. However, it has failed to demonstrate any effort to actually address its problems, other than by coming up with a restructuring plan for Kanaleneiland as well (which has, admittedly, now been postponed again).

For this restructuring of Kanaleneiland, Utrecht has signed a covenant with several housing corporations to carry out demolition and new-build plans for 2,400 dwellings in Kanaleneiland-Noord over a period of 15 years ('The Utrecht Project', 2001). It is thus no surprise that this plan is founded on a predominantly technocratic approach, primarily inspired by administrative and market standpoints. Indeed, the city will have to allow the corporations to build dwellings in a higher market segment with a large profit margin, and they can even keep a sizable portion of the profits from the land development. In return, the city is asking the corporations to take over the arrangement and management of public facilities (parking garages, pavements, et cetera). The dependence of municipalities on private capital for the development and management of such restructuring projects has become standard practice, and is definitely not unique to Kanaleneiland. It is telling that at a study day organized by the Ministry of Housing, Spatial Planning and the Environment on components of its big-city policy, only the issues of management technique in such covenants were highlighted by municipal officials. Covenants may well address the technical aspects of a restructuring project; the final responsibility for the quality of the living environment is difficult to pin down in such arrangements. Let alone there being any room for specifying an integral framework to serve as a guiding principle, which not only addresses issues of management technique but also formulates a social vision. The role of government as designer of the socio-cultural structure of the built environment seems to have been played out once (public) housing construction was turned over to the market. Even if the city of Utrecht, in a nostalgic burst of visionary social policy, were to come up with a sound social plan, its signing of the covenant has reduced its field of operation to that of rhetoric and the slippery terrain of image-making. A thankless task it prefers to relegate, as a recent example has shown, to the visual arts.

Art as Development Cooperation: <re-start>

The city of Utrecht's policy document *Stedelijk Ontwikkelingsplan* ('Urban Development Plan') (1999) formed the Cultural Affairs Department's framework for formulating the question of whether, in addition to physical possibilities for art in Kanaleneiland, there were also opportunities for art to enter the socio-cultural context of this post-war area. The city described this as 'employing art to improve the image of Kanaleneiland'. With the prospect that structural improvement in the area would take years, the department grabbed the opportunity to do something immediately in terms of image-making and public opinion.

It is remarkable that the city of Utrecht is giving the arts, of all things, the honour of changing this negative image. Art as a *deus ex machina*, unexpectedly engaging with the sensitive domain of image- and opinion-making. In a place where the government has failed to build up the confidence of residents by providing a positive vision of the future, the visual arts are being pressed forward as a relatively cheap alternative instrument that, based on public participation, must care for a new sense of collectivism and a fundamental upgrade in the experience of the area. Comparable projects in other cities, such as Jeanne van Heeswijk's project *De Strip* in Vlaardingen, apparently provided the inspiration for this administrative solution. As far as organizing the necessary support to generate this participation, the Cultural Affairs Department could offer little more than a few telephone numbers of community workers and steering committees and a gratuitous assurance of cooperation.

Following an exploratory assignment, the <re-start> project was launched within this loose set of parameters. The project, a work in progress by Jan van Grunsven and Ineke Bellemakers, extends over several years (2003–2007). The approach they have planned is based on the integration of those two tracks: the physical-spatial and the socio-cultural. Using a series of studies, explorations of the area and participation projects with residents, they intend to create not only a better picture of the problems in the area, and what the actual experiences of the residents are, but also offer alternative solutions along the way. For <re-start> does not consider the restructuring project to be necessarily what will rescue the area. These solutions may in fact be related to physical-spatial problems, for example the concrete design of solutions for run-down rest areas, but can also address the desires and future expectations of residents and be used in designing new forms of public space, in which a new collectivism is expressed. The plan upon which <re-start> is based is predicated on the capacity to learn of the project group as well as of the residents and the relevant institutions. Each project component forms the teaching material out of which the next project section will be constructed. This vision and approach is based on the ambition of <re-start> to make an in-depth investment in the socio-cultural structure of the area. In this series of project sections, <re-start> takes a 'mediating position' each time – as a mediator between area residents and the experts and professionals involved in the project (such as designers, architects, journalists, stylists or curators).

In an atmosphere of cultural segregation, permanent negative media coverage and a decimation of basic facilities (for instance secondary schools deserting the area) <re-start> being granted this mediating position is by no means a given. During an exploration project – one of the project sections – there was obvious suspicion, especially among young people of immigrant backgrounds, when one of the researchers took out a camera to take some pictures. One Moroccan boy vehemently explained that they were sick of random Moroccan youths being photographed for newspapers and magazines in which captions would say that these were criminal problem kids. It took some time and persuasion to reassure the lad that this was not the case this time. In this first phase of the project, it was made clear that organic forms of cooperation were to be sought out, which could only emerge through slowly gained trust. Creating support, a prerequisite to gaining access to the other face of the area, turned out to take more than good intentions and exciting plans. Only by acknowledging the sensitivity concerning this point could the plan have any chance of success. Therefore it was decided to consider the public visibility of the project primarily in conjunction with projects that were conducted in cooperation with residents.

Photographs taken by pupils of De Kaleidoskoop primary school, research group 1, 2, 3.

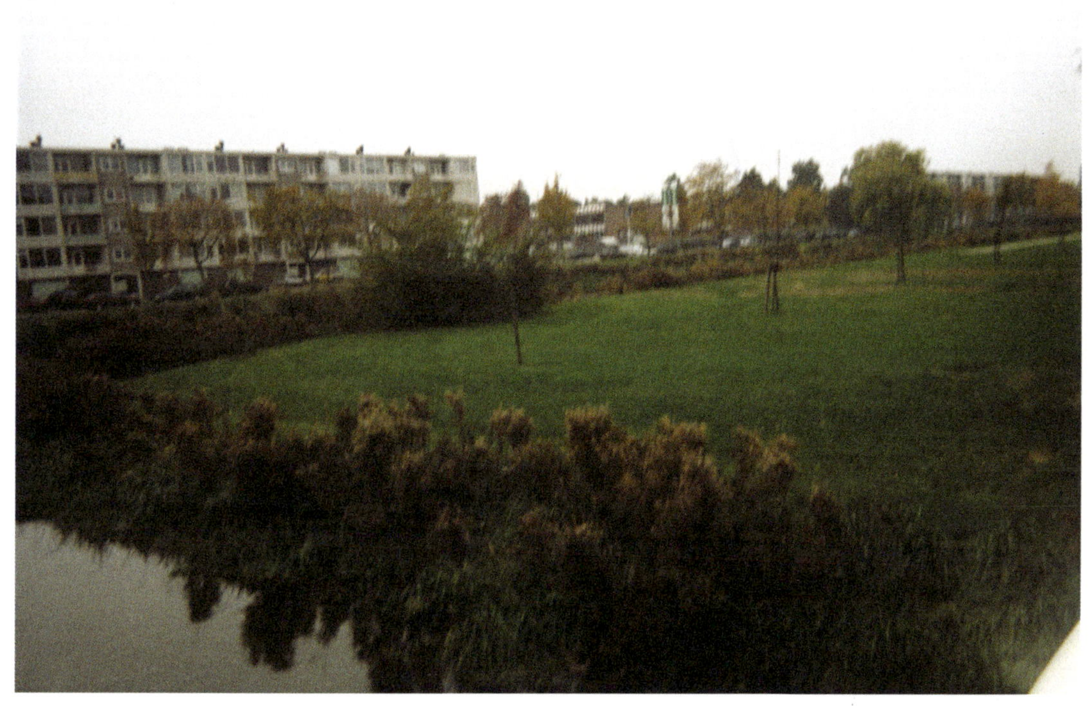

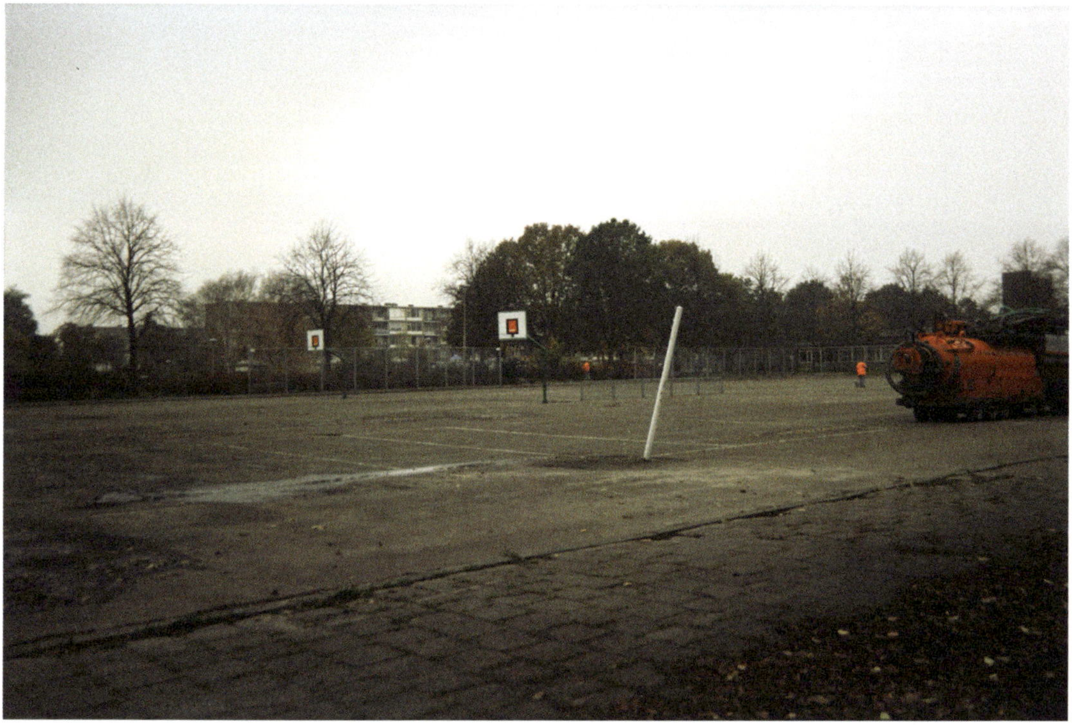

Photographs taken by pupils of De Kaleidoskoop primary school, research group 1, 2, 3.

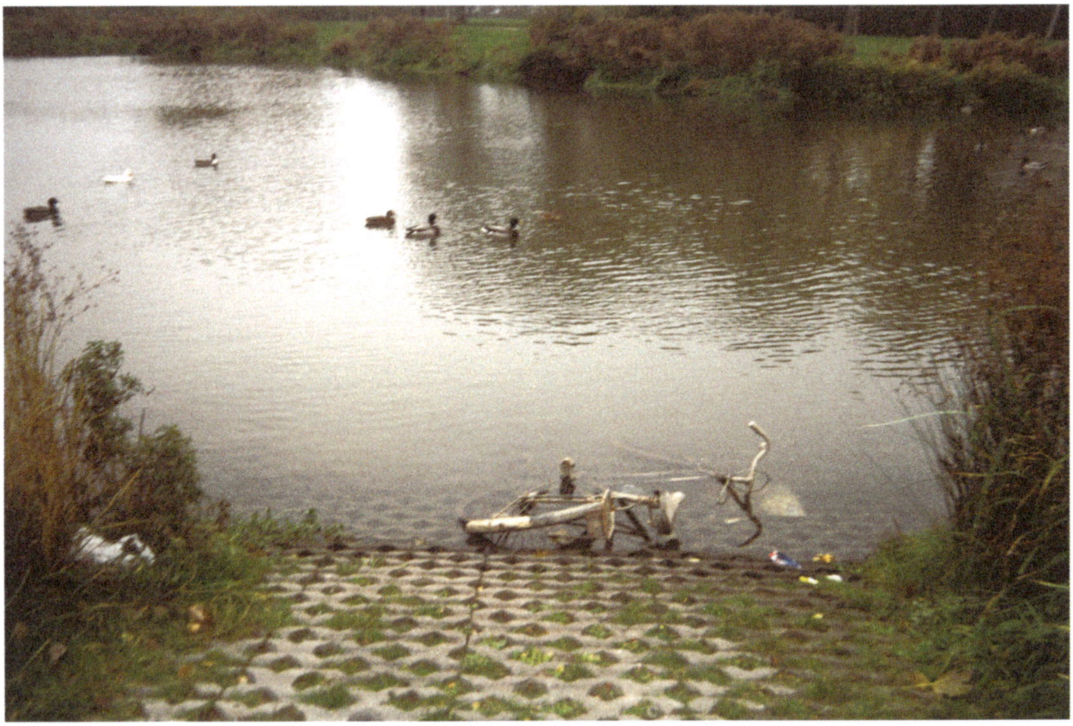

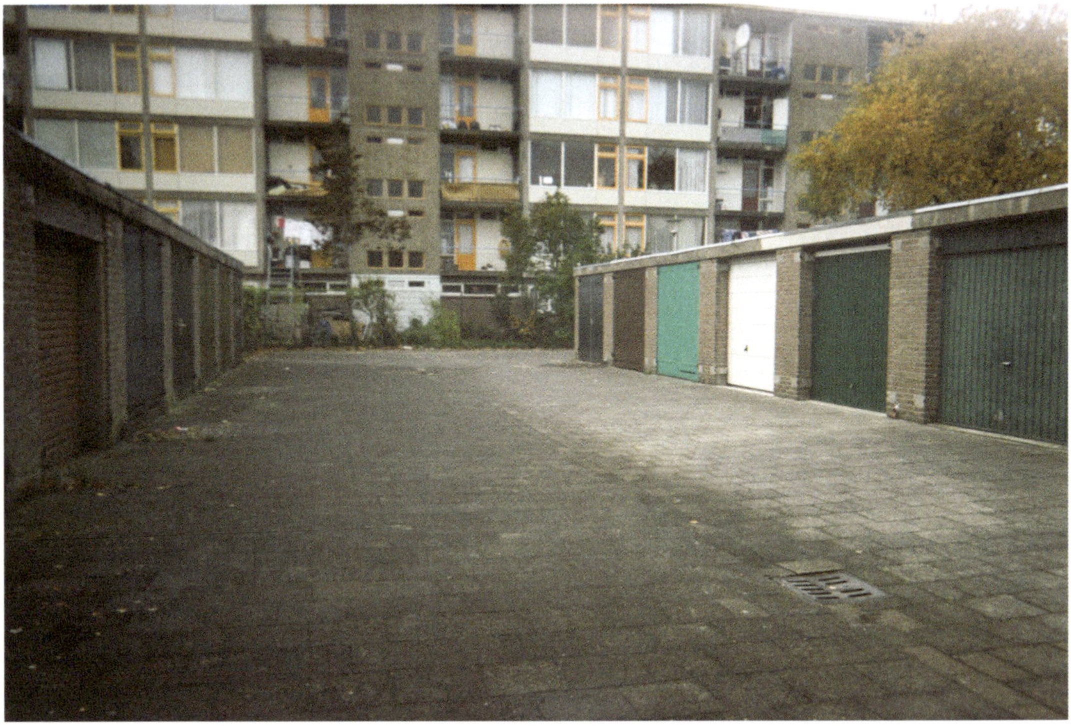

Photographs taken by pupils of De Kaleidoskoop primary school, research group 1, 2, 3.

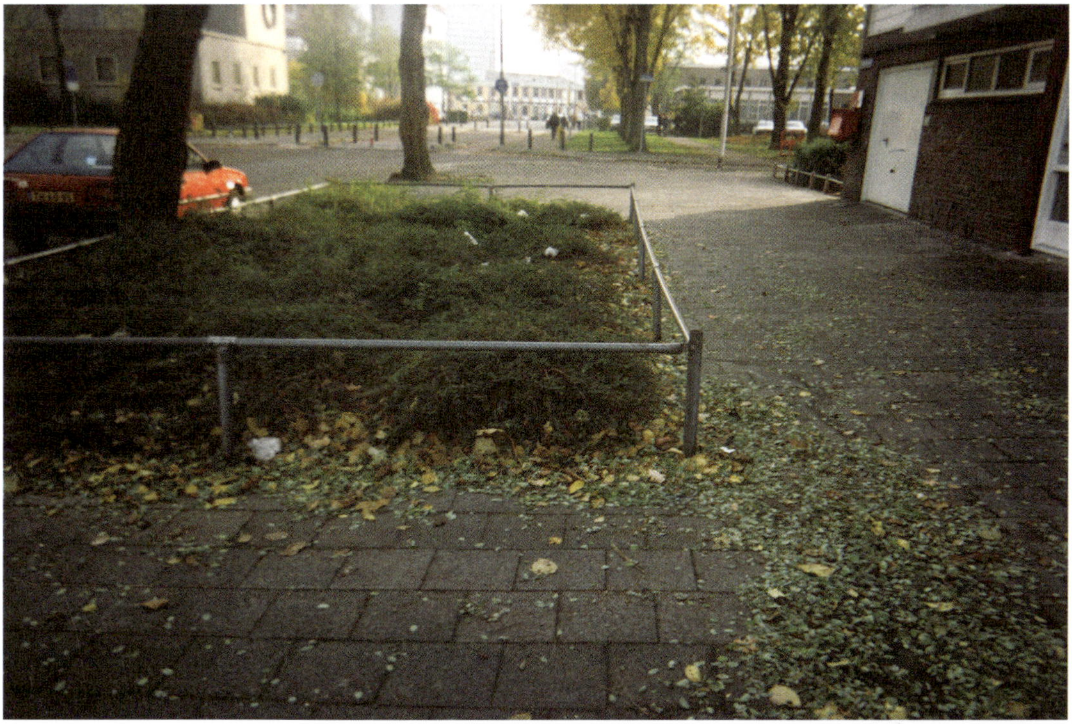

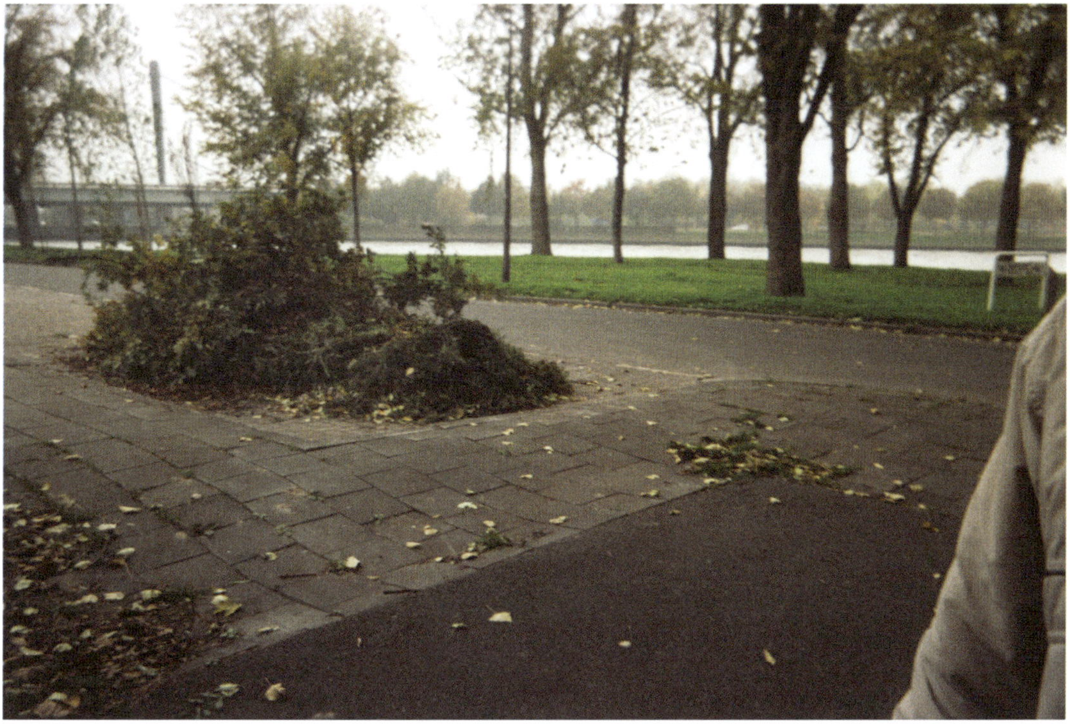

Preliminary field research by pupils of De Kaleidoskoop primary school.
Videostills by Erik Weeda/dc158.

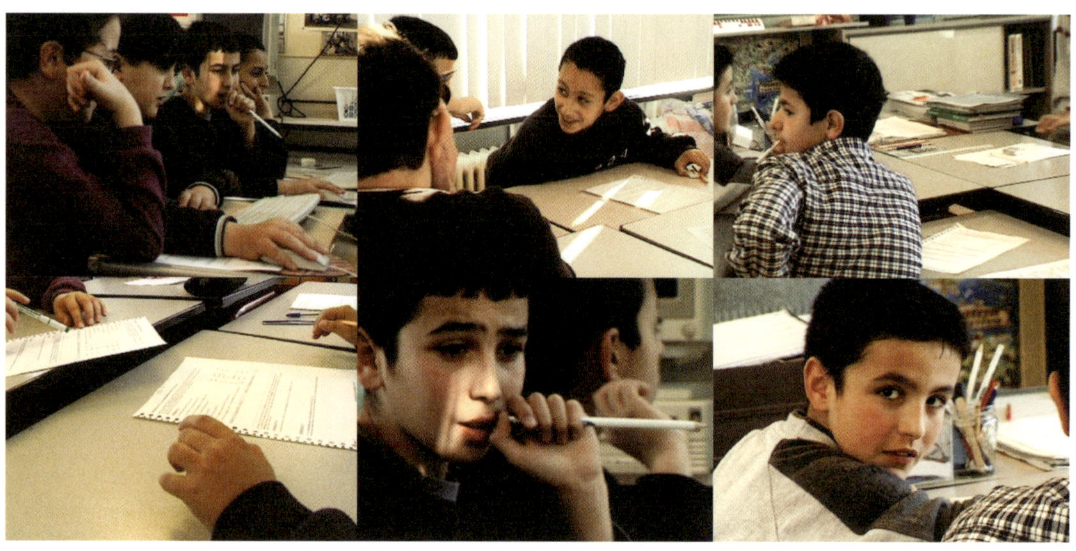

Pupils of De Kaleidoskoop primary school carrying out field research.
Videostills by Erik Weeda/dc158.

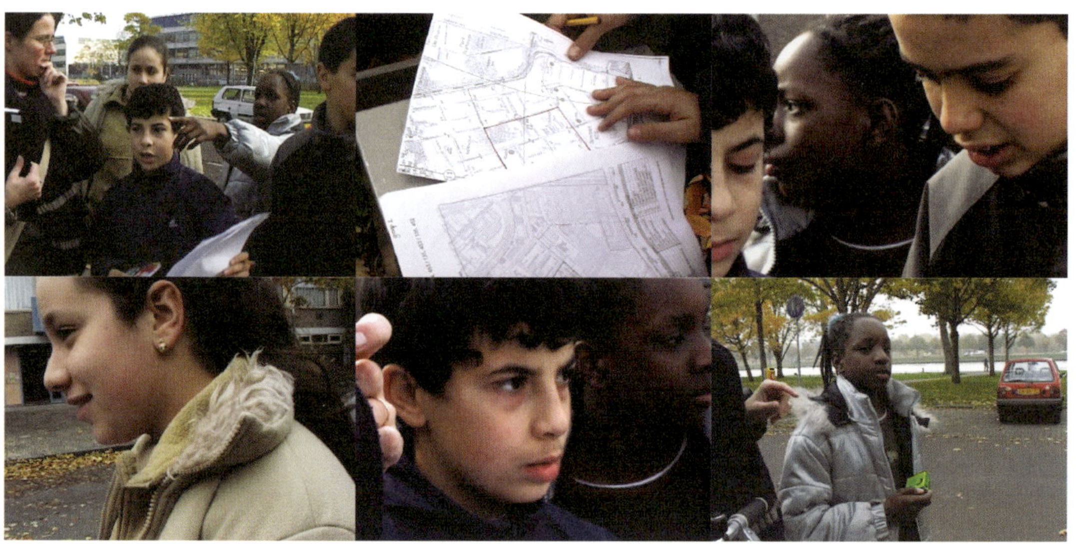

Processing of the data and evaluation of the field research by pupils of the De Kaleidoskoop primary school. Video stills by Erik Weeda/dc158.

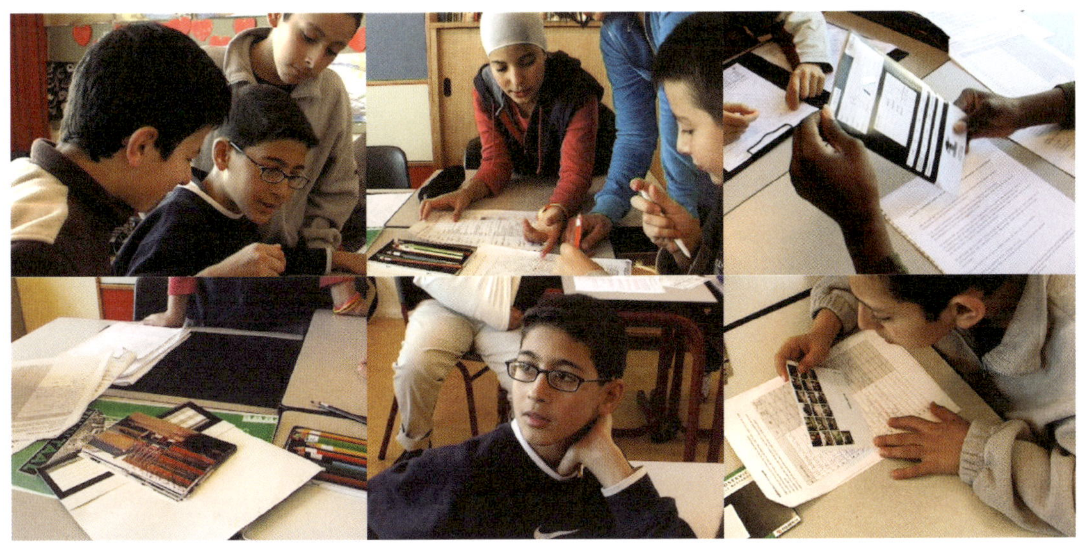

Pupils preparing for the interview they are going to record. Video stills by Erik Weeda/dc158.

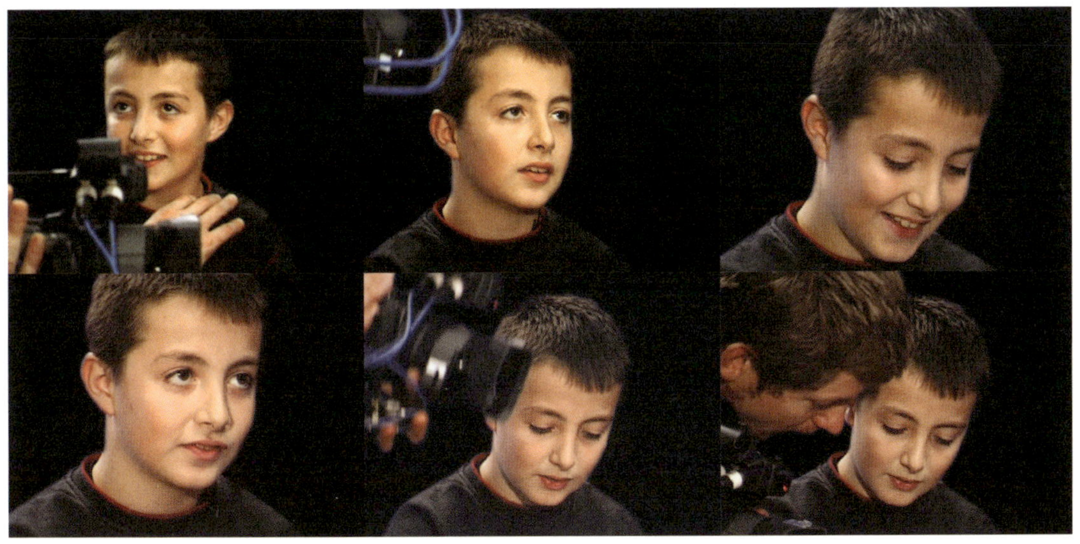

This made the legitimacy of <re-start> as a 'product' no longer the formal representation of third parties (for example the client, in this case the Cultural Affairs Department), but the contributing to making visible those who in an atmosphere of insecurity are increasingly less visible.

Diane project

One of the projects adopted by <re-start>, in part in order to build support, is the Diane project. This is a national education project begun four years ago. It is an initiative of the HHIT (Expertise Centre for Education and Information Technology of the Hogeschool Holland). Participating school classes (starting with Year 5) conduct research into the liveability of the school's immediate surroundings. The research area is one square kilometre. Topographic maps of each of these quadrants are made available. The data provided by the children are centrally processed for the Netherlands Internet@tlas, which is also available online.

To gather the information, the pupils must carry out field research, including conducting interviews with residents and taking photographs. <re-start> found several primary schools in Kanaleneiland were prepared to participate in this project. In addition they are also prepared to work with <re-start>, which aims to use the Diane project as a lever for image-making projects involving the children. These are workshops (led by Joke Roobaard, among others) in which the pupils are asked to contribute to the production of a picture archive. This consists of pictures of the pupils themselves, through which they wish to present themselves to the outside world. They will look into whether the image that others have of you can be influenced by your own intervention. The workshops are about more than simply a form of re-styling: they are about 'image-making' and what you yourself can do about it; they provide direction for the development of a visual idiom of and for the area.

From the reactions of the schoolchildren in the first phase of the project it was clear that they were highly reticent to conduct so many interviews with residents, but also to be photographed themselves. After a little practical experience the fear turned into enthusiasm. This project, which is to continue for several years and follow the pupils through secondary school, can be the beginning of a media emancipation that is currently lacking. It can make the young residents of Kanaleneiland media literate, which seems to be a requisite for survival in the present 'mediacracy'. It can enable the kids to effect an expressive correction to the images pandered by the regular media, which represent this 'insecurity'. For the politics of 'insecurity' are primarily the politics of the image.

Sources

Jan van Grunsven, 'De noodzaak van een tegenbeeld, <re-start> in Kanaleneiland', *Lucas x*, no. 1 2004, p. 28-40.

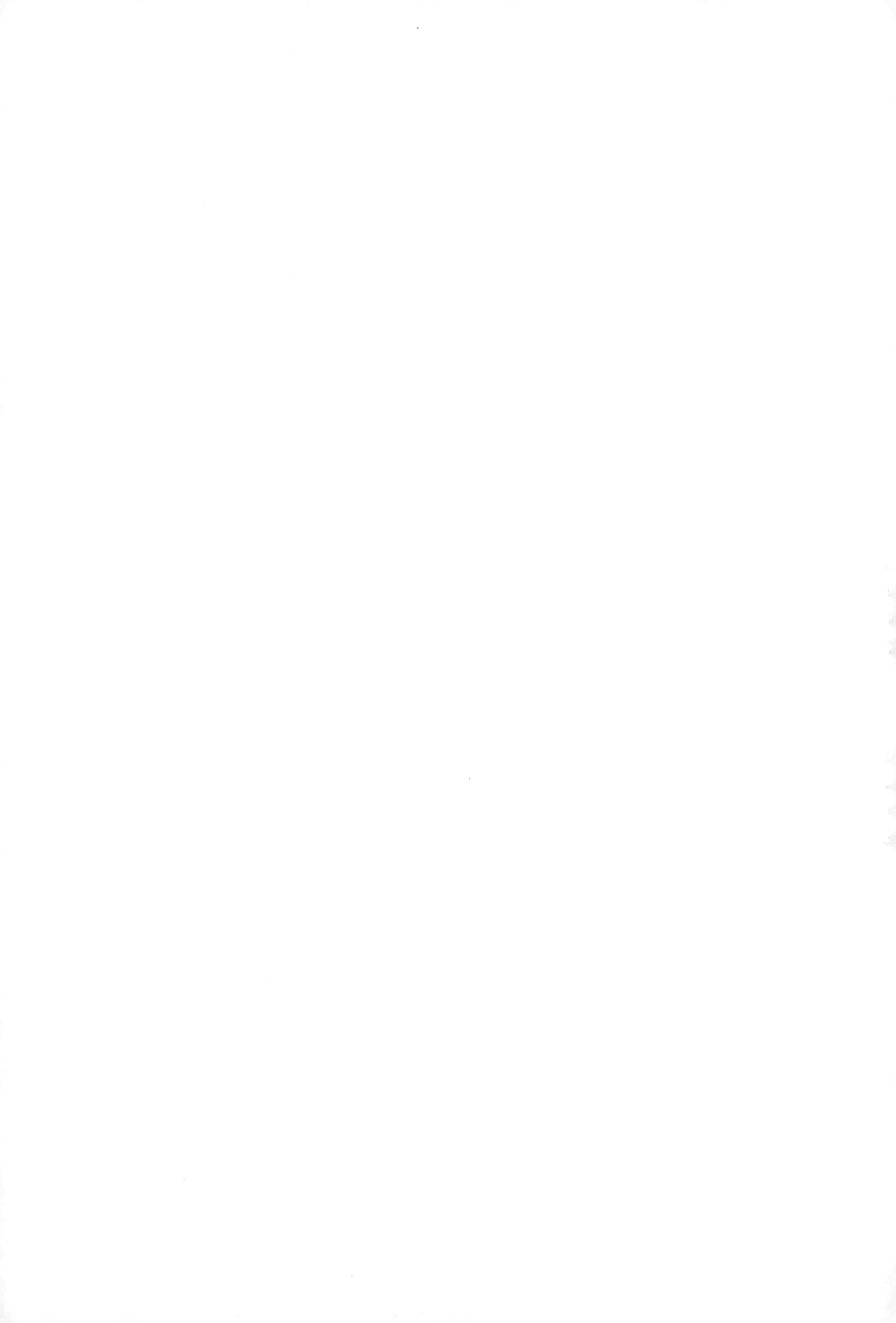

Q.S. Serafijn

Emotional Landscapes in the City

D-Tower in Doetinchem by Q.S. Serafijn and NOX/Lars Spuybroek

D-Tower measures the emotions of the inhabitants of Doetinchem. D-Tower measures hate, love, fear and happiness and draws the emotional map of the city. D-Tower includes three podia: a survey, a website and a physical tower.

The project is based on the map of the city and its division into postal code areas. In each postal code area, a cross-section of the population participates over six months in a survey totalling 360 questions and statements. The questions and statements are general at the start ('I am afraid') and become more specific over the course of the survey period ('I am afraid (a) that something will happen to my lover (b), my lover will get sick (c) and will die of cancer (d)'). Every six months a new group of participants are commissioned for the survey.

All participants are given a password that allows access to the survey. Each password is linked to the individual postal code of the participant. In this way, D-Tower can localize emotions on the map of the city down to the street level: 'In the Korte Kapoeniestraat people like pets, and dogs the most.'

D-site displays answers on to the lists of questions as 'emotional landscapes'. In hand-drawn animations the results unfold in peaks and troughs across the screen. Each landscape visualizes the 'emotional score' by subject, by postal code, by street.

The emotional tics of the city are entered into a database and transmitted to the physical tower. The physical tower is a semi-transparent 'polyp', 12.5 metres high, at the edge of the city centre.

Each emotion is linked to a colour: hate is green, love is red, happiness is blue, fear is yellow. Depending on the 'score' of the day, the tower glows red, yellow, blue or green. If the tower was blue, people in Doetinchem were happy. If the tower was red, Doetinchem was full of love.

Every visitor can send D-Tower a letter or participate in a discussion. In cases of explosive hate, extreme fear or total absence of happiness or fear, D-Tower sends a bouquet of flowers with a card to the relevant address.

———————

Project details: D-Tower (1998–2004)
Design: Q.S. Serafijn & NOX/Lars Spuybroek
Commissioned by: City of Doetinchem

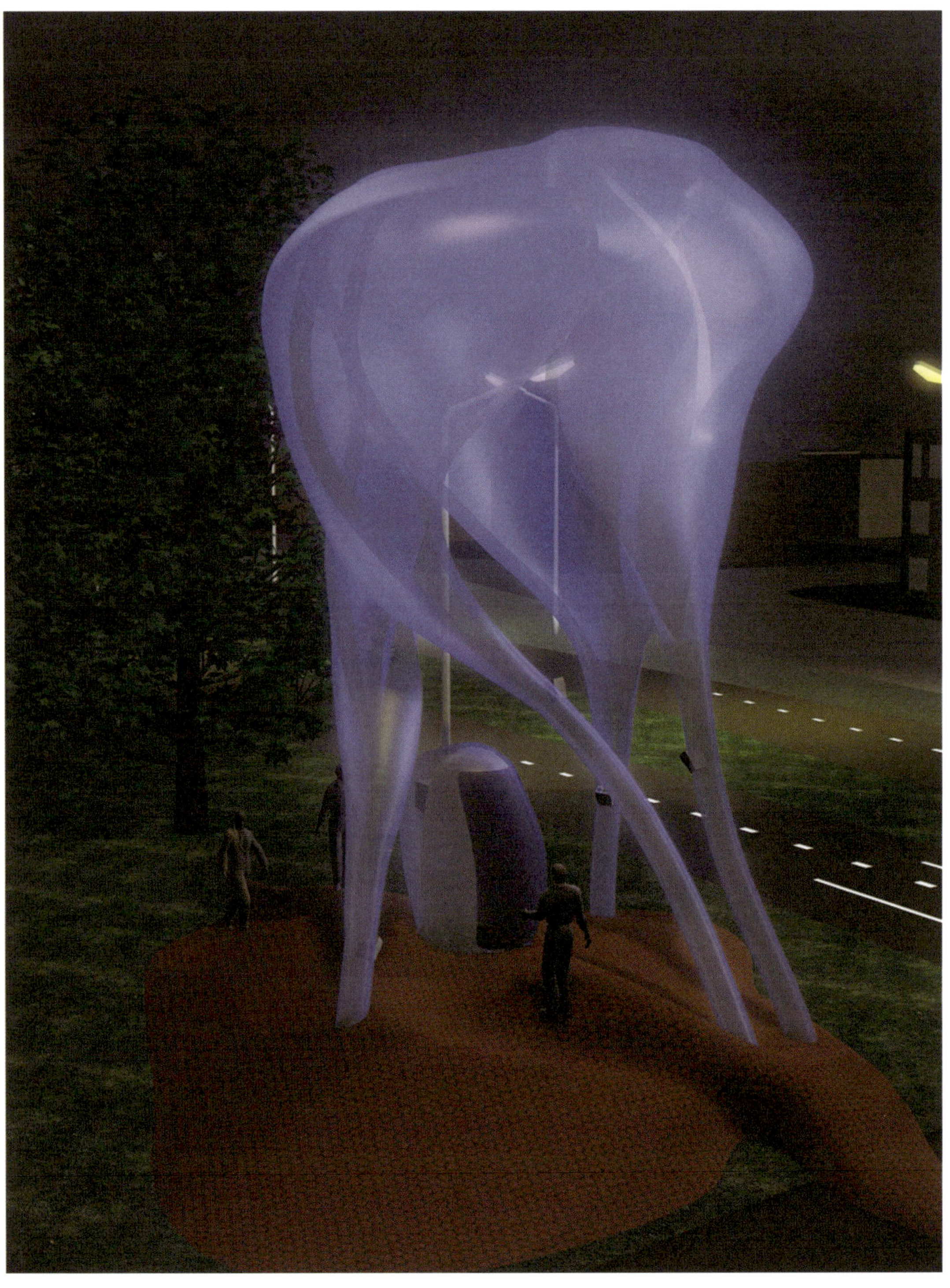

Insecurity is an Economic Impulse

00

A significant portion of the world is designed for the daytime. Therefore a significant portion of the world is perceived as unsafe at night. This is good for the economy. Insecurity is an economic impulse.

01

Public space is a territorial space. In the past, city ramparts, city watchtowers and military units protected the territory. Now public space is protected by legislation and jurisprudence. Criminals are testing the limits of the legal state. Public space is a legal space.

02

Virtual space initially seemed untouched by legal space. Now it erects firewalls and bolts its digital ramparts with passwords. Not just in terminology, in regulation and behaviour as well, virtual space is becoming more and more a copy of the physical public space.

03

City ramparts, watchtowers, legislation and jurisprudence are territorial markings of the power that protected the community as a collective. In the screen culture the protection is individual and private.

04

A friend once described his worst nightmare to me. He was a pea in a jar of peas. The fact that he was a pea in jar of peas did not worry him so much. The fact that as a pea he was not 'by the window' was his nightmare. The idea of spending his life in the dark centre of the jar frustrated him.

05

The fear that haunts people in a screen culture is the fear of not sitting 'by the window'. The attention and space that media (TV, magazines, newspapers, Internet) devote to the average citizen is an answer to this fear. Those sitting by the window of the media imagine or consider themselves safe.
Whereas security was once linked to invisibility and going underground, at present security seems increasingly linked to visibility and being out in public.

06

As a vertical tower symbol, D-Tower recalls the longing for collective security. As a horizontal medium, D-site projects the fears and triumphs of the individual citizen. The community of Doetinchem has placed itself as a collective sum at the window. By making itself visible in this way, the community of Doetinchem keeps watch over itself without mediation by the government or other parties.

07

D-Tower is the interactive heart monitor of Doetinchem. Arjen Mulder wrote about this interaction between man and machine: 'Yet interactive art does not flow unilaterally from man to machine, but in reverse as well. It is after all the machine that is meant to inspire the visitors to all manner of actions, ideas and experiences. By providing answers – honest or not – about your relations with yourself, your family, your lover(s), your pets, et cetera, you change the tower. But when the D-Tower turns green or yellow (much fear or hate), this might well elicit reactions from others that would rather see it coloured red or blue. You can become afraid of that weird D-Tower, or hate it, or love it, or be very happy with it. The D-Tower measures emotions and sets off emotions.'[1]

---

1. Arjen Mulder, *De emotionele toren van Doetinchem/de toren van emotioneel Doetinchem*, City of Doetinchem, 2000.

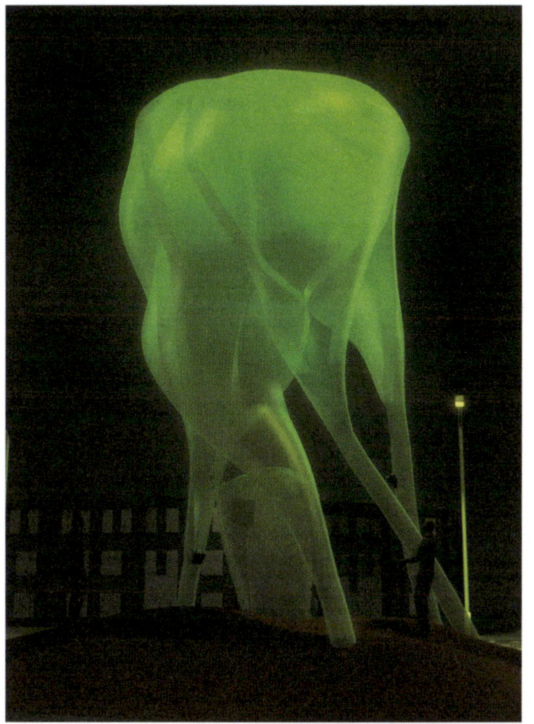

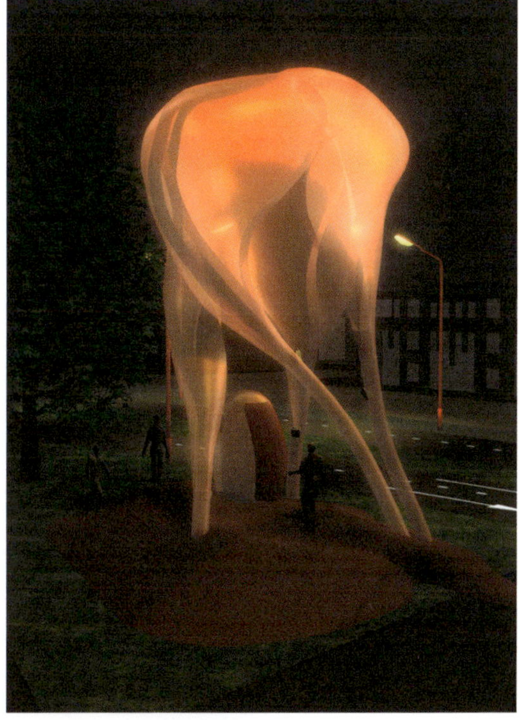

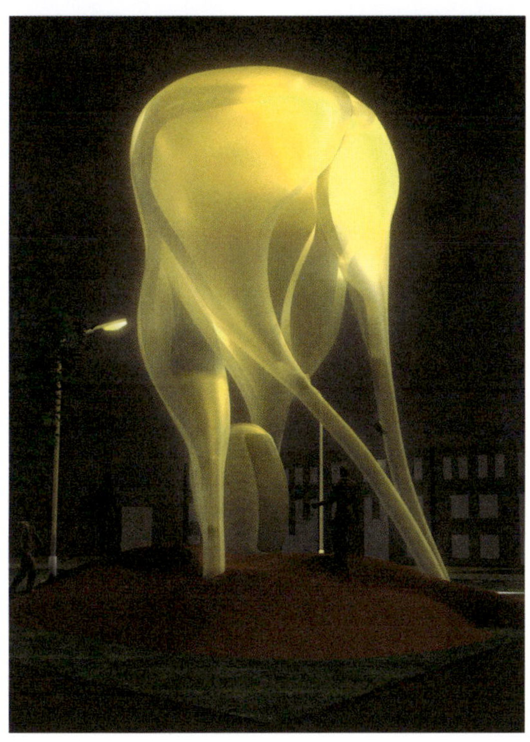

... ...

Are you happy?

... ...

Are you afraid?

... ...

Do you feel hate?

... ...

Are you satisfied with
your free time?

... ...

Does your religion make you happy?

... ...

Do you like dogs?

... ...

My partner and I have good sex.

... ...

Are you happy as a
housewife/husband?

... ...

Are you dissatisfied because you
smoke too much?

... ...

Do you like pigeons?

... ...

Are you afraid of dying of AIDS?

... ...

Are you depressed about the world
and the environment?

... ...

Is your IQ between 120 and 140?

... ...

Does being creative
make you happy?

... ...

Are you troubled by constipation?

... ...

Are you jealous of people
with money?

... ...

Have you and your partner been
happy together for more than
15 years?

... ...

Are you jealous of people who are
more beautiful than you?

… … … … … … … … … … … …
My friendships last longer than five
years on average.

… … … … … … … … … … … …
I earn more than 25,000 Euro after-
tax per year. I am happy with that.

… … … … … … … … … … … …
Do you feel good because you do
not use medication?

… … … … … … … … … … … …
Are you afraid that foreigners in the
city are contributing to crime?

… … … … … … … … … … … …
Do you have more than two friends?
I am afraid of rats.

… … … … … … … … … … … …
We are happy that our children are
going/went to college.

… … … … … … … … … … … …
Do you go through life with a smile?

… … … … … … … … … … … …
Do you love yourself because you
are well-endowed?

… … … … … … … … … … … …
Are you (too) much concerned with
your own happiness?

… … … … … … … … … … … …
I hate it when I get aggressive after
I have been drinking.

… … … … … … … … … … … …
I am afraid that my partner will die
in a traffic accident.

… … … … … … … … … … … …
I work 40 hours a week in paid
employment and I am happy
with that.

… … … … … … … … … … … …
Do you hate the children when they
are boisterous and loud?

… … … … … … … … … … … …
Does walking and/or cycling make
you happy?

… … … … … … … … … … … …
Do you like to tell jokes?

… … … … … … … … … … … …
Are you a fan of German cars?

Screenshots of D-Tower website, design by Q.S. Serafijn and NOX/Lars Spuybroek

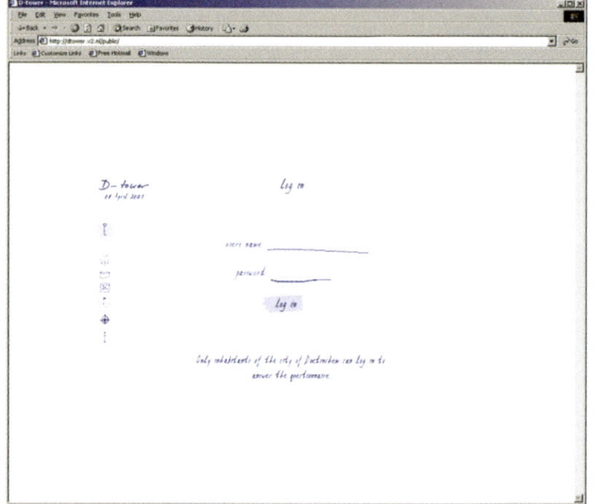

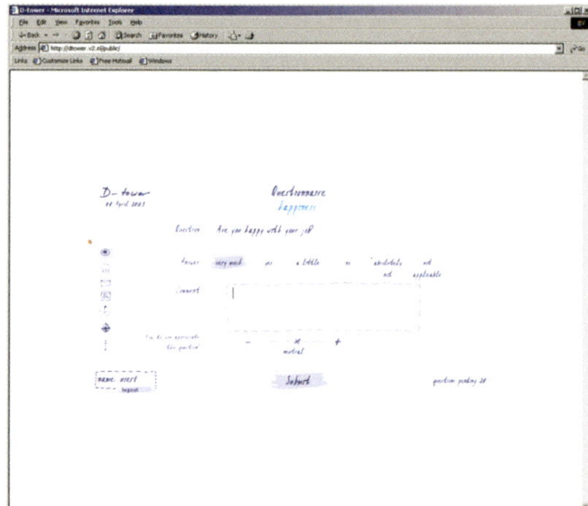

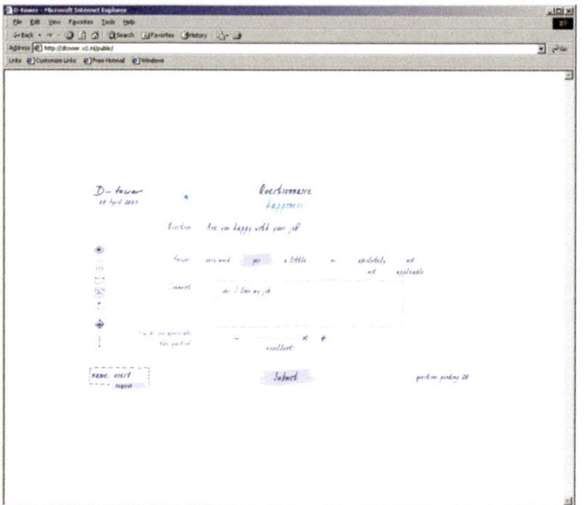

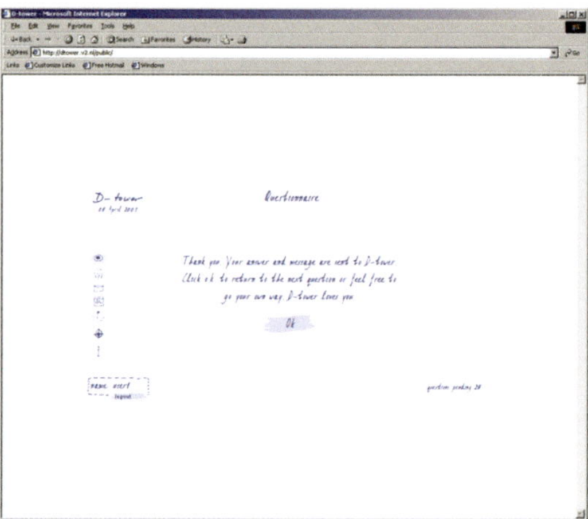

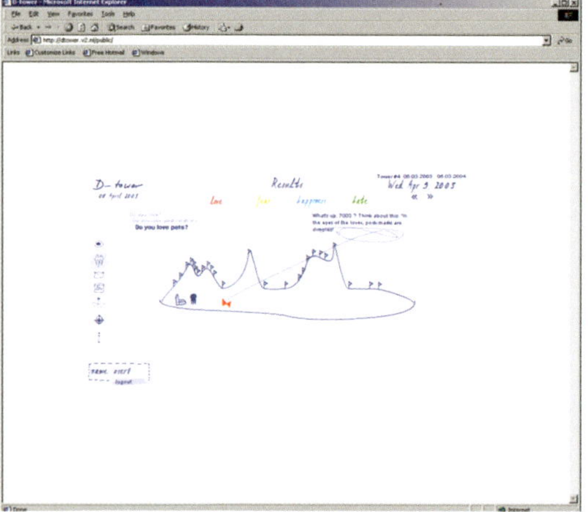

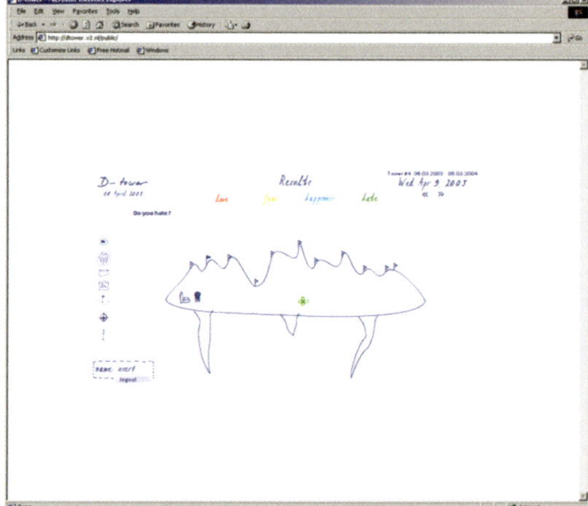

Mark Wigley

Cabin Fever

The Home of the Unabomber

At the end of the 1990s, the Unabomber was put on trial in the United States. His defence team tried to present his cabin as one of the most significant pieces of evidence of his insanity. The strict aesthetics of simplicity, natural materials, craftsmanship and geometric purity have since become symbolic of disturbing acts of terror, forever blemishing the image of the idyllic little house on the prairie.

December 2nd 1997. A small hut that had been hidden in the sparsely populated woods of Montana is lifted onto a flat-bed truck, covered with a black tarpaulin and transported 1100 miles to Sacramento. Shadowed by a caravan of photographers and a swarm of helicopters, it takes three days for the 10 by 12 foot wooden box to make the epic journey from isolation to metropolitan centre. For the first time, a whole building is to be presented as evidence in a court case. Architecture is brought to trial. A seemingly innocent structure is accused of sheltering the target of the biggest manhunt ever, the infamous Unabomber who had terrorized the nation for 18 years.

Not much for the jurors to look at, though. Everyone can picture the building before seeing it. Any child could draw it. Indeed, people are always drawing it, dreaming about it. The simple form plays a key role in the American imagination. The cabin in the woods is the generic retreat that is meant to tame restless city dwellers and has long been institutionalized in the camp hut, the holiday house, the fishing lodge. In fact, the Unabomber's building is a copy of the cabin in which Thoreau so famously withdrew from the city between 1845 and 1847. It self-consciously participates in a long cultural tradition.

Yet the unique power of this form is precisely that it is not seen as a cultural artefact. It is understood to be the form that precedes the arrival of culture. The retreat is always a retreat in time, a withdrawal to a lost simplicity, purity, immediacy, harmony... a lost beginning. In the romanticized national mythology of the immigrant pioneer, the domestication of the wild by the independent settler begins with the construction of a simple domestic space using primitive means. The wooden box with a pitched roof symbolizes the moment of settling down, the erection of an isolated house in the wilderness that precedes collective settlement. The cabin is that which precedes pattern, a solitary point in an unmapped terrain. Indeed, it is the pattern of the house itself, the newly defined limits of an interior carved within an unlimited and threateningly mysterious space, that makes possible the domestication of territory and the eventual rise of settlements.

This is not simply an American fantasy. It is a generic fantasy about a generic form. Each culture dreams of the mythical isolated hut, and each has its symbolic retreats, its designated sites of withdrawal from the dominant patterns. It may not even be possible to think about the patterns without thinking of these sites. Settlement is always conceived in terms of its other.

Technology as the Enemy

The Unabomber used his settler's cabin to unsettle the dominant pattern. His carefully written manifesto on the horrors of industrialized life condemns the modern city for its stressful, crowded existence in which people are kept prisoner under constant surveillance by police, cameras, and the manipulations of social programming. The enemy is technology, as exemplified by the computer that has united the world into a single social and spatial organization. The best solution is to go back to the purity of 'wild nature' in the age of the humble log cabin. Everyone should withdraw from the computer to the cabin. Within such a retreat, sixteen bombs were built and targeted with deadly effect against symbols of the technological order: computer scientists, airline executives, biogeneticists, electrical engineers. The point of the violence, said the ex-professor of mathematics, was to break society down into small units, to break the pattern.

The cabin itself is a manifesto, a puritanical polemic. No electricity or water softens the bomber's life or connects it to the national infrastructure. The only furniture is a single chair, a small table and a bed made of a sheet of plywood covered with a thin layer of foam. There are two tiny windows. Neither provides a scenic view. One is at the top of a wall and offers a square of sky. The other, a little lower on the facing wall, monitors the access path. There is a single door at the centre and a storage loft suspended under the roof. Built by its occupant with simple tools and reused wood from an abandoned cabin, the house is immaculately constructed. The dark stained wall boards are neatly matched. Roof joists are rhythmically arranged. Windows, door and air vent are triumphs of minimalist anti-detailing. Every nail pinning down the green tar paper on the roof is exactly spaced. The house is a display of control – even if it was never meant to be seen by anyone other than its reclusive occupant.

Likewise the bombs. They had exactly the aesthetic of the house they were built in. Most were hand-crafted boxes that were carefully carved, sanded, polished and repolished – even if they would only be seen for a few moments by the victim before their devastating disintegration. Each was repeatedly taken apart, rebuilt and refinished with fetishistic but deadly care. The mechanism of the fifth one did not work and the ninth one looked suspicious, so the boxes survived. X-rays revealed that their delicate interior organization was assembled out of recycled materials held together with handmade screws and fittings. Many of the key parts were made of wood. The rest were reworked household items – untraceable because generic. The everyday as a weapon.

Symptomatically, the cabin too had to be x-rayed for fear that it was booby-trapped. Every surface was scanned for 'secret spaces'. After all, no piece of wood could be trusted. Two of the most deadly bombs had been designed to look like simple blocks. For days, the cabin could not be entered normally. Robots were sent in through the end walls to scan each of the 700 objects found inside and, sure enough, detected a finished bomb ready for delivery. The very technologies that the Unabomber rebelled against were brought to bear on his hideaway.

The Unabomber's cabin is stored in a warehouse in Sacramento.
Photo Richard Barnes

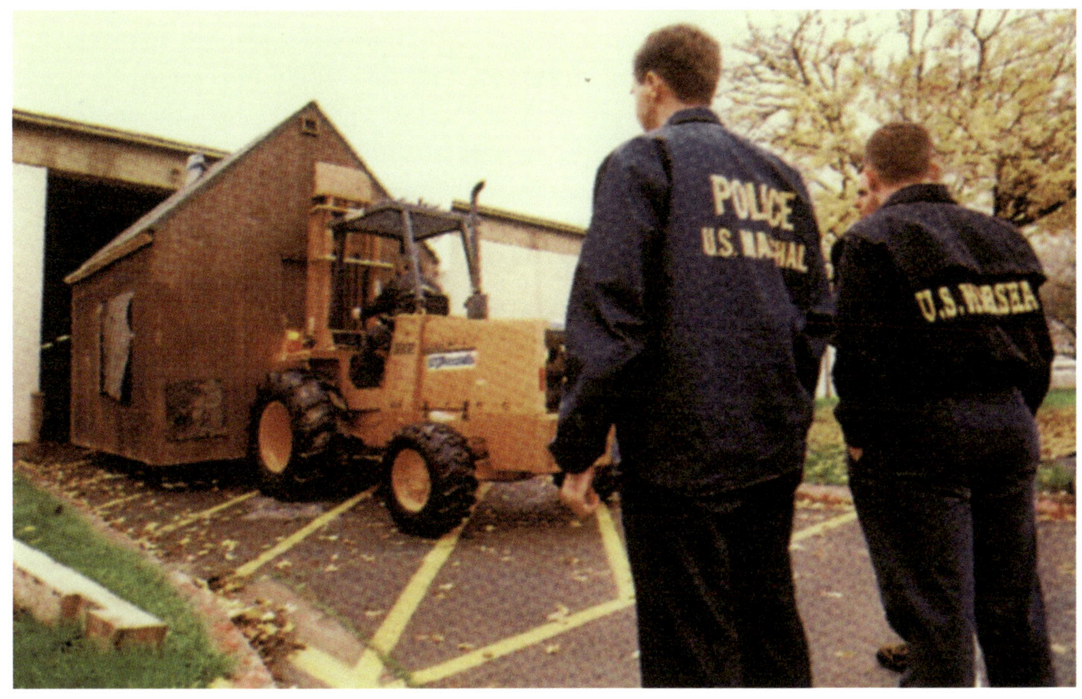

In 1998, the whole cabin was packed up and transported from the woods
of Montana to Sacramento. Photo Richard Barnes

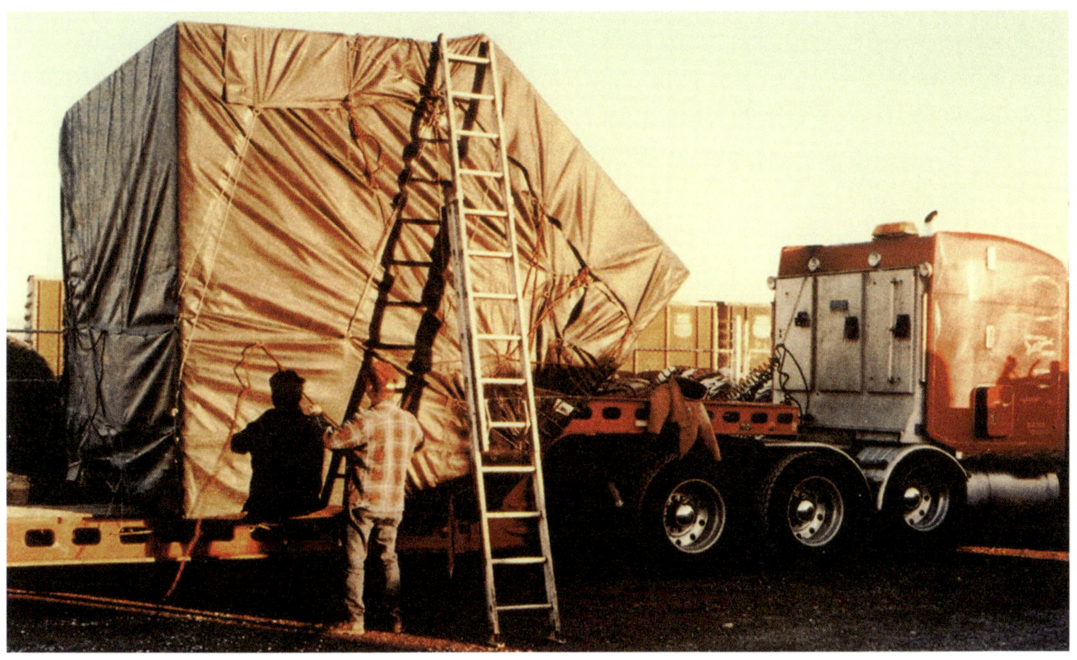

Even the woods were scanned. The FBI had taken detailed pictures from a spy satellite and laced the trees with motion detectors, microphones, television cameras and infrared scopes before waiting two months for their chance to move in. This was not simply the sudden intrusion of contemporary technology into an isolated place. Retreats are already part of the technological network, part of the pattern they seem to have escaped. Thoreau was never really isolated. On the contrary, his withdrawal was a very public act described in a best-selling book. The ideology of his cabin was actually constructed in the urban milieu. The settlement always includes within itself what it nominates as its other. 'Isolated' is an urban concept. It is a product of the city. To leave the map behind is a uniquely urban fantasy. It is those at the centre of the pattern that talk the most about escaping it. But their escapes are usually just extensions of the pattern, demonstrations that the city knows no limit. [*This has become ever more obvious today with the rise of ecotourism, off-the-road vehicles, and wireless communication links to any point of the globe. All interiors – whether of a suburban house, a university, an airliner, or the jungle – are interconnected in multiple ways. Radical disconnection from the networks can of course occur, but anywhere, by definition. It is not a matter of leaving the city but of using the gaps in its fabric.*]

The cabin in the woods is actually at the centre of the city. Far from disconnected, the terrorist ruthlessly exploited the ever-present intimate ties between isolated cell and dense urbanization. His frightening talent was the ability to hide his points of connection. While refusing to attach himself to the telephone, water and electricity lines that were only a quarter of a mile away, he kept his rural mail box on the roadside nearby, using the mail network to distribute his terror and get his manifesto published in national newspapers.

This is why a seemingly isolated hut could exemplify one of the greatest fears of urban life. The cabin has always belonged to the downtown to which it was eventually brought. It is quite at home in the public spaces of the media, including the pages of this journal. In the striking images by Richard Barnes that are presented here, the anti-technological wooden house has been lit by electronically controlled lights and photographed with a computerized camera. Every detail is ruthlessly exposed. The Sacramento warehouse in which the building still remains has been blackened out. This remobilizes the house, sending it on countless more epic journeys as we can easily see it standing on any of the sites where the archetypal form has typically been installed – whether real or imaginary.

But the all-important interior remains hidden, mysterious, threateningly obscure. The photographer, like all the journalists visiting the original site, was not even allowed to look through the windows. In over 25 years, the bomber had

Exterior of the cabin in the Montana woods the Unabomber built and operated from for years. Photo Richard Barnes

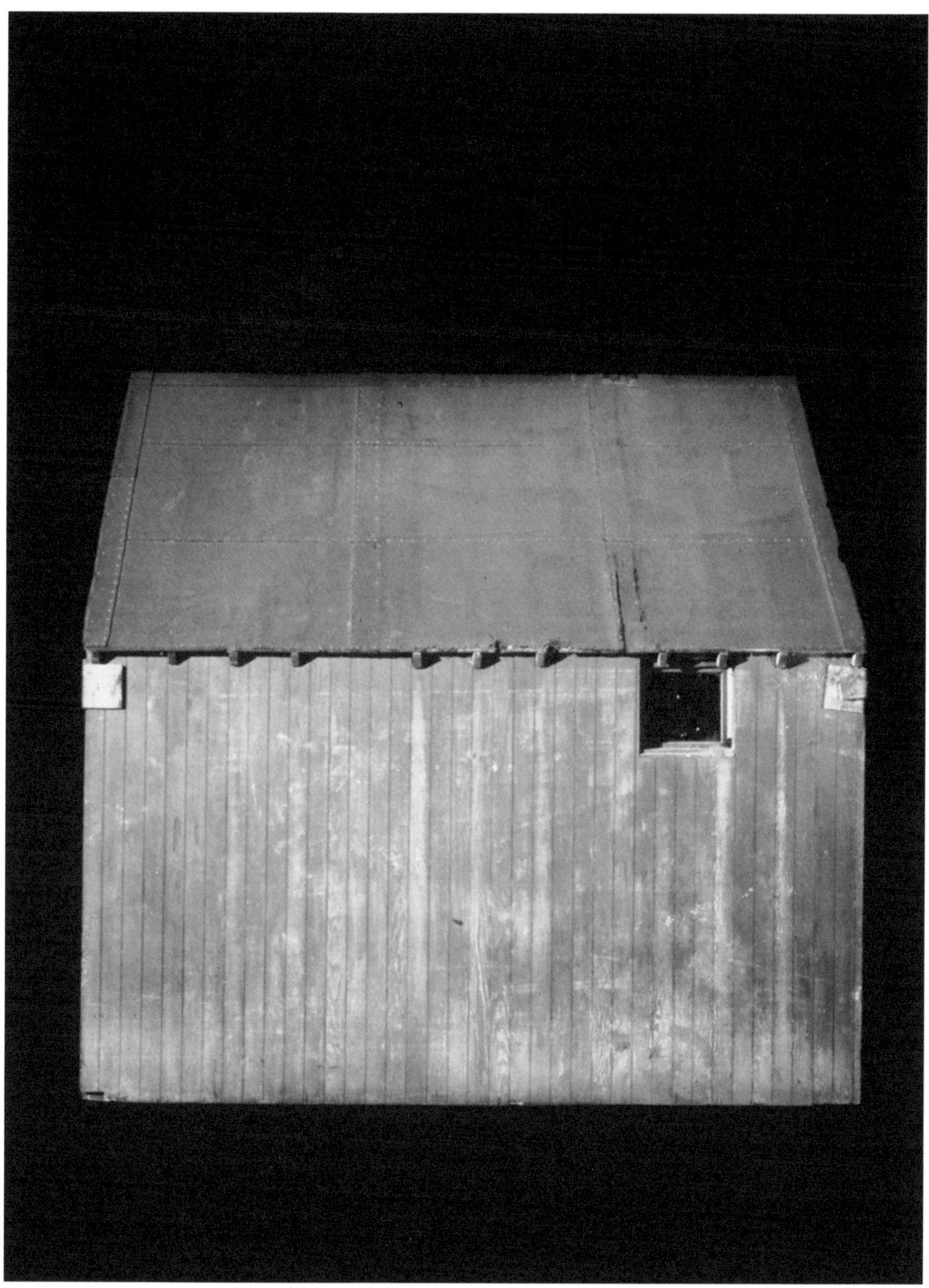

Exterior of the cabin in the Montana woods the Unabomber built and operated from for years. Photo Richard Barnes

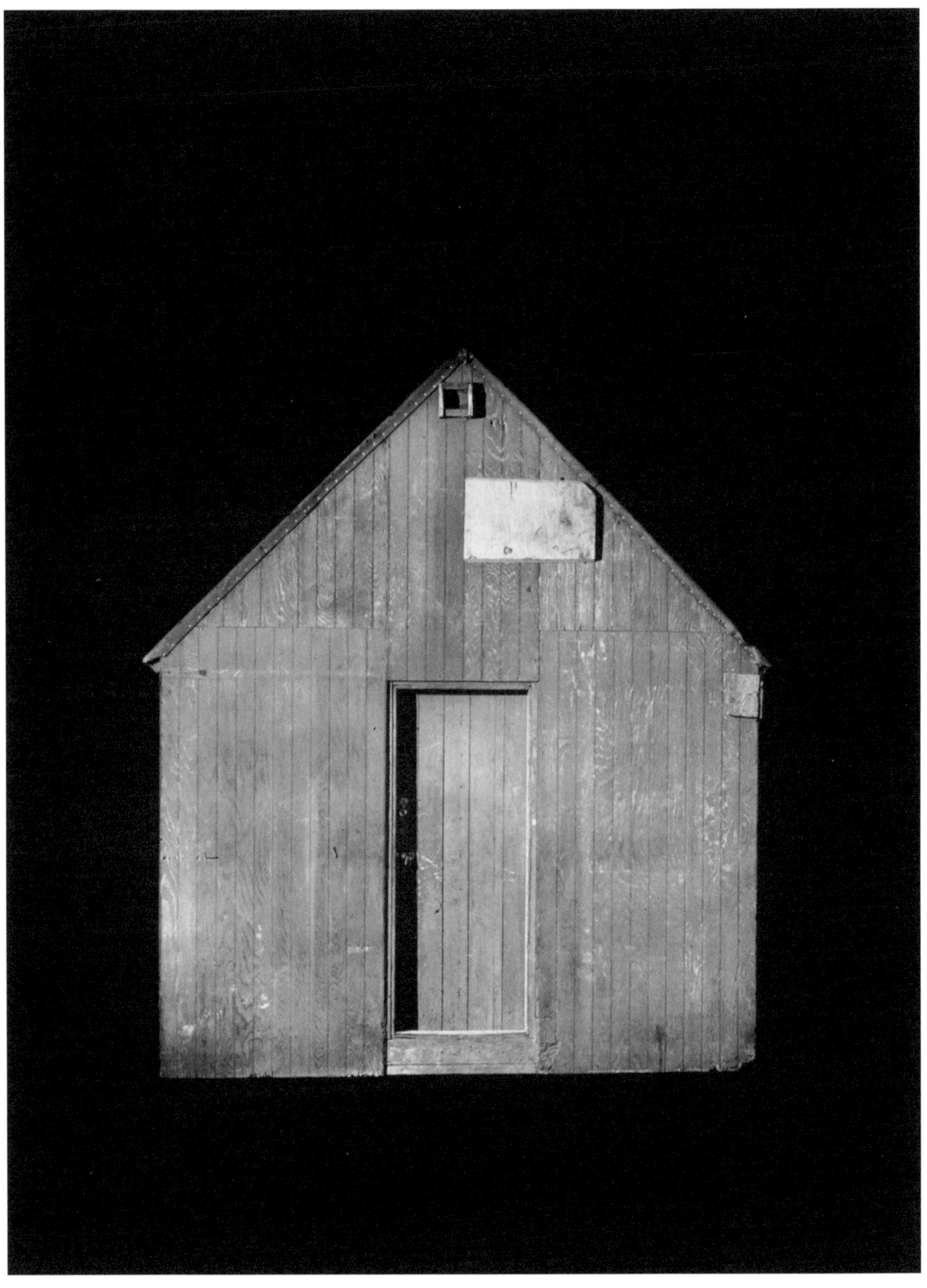

let only two people see inside. And it would be the interior that was on trial. The terrorist's lawyers wanted to exhibit the actual cabin to demonstrate his insanity. They rejected the prosecutor's conventional scale model, arguing that to be taken inside the brutally minimalist building was to be taken inside a deranged mind. The prosecutors were going to counter with photographs of the space at the time of the arrest. It was, they said, as well organized as an all-too-sane calculating mind. But the defendant preferred to plead guilty than be judged insane. The cabin was not entered and no images were ever released. The interior escapes us.

To look at these photographs is to scrutinize the exterior surfaces of an archetypal architecture for clues as to its explosive contents. The rigorous aesthetic of simplicity, natural materials, craftsmanship, and geometric purity has become an unsettling agent of horror.

bookreviews

Slow-Motion Film with Crash-
Test Dummies

Willem van Weelden

*Internet Art, The Online Clash of
Culture and Commerce*
Julian Stallabrass
Tate Publishing, Londen 2003,
ISBN 1854373455, € 30,95

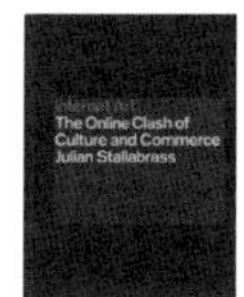

It has become the norm to judge a work of art on the connections it has with 'lifestyle', 'identity' or 'ideology'. The work of art is seen as a 'product' that derives meaning and effect not merely from strictly formal character-istics, but also from the way in which is communicates an identifiable vision or identity within a specific context or market. Viewed in this way, the artwork, in the first instance, communicates its brand quality. The brand is a closed system of values that primarily refers to this self-assigned and designed 'identity'. In regular marketing it has long been recognized that a product cannot be sold purely on the basis of its strictly formal characteristics. A successful product must communicate a message and appeal to a recog-nizable identity. It must be an incarnation of an ideal world, which becomes accessible by purchasing it. By buying a product (a logo) one shows that one identifies with the identity that the brand expresses. This principle has by now been so thoroughly developed that a brand is designed as if it were a flesh-and-blood human being. It must prove and fulfil its credibil-ity at all times. Its users or buyers not only expect the brand to have human qualities, but also to be able to come into contact with it. The product must have

an open connection to the end user, must be interactive. In the world-*cum*-market you must be able, just as in love, to merge as a lovesick mortal with your sweet-heart. This form of emotional and economic swindle is called branding.

In the introduction to his recently published book *Internet Art, The Online Clash between Culture and Commerce* Julian Stallabrass describes how ®™Mark (http://www.rtmark. com), a group of 'anticorporate' saboteurs operating in the grey area between activism and performance art, responded to its selection for the prestigious 'Whitney Biennial' in 2000. The invitations sent to ®™Mark, including the accompanying letter which stated that the group now belonged to the elite of the American art world, was put up for sale by ®™Mark on the Internet auction site eBay. The auction raised $4,000, which ®™Mark immediately put into its project fund. The group's action left the Whitney Biennial institu-tion completely perplexed about whether this act was part of a serious artistic concept, or a clear act of sabotage, or perhaps simply a tasteless joke. Stallabrass describes this incident as 'symp-tomatic' of the dispute between the complacent art world and online activists. In his view, it demonstrates that the official art

world attempts to 'brand' the culture of activists, hackers and net artists as art, but also shows that this alternative culture is in turn hostile and evasive toward the archaic, elitist and appropriat-ing practices of the art world. The question of whether Stallabrass is making a more cunning attempt to brand this volatile phenomenon must be weighed against the evidence he submits and the argument he develops.

What counts in Stallabrass' favour is that he is thoroughly conscious of the unstable character of what can be defined as Internet art. He makes a reasonable case for the proposi-tion that this instability is not just the result of the deliberately evasive tactics of its makers, but is also determined by the nature of the Internet itself, as a highly changeable technological communication platform. In the first two chapters, he delves into the structure of the Internet and of data. In doing so he does not allow himself to be seduced by idealistic futuristic visions, as is the case in a lot of cyber theory. He primarily attempts to reflect on the potential contained in the phenomenon. His assumption is that this 'art', from a conceptual and social point of view, is the most evolved and contemporary. Amazingly, in this context, he insists on confining himself to 'fine art'. Stallabrass argues that 'fine art' has condemned itself to marginality (in contrast with literature, music and film) and that the Internet is the ideal medium by which to escape the archaic shackles of the traditional production and distribution of artworks. For Stallabrass, art will only become socially relevant again once art has emancipated itself from the 'old economy'. In itself this reasoning still makes sense, but it is disturbing and confusing to find the author seems not to be conscious of the fact that if this reason for existence is genuinely undermined, then the whole idea of 'fine art' no longer exists – something that should not have to matter anyway.

In the chapters on the political character of Internet art and the tradition of media tactics that is inextricably linked to it, he shows himself to be reasonably up to date, and in this light his book is a handy overview of the illustrious history of online art. Yet what is very regrettable in his story is his need to apply the old parameters of 'art' to Internet art, with considerable confusion as a result. What he particularly seems not to understand is that many of the groups and projects he describes are deliberately ambiguous. In virtually not a single instance is it something that the makers unequivocally intended as art. For ®™Mark, for example, it is just as important that business magazines or online sport fanzines write about them as renowned art journals. ®™Mark's projects are after all about resistance to global capitalism, and whether some see them as an activist or anarchist group, and others as art, or even as net entrepreneurs, makes no difference to them, as long as it contributes to their objective, and this is not to rescue 'art': that seems to be mainly Stallabrass' own quest. Stallabrass' treatment of the clash between net artists, activists and the established art world is akin to a slow-motion film with crash-test dummies. Sterile, and completely outside actual practice, with all its coincidences, static and everyday delusion. His case, despite all his attempts to call attention to the phenomenon of Internet art in an enthusiastic way, is nevertheless dominated by a concession to the established art world and its problems in classifying and conserving net art. A conservative attitude that, given the history of the innovative and the critical – whether in art or not – is hardly new. Stallabrass seems not to realize that the conflict he presents between net art and the established order has already been undermined from the inside out, and that changes usually occur not in great collisions, but through stealthy infiltrations, which destabilize the established order, causing it to continually mutate.

Das war einmal

Max Bruinsma

New Commitment: In architecture, art and design
Reflect #01, NAi Publishers, Rotterdam, 2003,
ISBN 90-5662-347-8, € 19,50

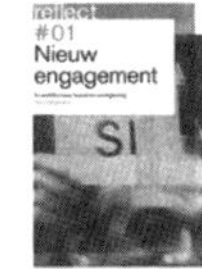

The new NAi series *Reflect*, a series of 'books without preconceived notions', aims to address a demand for reflection on meta-questions left unaddressed or merely mentioned in passing in many other books on architecture. In his introduction to the first instalment, on engagement (or commitment), publisher Simon Franke reveals the conclusion straight away: 'Commitment is difficult, so much becomes clear after reading the articles in this book; much more difficult than in the past, that is, in the 1960s and 1970s.'

Franke summarizes it well: for the majority of the writers in this collection the 1960s are *the* problem of contemporary engagement. Seldom have I read such agreement among such divergent authors in relation to a concept open to so many interpretations. This like-mindedness has less to do with the forms of engagement described in the book – these vary significantly – and more with the general tenor of the vast majority of the articles: 'After postmodernism, engagement as in the 1960s is no longer possible. That engagement was after all based on naiveté and we are not naive anymore.' I'm summing it up somewhat crudely, but that is what I got after reading this first instalment of *Reflect*.

In the opening essay René Boomkens describes postmodernism as the neurosis of a generation of spoiled airheads, who find a refreshing sense of 'new

seriousness' in 'new engagement'. Based on his mistaken
notion that 'engagement is not
an individual choice, but the
expression of collective commitment to a crucial movement or
development', Boomkens gives
'the errant individual' one last
hope: a new kind of collectivism,
which actually implies an accept-
ance of the dissolution of the
individual, as we thought we
knew him, into a kind of collective individuality entirely put
together from the shelves of the
consumer society. In opposition
to this stands the individual scepticism of what used to be called
the 'establishment', now consisting of Baby Boomers disap-
pointed with their own 1960s
engagement. The disillusionment
of these ex-revolutionaries
expresses itself as scepticism
toward any form of enthusiasm
and thus erodes the seed-bed of
any personal engagement.
Boomkens goes rather far, but
his linking the 'failure' of 1960s
engagement with the resulting
quasi-impossibility of engagement in the present is echoed
repeatedly by this congregation,
which consists for the most part
of (post-) Baby Boomers. Lieven
De Cauter: 'Perhaps even this
new commitment is no more
than a trend...' Hilde Heynen:
'...a theme that seems to have
been out of sight for long
enough for it to be presented as
something fresh and new today'.
Ole Bouman: '...how architecture, after years of postmodernist
dis-engagement, of philosophical
deconstruction and digital experiments with form, can recover
some measure of social significance'. The only one who makes
a brave attempt to formulate the
conditions for a renewed engagement is the pre-Baby Boomer

Henk Hofland, the journalistic
conscience of engagement in the
Low Countries. He is also the
only one who gives it a genuine
definition, and one still quite
applicable: 'Commitment, in the
original sense of the word, means
being rationally involved in the
world in which one lives, appreci-
ating the human condition and,
consequently, taking sides.' Clear.
And he concludes: 'New commitment rests in (...) the outline of
a new Utopia in which, in the
first instance, those capable of
independent thought will break
out of the prison into which they,
as consumers, have locked themselves.'
This is a simultaneously encouraging and discouraging conclusion. Encouraging, because the
old man, virtually alone, adopts
an actively critical attitude toward
the consumer society, an attitude
one also finds among the newest
generation, whereas the intervening generation of Baby Boomers
surrender, disillusioned, to the
inevitable triumph of the
shopping culture. Because, alas!,
Utopia, the Blochian *noch nicht*,
the distant vision of man
liberated! If one thing is clear
from the articles by Hofland's
juniors, it is that we should in
fact be liberated by now from
such illusions as 'Utopia' and
'liberation', and that engagement
has become an institutionalized
consumer product. There seems
little hope that Hofland's
'prisoners' will revolt. The 'revolt
of the masses' has been turned
into a mass of lifestyle rebels.
The uneasy engagement of the
Benetton generation, let's say.
The institutionalization of social
involvement is a potentially
suffocating factor for the rise of a
'new engagement', not just in
the form of consumer idealism.

In the Netherlands 'engagement
has now penetrated into every
facet of society', Lucas Verweij
and Ton Matton observe. 'It is a
fixed component in diverse
government bodies, in associations, foundations, political
parties and subsidy providers.
Urban renewal, public safety
policy and the Dutch government's "Postbus 51" central
information services are all semi-
institutionalized forms of engagement that flowed from a process
of engagement's social embed-
ding.' And more particularly in
reference to the arts, Jeroen
Boomgaard remarks: 'Commitment has become so general in
form and content that it lends
itself without any difficulty to
a prestigious existence in the
official arts circuit.' And he goes
on to remind us that art institutions and engaged art have
always had very difficult relations.
Is there hope? Is there really a
'new engagement'? From this
book, I wouldn't know. For
intellectual debate it is of course
good that more questions are
raised than answered, but I
would have liked to have seen
more variation. Or a glimmer of
analysis of *contemporary* engagement, instead of yet another nail
in the coffin of the engagement
of the past. For the moment, as
far as the present is concerned, it
basically comes down to 'we
don't really know what to do,
but if we don't do anything it's
going to get a lot less pleasant,
so "new engagement" will do...'
A rather meagre sequel to the
'doom thinking' of the 1970s,
which at least still offered hope
of (radical) change and improvement. Is this all the result of the
postmodern thinking that has
declared ideology dead and
proclaimed irony as its new idol?

Probably. When the only one who dares to use the word 'liberation' in the context of renewed engagement is a man around 80 years of age, I fear for my own generation and pin my hopes on the newest generation, who know irony and disdain for 'dogmatic do-gooders' of the past only as historical phenomena. Why should we keep on whinging about an unresolved trauma from the 'failure of '68', when the *present* compels us, as Hofland says, to 'take sides'. Putting off this choice in favour of an endless rehashing of the disappointment with what 40 years ago was *as* beautiful as it was impossible, is worse than repression – it is denial.

A Call for a New Relationship between Art and Place

Mariska van den Berg and Dees Linders

One Place after Another. Site Specific Art and Locational Identity Miwon Kwon
MIT Cambridge Mass., Londen 2002, ISBN 0-262-11265-5, € 43,69

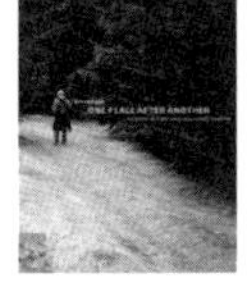

In her book *One Place after Another: Site Specific Art and Locational Identity* (2002) Miwon Kwon outlines a unique view of the evolution of 'site specific art' from the 1960s onwards. The way in which she lumps the most divergent art practices with a conscious relationship to 'place' into the 'site-specific' category takes some getting used to. In the process she uncovers a complex battleground of the evolution of the concept and practice of 'site specificity'. After a fascinating historical description, she turns to the development of site-specific art in the public domain. She relates her research and her findings to urban theory, postmodern criticism in art and architecture, and especially the present-day debate on the vanishing city and the unstable relationship between place and identity: the 'disappearance of site'. Kwon makes clear the importance of art's relationship to place. And with a thorough analysis, she hopes to create room for the representation of new coordinates for the relationship between art and 'site'. Kwon describes the development of 'site specifity' using three paradigms, in which she attempts to sum up history and the present. The first, 'phenomenological' paradigm is related to the original site-specific art of the late 1960s and early 1970s, in which the 'site' was the starting point and reason for being of the artwork. The physical place and artwork were inextricably linked. Within the second, 'social' or 'institutional' paradigm, 'site' is formed by a much broader framework, with the focus on the social, economic and cultural-political conditions in which art is produced and presented. The dematerialization of the 'site' and of the artwork which begins here continues in more recent art practices, summed up in the third, 'discursive' paradigm. Within this, artists expand their field of operation, in the sense of location, form, content and function, far beyond the context of art. Often social issues are the focus. 'Site' can now also be an area of knowledge, an intellectual exchange or a cultural debate. Kwon sums up the evolution she describes as a shift from a sedentary model to a nomadic model, a shift from a close relationship to a steadily looser, more unstable relationship between subject/object and place.

Because her theory encompasses not only the artwork but also the artist's practice, this leaves room for experimental artistic practices that, measured by traditional criteria of artworks, fall outside the boundaries of art.

Three extensive case studies, Richard Serra's *Tilted Arc*, a John Ahearn commission for *South Bronx Sculpture Park*, and the exhibition 'Culture in Action' (1993, Chicago) bring Kwon to call for a reconsideration of previously outlined models of 'site specificity'. The cases show the precarious relationship of the art projects to a stubborn practice within the public domain. To Kwon, treating 'community' as a social coherence is a serious misconception. This misconception is due to the failure of many of these interactive practices.

She elaborates this using the exhibition 'Culture in Action' by Mary Jane Jacobs, to her a textbook example of the political and activist 'New Genre Public Art', which lays a strong emphasis on interaction between artists and 'communities'. The practice of New Genre Public Art is based on a protest against the exclusion of individuals and groups. A political aspiration to democratization is of fundamental importance here, 'to empower the audience'. Art should also become the property of the man in the street: 'real place', 'real people', 'real problems'. It is a form of public art that, at this level and with this political aspiration, is inconceivable in the Netherlands. In her analysis of the eight projects comprising 'Culture in Action', Kwon thus focuses acutely on the way in which the relevant groups/communities were assembled, defined and approached by the artist, curator or art institution. Was the group approached as socially coherent? To what extent did a reductive picture of the identities of the participants emerge, whereby essential differences, particular characteristics and interests were left out? Difference, heterogeneity and instability, to Kwon, are by definition intrinsic to every community. This realization must serve as the basis for any interaction between art and a community.

Based on this realization, Kwon proposes a different model of collectivism and 'belonging', conceived not out of 'common-being' but out of 'being-in-common'. She outlines a collective artistic practice she dubs 'Projective Enterprise': this is also predicated on the groups assembled for the occasion, whereby she calls for the people involved to be constantly conscious that every aspect of the interaction is constructed and mediated. However, Kwon's 'Projective Enterprise' seems closely modelled on New Genre Public Art as she describes it. She makes a stand for the further development and reconsideration of 'community art', but it is too early to speak of a new model. In the closing chapter Kwon draws a direct link between the disappearance of the physical place in 'site-specific' art practice and the unravelling of the relationship between subject/object and place. Kwon sees a task for art to fulfil within the problems of contemporary existence and the significance of the modern city against the background in which this unravelling is taking place, as long as art is capable of inventing a new model for the art-place relationship. Site-specific art can function as a cultural mediator, although Kwon is also conscious of the risk of interpreting site-specific art as a melancholic discourse: the recognition of the loss of 'place, but no solution for the loss of place'.

According to Kwon, it seems historically inevitable that we discard the nostalgic notion of 'site' and identity, connected in essence to an actual place. At the same time, the yearning for this close constant relationship, which is related to the experience of identity and safety, will never go away. The model that Kwon proposes for art therefore encompasses the nostalgic yearning for 'place and identity' as well as the recognition of an unstable (nomadic) relationship between subject and place: the notion of 'the wrong place, belonging in transience', 'to be out of place with punctuality and precision'.

So far Kwon's proposal is easy to follow and interesting. From this point, however, her argument becomes unclear. To apply this model within the public domain, she seems to bring out the traditional, presumed expertise of art: 'Thus, in its final pages the book can only conjure up the critical capacity of intimacies based on absence, distance, and ruptures of time and space.' Does she mean the presumed capacity of art to reinforce emotions and experiences to the point that can be exercised within the 'safe' area of art? Is she identifying an art in the public space that, through models, can teach a critical attitude toward the proximity of absence, distance, ruptures in time and space? That would be worth reflecting upon. But is this in fact what she has in mind? Her examples, after all, show that art is not easily tolerated in the urban public space, and perhaps cannot help developing as a 'democratic art'. And does this not mean that, by definition, art must sacrifice its instability, unrest and unease in favour of accessibility – qualities that are characteristic of a nomadic constellation?

Kwon's exposition elicits yet more questions. For instance, does she not excessively ascribe her theory to a supposed practice? It is also odd that Kwon's research into art practice stops in 1993, while she is proposing a different model for art in the public space based on this research in 2002. In that intervening decade, in facet, an entirely new model for art and participation has been developed by a new generation of artists and theorists such as Nicolas Bourriauld, Hans Ulrich Obrist, Rirkrit Tiravanija, Jeanne van Heeswijk, Alicia Framis, Marius Babias, Florian Waldvogel, to name but a few.

Nevertheless Kwon's book offers clarification and food for

thought, especially in relation to interactive/participative art and public space. Perhaps her method of 'Projective Enterprise' and her essential model of 'the wrong place' is not suited to the great public urban domain; perhaps its potential rests primarily on small communities, in fact.

<u>PERSONALIA</u>

MARISKA VAN DEN BERG is a project coordinator with SKOR in Amsterdam.

HANS BOUTELLIER is the director of the Verwey-Jonker Institute whose writings include <u>De veiligheids-utopie. Hedendaags onbehagen en verlangen rond misdaad en straf</u>.

MAX BRUINSMA is a design critic based in Amsterdam and Basel, author of, among others, <u>Deep Sites. Intelligent innovation in contemporary webdesign</u> (2003), and editor of, among others, <u>STIFF, Hans van Houwelingen vs. Public Art</u> (Artimo, Spring 2004).

LIEVEN DE CAUTER is a cultural philosopher whose writings include <u>Archeologie van de kick. Verhalen over moderniteit en ervaring</u> (1995). He teaches in the department of Architecture, Urban Planning and Spatial Planning at the Catholic University of Leuven, the Rits film school and the Parts dance school in Brussels and the Berlage Institute in Rotterdam.

JOUKE KLEEREBEZEM is a visual artist, author and advising researcher with the design department at the Jan van Eyck Academie. His work is oriented to the Internet; www.ref.: www.nqpaofu.com.

THOMAS Y. LEVIN is a professor at Princeton University, where he teaches culture and media theory

DEES LINDERS is a project coordinator with SKOR, Amsterdam.

SVEN LÜTTICKEN is an art historian and art critic. He teaches art history at the Vrije Universiteit in Amsterdam and is a member of the editorial board of <u>De Witte Raaf</u>.

GIJS VAN OENEN is a political scientist and legal philosopher and university lecturer in the Faculty of Philosophy at the Universiteit Rotterdam.

Q.S. SERAFIJN is a visual artist based in Rotterdam.

SEAN SNYDER is a visual artist. He is originally from the United States and lives and works in Berlin.

HARM TILMAN is editor in chief of <u>de Architect</u>.

WILLEM VAN WEELDEN is a visual artist/researcher/writer who lives and works in Amsterdam.

MARK WIGLEY is a professor with the School of Architecture, Planning and Preservation at Columbia University whose writings include <u>Constant's New Babylon. The Hyper-Architecture of Desire</u> (1998).

OPEN

Editing Jorinde Seijdel (editor
in chief), Liesbeth Melis
Final Editing Liesbeth Melis
Editorial Board Max Bruinsma,
Jan van Grunsven, Dennis Kaspori,
Dees Linders

Dutch-English Translation
Pierre Bouvier (except Levin,
Lütticken, Snyder, Wigley)

Graphic Design Thomas Buxó in
collaboration with Klaartje
van Eijk
Printing and Lithography
Die Keure, Bruges

Project Coordinator Brecht Bleeker,
NAi Publishers
Publisher: Simon Franke,
NAi Publishers

SUBSCRIPTIONS
NAi Publishers
Mauitsweg 23
3012 JR Rotterdam
Tel +31 (0)10 2010133
Fax +31 (0)10 2010130
info@naipublishers.nl

EDITORIAL ADDRESS
SKOR
Ruysdaelkade 2
1072 AG Amsterdam
T +31 (0)20 6722525
F +31 (0)20 3792809
open@skor.nl

open is published twice a year.
open 7 will be published in
October 2004, with memory in art
and the public domain as its theme.

SUBCRIPTIONS
Netherlands: € 37,50
Within Europe: € 45,00
Outside Europe: € 50,00

Available in North, South and Central America through
D.A.P./Distributed Art Publishers Inc, 155 Sixth Avenue
2nd Floor, New York, NY 10013-1507, Tel 212 6271999,
Fax 212 6279484.

Available in the United Kingdom and Ireland through Art Data,
12 Bell Industrial Estate, 50 Cunnington Street, London W4
5HB, Tel 208 7471061, Fax 208 7422319.

The editors and NAi Publishers have made every effort to
fulfil their legal obligations in regard to copyright holders.
Should there be work included in this issue by copyright
holders unknown to the editors, interested parties are
requested to contact NAi Publishers.

NAi Publishers is an internationally orientated publisher
specialized in developing, producing and distributing books
on architecture, visual arts and related disciplines.
www.naipublishers.nl info@naipublishers.nl

SKOR is an Amsterdam-based organization whose objective is to
realize special art projects in public and semi-public
settings throughout the Netherlands.www.skor.nl, info@skor.nl

ISSN 1570-4181
ISBN 90-5662-382-6

Photo cover: Henrik Plenge Jakobson, Angst, 1999.
Courtesy Galleri Nicolai Wallner.